Lecture Notes in Computer Science 10618

Commenced Publication in 1973
Founding and Former Series Editors:
Gerhard Goos, Juris Hartmanis, and Jan van Leeuwen

More information about this series at http://www.springer.com/series/7408

Issa Traore · Isaac Woungang
Ahmed Awad (Eds.)

Intelligent, Secure, and Dependable Systems in Distributed and Cloud Environments

First International Conference, ISDDC 2017
Vancouver, BC, Canada, October 26–28, 2017
Proceedings

Springer

Editors
Issa Traore ⓘD
University of Victoria
Victoria, BC
Canada

Ahmed Awad
New York Institute of Technology
Vancouver, BC
Canada

Isaac Woungang ⓘD
Ryerson University
Toronto, ON
Canada

ISSN 0302-9743   ISSN 1611-3349 (electronic)
Lecture Notes in Computer Science
ISBN 978-3-319-69154-1   ISBN 978-3-319-69155-8 (eBook)
https://doi.org/10.1007/978-3-319-69155-8

Library of Congress Control Number: 2017956716

LNCS Sublibrary: SL2 – Programming and Software Engineering

Printed on acid-free paper

This Springer imprint is published by Springer Nature
The registered company is Springer International Publishing AG
The registered company address is: Gewerbestrasse 11, 6330 Cham, Switzerland

Welcome Message From ISDDC 2017 General Co-chairs

Welcome to the proceedings of the First International Conference on Intelligent, Secure and Dependable Systems in Distributed and Cloud Environments (ISDDC 2017).

We were happy to present an impressive technical program thanks to the work of many volunteers. We would like to thank all of these volunteers for their contributions to ISDDC 2017.

Our thanks go to the authors, and our sincere gratitude goes to the Program Committee, who gave much extra time to carefully review the submissions. About 43 technical papers were submitted from around the world, and were thoroughly peer reviewed; 30% were accepted for presentation at the conference and publication in the conference proceedings. Papers were peer-reviewed by three or more Program Committee members, in a single round of review.

In addition to the technical paper presentations, ISDDC 2017 invited select guest speakers to provide stimulating presentations on topics of broad interest. This year's distinguished speakers were:

- Lloyd Jura, CISSP, Director, Information Security, Vivonet
- Ian Paterson, CEO, Plurilock Security Solutions Inc.
- Leo de Sousa, Director, Enterprise Technology, City of Vancouver Adjunct Faculty, New York Institute of Technology, Vancouver

We are pleased that authors of selected papers were invited to submit extended versions for publication in Wiley's *Journal of Security and Privacy*.

Finally, we thank the larger ISDDC community for their continuing support, by submitting papers and by volunteering their time and talent in other ways. Whether you attended ISDDC in person this year or are reading these proceedings, we hope that you find these papers interesting, inspiring, and relevant. Enjoy!

September 2017
Issa Traore
Isaac Woungang

Welcome Message From ISDDC 2017 Program Co-chairs

Welcome to the proceedings of the First International Conference on Intelligent, Secure and Dependable Systems in Distributed and Cloud Environments (ISDDC 2017), which was held October 26–28 in Vancouver, BC, Canada.

The purpose of the ISDDC conference is to bring together developers and researchers to share ideas and research work in the emerging areas of intelligent, secure, dependable systems, and cloud environments.

The contributions included in the proceedings of ISDDC 2017 cover many aspects of theory and application of effective and efficient paradigms, approaches, and tools for building, maintaining, and managing secure and dependable systems and infrastructures, such as botnet detection, secure cloud computing and cryptosystems, IoT security, sensor and social network security, behavioral systems and data science, and mobile computing.

In this edition, 43 submissions were received from all over the world. Each submitted paper was peer-reviewed by the Program Committee members and external reviewers who are experts in the topical areas covered by the papers. The Program Committee accepted 13 papers (about 30% acceptance ratio). The conference program also included three distinguished keynote speeches and two tutorials.

The organization of an international conference requires the support and help of many people. First, we would like to thank all authors for submitting their papers. We would also like to thank the Program Committee members, who took care of the most difficult task of carefully evaluating the submitted papers. We would like to thank the ISDDC 2017 local arrangements chair for the excellent organization of the conference, and for his effective coordination creating the recipe for a very successful conference.

September 2017

Isaac Woungang
Issa Traore
Sanjay K. Dhurandher

ISDDC 2017 Organizing Committee

General Co-chairs

Issa Traore — University of Victoria, Canada
Isaac Woungang — Ryerson University, Canada

Publicity Co-chairs

Isaac Woungang — Ryerson University, Canada
Issa Traore — University of Victoria, Canada

Program Co-chairs

Isaac Woungang — Ryerson University, Canada
Issa Traore — University of Victoria, Canada
Sanjay Kumar Dhurandher — University of Delhi, India

Local Arrangements Chairs

Ahmed Awad — New York Institute of Technology, Vancouver, BC, Canada
Issa Traore — University of Victoria, Canada

Tutorial Chair

Ahmed Awad — New York Institute of Technology, Vancouver, BC, Canada

Technical Program Committee

Isaac Woungang — Ryerson University, Canada
Ahmed Awad — New York Institute of Technology, Vancouver
Glaucio Carvalho — Ryerson University, Canada
Issa Traore — University of Victoria, BC, Canada
Sanjay K. Dhurandher — University of Delhi, India
Bharat K. Bhargava — Purdue University, USA
Xavier Fernando — Ryerson University, Canada
R.K. Pateriya — MANIT, India
Petros Nicopolitidis — Aristotle University of Thessaloniki, Greece
Ilsun You — Soonchunhyang University, Republic of Korea
Wei Lu — Keene State College, USA
Babak Beheshti — New York Institute of Technology, New York, USA

ISDDC 2017 Keynote Talks

What are the Current Cyber-Threats?
Exploring the Trend in Yesteryear

Lloyd Jura

CISSP, Information Security, Vivonet

Abstract. With the ever-increasing number of devices online, ever increasing sophisticated human attacks, have we reached the peak of cyber threats? With the perimeter almost vanished, could it be time to shift the battle inside? It is not a secret that even organizations with the deepest pockets cannot keep up with the speed of cyber attackers out there. This session will highlight the following:

- Internet Security Threats of 2016
- The bad guys
- Targeted attacks
- Email attacks
- IoT and the Cloud
- Ransomware
- Best Practices

Disrupting the Paradigm of Authentication: Leveraging Continuous Authentication to Replace out Point-in-Time Solutions

Ian Paterson

Plurilock Security Solutions Inc.

Abstract. Passwords are notoriously known to be flawed. They can be broken through automated attacks, social engineering, phishing, and related attack vectors. As a result, in the last decade, much effort has been invested in reinforcing passwords, primarily through multifactor authentication solutions. Despite encouraging progress made in this front, we have witnessed exponential increase in the number and sophistication of hacking incidents rooted in the circumvention of authentication methods. Now there is a push to replace passwords altogether. In this context, there is an urgent need for a paradigm shift. Continuous authentication provides a foundation for such paradigm shift. This talk will present and discuss industry advances and perspectives in leveraging continuous authentication toward replacing out point-in-time authentication solutions. The talk will discuss perception from real-world deployments and end-users, and will identify some challenges in research toward achieving the ultimate goal of a password-free world.

Building a Cybersecurity Practice to Support Smart Cities

Leo de Sousa

Enterprise Technology, City of Vancouver Adjunct Faculty,
New York Institute of Technology, Vancouver

Abstract. Governments are on a journey to leverage information technology to improve citizen engagement, service delivery and manage ever increasing costs. This session provides practical approaches to building a Cybersecurity Practice to address the risks facing governments in the "Smart City" context. The Canadian Federal Government issued the Smart Cities Challenge (http://www.infrastructure.gc.ca/plan/cities-villes-eng.html) to all Canadian municipalities, regional governments and Indigenous communities in June 2017. The Smart Cities Challenge offers several prizes from $5M to $50M CAD to winning submissions. The City of Vancouver has created an internal working group to respond to this opportunity. As part of the working group, we recognized the need to build a Cybersecurity Practice to ensure that we can securely adopt "smart" technologies to support the City's strategic direction.

ISDDC 2017 Tutorials

Ransomware: Emerging Threat and Anatomy

Asem Almekhlafy

Abstract. Among the various forms of malware, ransomware is currently one of the most common forms of cybercrime. Ransomware works on encrypting victim's data or locking victim's screen until extortionist's demands are met usually by paying a sum of money as ransom. The prevalence of ransomware attacks continues to grow and the number of reported ransomware incidents increased significantly in the past few years. Reports stated that more than 4,000 ransomware attacks happen every day and there is a massive increase at rate of 300 percent annually in the volume of ransomware attacks. The first half of the year 2017 witnessed the emergence of ransomware attacks, e.g. Wannacry, which infected hundred thousand of machines across the world. This massive growth of ransomware attacks is accompanied with an increase in the number of attacks particularly targeting organizations at rapid pace. The shift toward business sectors rather than individual victims is a profit-driven endeavor and represents a bigger potential gain especially when attacks can result in exposing confidential information or disturbing critical services. In this tutorial, we will highlight the ransomware phenomenon and the impact of ransomware on individuals and businesses, and illustrate ransomware attack anatomy through a case study. In addition, we will discuss the new advances in ransomware detection and defense techniques and mitigation of ransomware risk. We will talk about what are the important trends and forecasts.

Emerging Biometrics Technologies

Mohammed Alshahrani

Abstract. Nowadays, technological resources, devices, and services are being widely used by humans. In fact, technologies are infiltrating every part of modern living. In this context, critical resources that were accessible only through physical perimeters, are now available in digitized forms, and can be accessed from anywhere, by anybody. Traditional identification technologies like passwords and PINs are used as primary means of protection for these technologies and digitized resources, but they are no longer reliable or able to resist security threats. Therefore, security researchers and professionals have started thinking seriously about a strong alternative solution to replace or reinforce resiliently these technologies. Biometric technologies are commonly considered by security practitioners as one of the strongest contenders in achieving the aforementioned goal. Biometric refers to metrics related to human's characteristics such as gait, DNA and iris. These characteristics are unique and hence can be used to identify and distinguish people from one another. Some biometric technologies have already been deployed and implemented in the last decades such as fingerprint and iris, and others might emerge in the next few years or are recently emerging such as body odor and gait. The purpose of this tutorial is to explore and present the emerging biometric technologies along with their different foundational techniques to highlight recent advances and potential challenges these technologies face in their development. In this context, we will briefly review several new biometric technologies including DNA, EEG, ECG, PPG, Gait, Body odor, Lip, keystroke and Ear recognition. Also, biometrics performance and convenience will be discussed. This work derives from an in-depth study of various biometric research papers that have been published so far. Participants will gain a better understanding of biometric systems and their recent advances. The intended audience of this tutorial are those with a general computing background and researchers from all fields. There is no specific background knowledge that will be required because this tutorial.

Contents

Holistic Model for HTTP Botnet Detection Based on DNS Traffic Analysis

Abdelraman Alenazi[1], Issa Traore[1], Karim Ganame[2],
and Isaac Woungang[3(✉)]

[1] ECE Department, University of Victoria, Victoria, BC, Canada
aalenazi@uvic.ca, itraore@ece.uvic.ca
[2] StreamScan, 2300 Rue Sherbrooke E, Montreal, QC, Canada
ganame@streamscan.io
[3] Department of Computer Science, Ryerson University, Toronto, ON, Canada
iwoungan@scs.ryerson.ca

Abstract. HTTP botnets are currently the most popular form of botnets compared to IRC and P2P botnets. This is because, they are not only easier to implement, operate, and maintain, but they can easily evade the detection. Likewise, HTTP botnets flows can easily be buried in the huge volume of legitimate HTTP traffic occurring in many organizations, which makes the detection harder. In this paper, a new detection framework involving three detection models is proposed, which can run independently or in tandem. The first detector profiles the individual applications based on their interactions, and isolates accordingly the malicious ones. The second detector tracks the regularity in the timing of the bot DNS queries, and uses this as basis for detection. The third detector analyzes the characteristics of the domain names involved in the DNS, and identifies the algorithmically generated and fast flux domains, which are staples of typical HTTP botnets. Several machine learning classifiers are investigated for each of the detectors. Experimental evaluation using public datasets and datasets collected in our testbed yield very encouraging performance results.

Keywords: HTTP botnet · Botnet detection · Machine learning · Passive DNS · DGA domains · Malicious fast flux DNS

1 Introduction

A botnet is a network of enslaved machines, distributed geographically, which may be directed to perform malicious actions against potential targets at a large scale [12, 14, 18, 19]. The enslaved machines are compromised hosts known as bots. The individual or group of individuals controlling those machines are known as botmaster. Early botnets used centralized architecture for exchanging command and control (C&C) messages. The most prevalent communication protocols used in those earlier botnets was the Internet Relay Chat (IRC). However, this type of botnet is easy to detect and disrupt due to the single point of failure embodied by the IRC server, which manages

© Springer International Publishing AG 2017
I. Traore et al. (Eds.): ISDDC 2017, LNCS 10618, pp. 1–18, 2017.
https://doi.org/10.1007/978-3-319-69155-8_1

the C&C communications. Once the server is shut down, the botmaster loses control of the network of bots.

The next generation of botnets, which appeared a decade ago, addressed the aforementioned weakness by using peer-to-peer (P2P) protocols for command and control. Due to its distributed and resilient control structure, a P2P botnet is harder to shut down than an IRC-controlled botnet. However, in the recent years, as more knowledge has been acquired about P2P botnets, more effective solutions have been proposed to detect them and mitigate their impact. Furthermore, P2P botnets are more complex to implement, deploy and operate. As a result, there have been a shift in the C&C protocol of modern botnets from IRC and P2P channels to websites, using HTTP [6].

The advent of HTTP botnet can be linked to the development of exploit kits (EKs). EKs are sophisticated malicious software platforms, often professionally developed and marketed in the dark web, which allow cybercriminals to readily build and operate botnets and other types of malicious software. Due to the prevalence of http communications and sites, detecting botnets that use HTTP protocols is much harder [3, 4, 7, 8]. Many organizations host websites for regular business activities, and as such, enable http communications. Hence, it is easy for http-based botnets to evade the detection by hiding their command and control messages in the huge volume of legitimate HTTP traffic occurring in most organizations.

Despite such challenge, HTTP botnets have certain characteristics which can be leveraged and used to detect them. Some of those characteristics are rooted in the central role played by the concept of domain names in any web communication. The domain name by design represents a user-friendly mechanism to identify the servers in the cyberspace. However, user friendliness matters only when humans are involved in both ends. Such consideration does not matter in the automated settings embodied by botnets. As such, HTTP botnets abuse as much as possible the domain name system (DNS) toward achieving their main purpose of evading the detection, by using mechanisms such as fast flux DNS and algorithmically generated domain names. Ironically, while the DNS is abusively used by HTTP botnets to escape the detection, they leave a number of trails in the generated DNS traffic as part of the C&C communications, such as the regularity in the type and timing of the DNS requests, which are clues about their presence.

In this paper, we propose, to capture and analyze passive DNS queries for HTTP botnets detection [16]. We take a holistic approach by investigating different detectors which are suitable for capturing specific patterns. The combination of these detectors in a multi-detection scheme can provide a powerful HTTP botnet detection system, which can cover different types of HTTP botnets.

The rest of the paper is structured as follows. Section 2 summarizes some related work on HTTP botnet detection and the use of passive DNS for detecting the malicious activities. Section 3 provides some background on DNS and discusses some key characteristics of HTTP botnets that can be useful in building an adequate detection scheme. Section 4 introduces our proposed holistic detection framework by describing the feature space involved in the different detectors. Section 5 presents our evaluation datasets and performance results. Section 6 concludes the paper and discusses some future work.

2 Related Works

2.1 On HTTP Botnets Detection

Tyagi et al. [13] proposed a technique, which detects HTTP botnets by tracking similar flows occurring at regular time intervals, from the C&C to the bots in response to HTTP GET requests. The similarity between two flows is determined by computing and comparing the corresponding byte frequencies, for given sequence of bytes of length N. Although, the authors claim to have proposed the first approach that can be applied to all types of HTTP botnets, it was tested using only the Zeus botnet, yielding a detection rate (DR) of 100%, and False Positive Rate (FPR) of 0% for traffic with static C&C IP addresses, and DR = 98.6% and FPR = 0% for traffic with dynamic C&C IP addresses (fast flux).

Haddadi et al. [8] extracted and analyzed some flow-based features of botnets using two different classifiers, C4.5 and Naive Bayes. The flows are extracted by aggregating the network traces using flow exporters and using only packets headers. The experimental was done by collecting the domain names, including regular domains from the Alexa site and the malicious botnet C&C domain names generated by two different HTTP botnets, namely, Zeus and Citadel. A dataset was generated by running a custom script to initiate the HTTP connections with the domain names from the compiled list. It is unclear, however, whether the corresponding traffic really captures the actual behavior of the corresponding botnets. The evaluation without/with HTTP filtering (i.e. removing non-HTTP related traffic) indicated that the latter yields improved performance. The best performance was obtained when using the C4.5 classifier with the HTTP filter, yielding a performance of (DR = 97%, FPR = 3%) for Citadel and (DR = 86%, FPR = 15%) for Zeus.

Cai and Zhou [3] proposed a model which starts by clustering the HTTP request data from the HTTP flows using the Levenshtein Distance metric. Their approach was validated by using a dataset that they collected by themselves, yielding a False Alarm Rates (FAR) ranging from 13.6% to 26.3%.

Khillari and Augustine [9] proposed an HTTP botnet detection technique by mining the patterns set from the network traffic using the Apriori algorithm. However, it is unclear how the proposed approach was validated experimentally.

Garasia et al. [7] also proposed an HTTP botnet detection approach by applying the Apriori algorithm to the network traffic generated from HTTP communications. Although an attempt was made to conduct some experimental validation, the focus was limited to a hypothetical example. No real malicious samples were involved in the study, and no performance results were provided.

Kirubavathi Venkatesh and Anitha Nadarajan [15] studied the detection of HTTP botnet by applying an Adaptive Learning Rate Multilayer Feed-forward Neural Network to relative and direct features of TCP connections. An experimental validation was based on a dataset consisting of botnet traces for Spyeye and Zeus, that was merged with normal web traffic collected separately. A performance of (DR = 99%, FPR = 1%) was obtained. Next, the use of C4.5 decision tree, Random Forest and Radial Basis Function, confirmed that the proposed neural network model showed promising results.

2.2 On DNS Traffic Monitoring

Piscitello [10] discussed about how DNS traffic monitoring can help uncover indicators of compromise (IOC) for malware such as Remote Access Trojans (RATs). Specifically, six signs and traffic patterns for suspicious activities were identified. One of these signs relates to DNS queries that request known malicious domains or names with characteristics common to Domain Generation Algorithms (DGA) associated with the botnet. Other signs are the abnormally high amount of query answers returning Non-Existent Domain (NXDOMAIN), the high amount of query responses with short time-to-live (TTL) for newly registered domain names, and responses with suspicious IP addresses.

Weymes [17] proposed an approach to detect suspicious DNS queries by considering three different features consisting of domain length, name character makeup and level domain (e.g. .com, .ru, .biz, etc.). Based on a traffic sample from the Zeus botnet, it was shown that the domain length can raise a red flag when it exceeds 12 characters long. According to Weymes, a typical Zeus query is more than 33 characters long whereas normal queries are less than 12 characters long. The name character makeup such as alphanumeric, numbers, or vowels only, was also considered as impactful.

No experimental models or performance results for malicious activities detection was provided for the above work on passive DNS, however, some signs and characteristics that can be taken into account when attempting to detect suspicious DNS queries were highlighted.

Da Luz [5] used passive DNS traffic to detect domain names related to botnet activities. In their proposed model, 36 different features are extracted from passive DNS data and processed using machine learning techniques. The extracted features consist of lexical features of the domain name (e.g. number of characters, number of digits, number of consonants, statistics of character n-grams, to name a few) and network features of the domain such as TTL and number of IP subnetworks. Three different techniques are studied, including the k-Nearest Neighbors (kNN), the decision trees and the Random Forests. Experimental evaluation conducted using a 2-week passive DNS traffic yielded an accuracy rate of 97%, and a False Positive Rate (FPR) of 3%.

Antonakakis et al. [1] proposed a dynamic reputation system for DNS called Notos, assuming that malicious DNS activities are distinguishable from legitimate DNS traffic. Based on passive DNS data, the system extracts and analyzes the network and zone features of domains, then it constructs models of known legitimate domains and malicious domains. A domain is classified as legitimate or malicious according to a reputation score computed from the constructed models. Their proposed system was evaluated on a large ISP network with DNS traffic of 1.4 million users. Notos detects malicious domains with TPR = 96.8% and FPR = 0.38%. It was also reported that Notos can identify malicious domains weeks before they go active.

In [2], Bilge et al. developed a system called *Exposure* for detecting malicious domains, which uses 15 behavioural DNS attributes distributed among four groups, namely: Time-based (e.g. short-life, daily similarity), DNS answer-based (e.g. number of distinct resolved IP addresses, number of domains sharing the same IP), TTL-based (e.g. TTL, average and standard deviation, and number of TTL change), and DNS name-based features (e.g. measuring the percentage of numerical characters in a domain name). For the design of such system, the J48 decision tree was used for classification purpose assuming that short-lived domains[1] are often malicious. The proposed model was evaluated on an ISP dataset of 100 billion DNS packets, and yielded a performance of DR = 98% with FPR = 1%.

Nazario and Holz [11] proposed a way to classify fast flux domains using a series of heuristic rules. Their detection model extracts nine different features from DNS resources records such as TTL values, the discovery of more than five unique IPs in a single A-record query response, the average distance between IP addresses in A-records query responses, to name a few. Domain names are classified as fast flux when they match four or more of the nine features. From this study, it was reported that over 900 domain names that are using fast flux technology can be identified.

3 Passive DNS and HTTP Botnet

3.1 DNS Overview

The Domain Name System is a hierarchical scattered system that is mainly responsible for translating and mapping meaningful domain names to IP addresses. It is a critical component of the Internet infrastructure that is currently being used in most of the network services. Besides the ease of domain name memorization, DNS makes it possible to link a domain name to a collection of services such as Mail Exchange server, Web server, File servers or other Internet resources in a meaningful and independent way. The domain name system provides stability in how Internet resources are referred and located even if the underlying infrastructure changes.

DNS communications are based on hierarchical recursive requests. When a user aims to establish a connection to a domain name (e.g. example.com), DNS client sends a query to a DNS recursive resolver, which may be hosted locally or by third-parties such as Internet Service Providers (ISPs). DNS recursive resolvers attempt initially to resolve the received queries using cached information from past queries. If such resolution is unsuccessful, the request will be forwarded to other servers iteratively until a match is found. Figure 1 shows the process of DNS resolving when no cached records are available.

DNS naming structure is shaped as tree data structure. A top-level-domain (TLD) is the node that comes after the root. For example, .com, .net, and so on, are known as TLDs. Each TLD is a registry that holds and manages a zone file. A prefix name or sub domain of each TLD is known as a second level domain (SLD) name. All second level domains are controlled by authoritative DNS servers. A domain name can have one or more hierarchical sub domains; each sub domain level is defined by the incremental second-level domain. For example, foo.example.com is a third level domain. Moreover, a complete domain name (e.g. www.google.com or blog.example.com) is referred to as a fully qualified domain name (FQDN).

---

[1] Short life refers the time interval between two queries of the same domain.

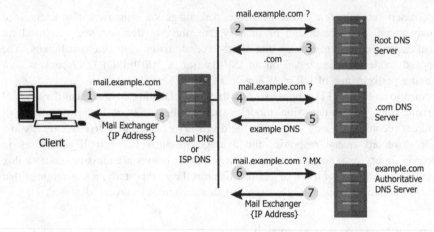

Fig. 1. DNS query cycle

DNS provides different types of records which map various resources such as web, mail servers, etc. Each DNS query contains a time-to-live (TTL) value that determines how long a machine caches a query. Normal TTL values, for an A record are between 3,600 to 86,400 s.

Some web services use a technique known as fast flux DNS which sets TTL to lower values for the purpose of balancing the load between multiple servers. Fast flux DNS solves issues such as single point of failure, by distributing ingress traffic to multiple cloned servers or mapping several IP addresses to one domain name.

Cybercriminals use the same concept in order to evade the IP address blacklisting and achieve high-availability [19]. While fast flux techniques are used for legitimate purpose, cybercriminals have flipped this technology over its head, as they have found that a malicious usage of Fast Flux networks provides a very effective mechanism for hiding their C&C servers and ensuring resilience. This is done by using a short time-to-live TTL on DNS resources records, which allows swapping and rotating between servers efficiently. A key challenge faced by researchers is about developing effective approaches to differentiate between malicious and benign fast flux networks.

3.2   HTTP Botnet Architecture

Traditional botnet architectures such as IRC botnet and P2P botnets use push-style communications to exchange commands. The bots join the identified command and control channels to receive the commands from the botmaster, then remain connected to these channels. Such channels can be IRC servers for IRC botnet or other peers for P2P botnets. In contrast, HTTP botnets use pull-style communications to obtain the commands. Instead of being connected permanently to the channels, the bots regularly contact the HTTP C&C servers hosted on different sites in order to get the commands. The commands are embedded in web pages hosted on the C&C servers, and can be retrieved by the bots after requesting corresponding pages. While the HTTP bot does not remain connected to the C&C servers, it visits the corresponding sites on a regular basis, and at a pace defined by the botmaster. Such regularity can be leveraged in detecting the presence of the botnet.

Furthermore, HTTP botnet servers involve fewer web services compared to legitimate web servers. Typical HTTP botnet C&C server will provide a command download only while legitimate sites will support a wide range of services. The request parameters in HTTP C&C tend to be relatively stable or similar (e.g. images used as command files) while a variety of resources will be requested and exchanged in legitimate web communications.

4   Proposed Detection Model

4.1   General Approach

Our proposed detection model leverages the following key characteristics of HTTP botnets:

1. The reliance on pull-style communication model means that the bots initiate connections with the C&C server to get commands and updates. This will require issuing DNS queries, which could be tracked toward detecting the bots.
2. The regularity in the connection timing and characteristics. As connections to the C&C sites typically take place at regular time interval, analyzing the underlying timing information can help detect the presence of the bots.
3. The C&C domain names, selected only for the sole purpose of escaping detection, exhibit characteristics which are glaring departure from legitimate uses of domain names. Legitimate domains tend to be stable and user-friendly, whereas C&C domains are short lived and not intended for human consumption.
4. The extremely limited pool of requested web services by HTTP bots means predictable interaction patterns, which are different from what could be expected from legitimate applications' interactions. Such distinct interaction patterns can be captured in separate application profiles, and used to isolate and detect eventually botnets interactions.

Based on the aforementioned considerations, our approach involves multiple detectors, each capturing specific characteristics of the HTTP botnets. We propose specifically 3 different detectors as follows:

1. Time-series detector: its role is to detect the HTTP botnets by analyzing their timing characteristics.
2. Application detector: its role is to profile the individual applications running on the host based on their DNS interactions. This profile is used as a model to identify suspicious applications which eventually may be flagged as HTTP botnets.
   Domain Mass detector: its role is to analyze the characteristics of the domain names and identify the malicious domains that potentially could be part of the HTTP botnets.

These detectors work independently by extracting separate features from the data and classifying those features using a machine learning classification. We have investigated separately three different classifiers for all detectors, namely: the Random Forests, the J48 Decision Tree, and the Naïve Bayes.

Each of these detectors capture and analyze the packets flows over separate time windows. In our system design, we use time windows of 24 h, 1 min, and 10 min for the application detector, the domain mass detector, and the time-series detector, respectively.

In the sequel, we describe the features space for each of the aforementioned detectors.

4.2   Domain Mass Detector

The domain mass detector analyzes the characteristics of the domain name involved in the DNS queries and attempts to identify malicious domains such as algorithmically generated domains or domains associated with malicious fast flux DNS.

The underlying detection model extracts the following features:

– Total number of queries
– FQDN length (average, standard deviation, variance)
– Number of distinct DNS servers
– Number of geolocations of resolved IP addresses
– Number of A and AAAA records

One of the characteristics which stand out when comparing normal and malicious botnet traffic is the length of the involved domain names. As mentioned earlier, due to the use of DGAs, such domain names disregard basic DNS concepts such as user friendliness.

Normal DNS queries have varying domain lengths, which according to Weymes [17], are typically below 12 characters long. In contrast, botnets queries involving DGAs are often much longer, with limited variation. Therefore, we include in the feature set for the domain detector the *average domain length*, and the corresponding *standard deviation* and *variance* over a packet flow.

A recurring characteristic of a botnet architecture involving DGA is the relatively high number of non-existent internet domain name since the bot generates fake queries in order to evade detection. These fake queries trigger a high number of NXDOMAIN results (i.e. nonexistent domain names). If we consider the number of NXDOMAIN as a feature, it might work well on small networks, however, it may be lacking on larger networks.

Let *ScoreN* be the normalized ratio between the number of NXDOMAIN by the number of NOERROR (i.e. successful queries) observed over a time window, i.e.

$$ScoreN = \frac{(\text{Number of NXDOMAIN})}{(\text{Number of NOERROR}) \times 100}$$

Figure 2 shows the normalized score applied on the normal and malicious traffic samples, respectively. It is observed that there are some clear differences between malicious and non-malicious traffic based on the *ScoreN* metric. Furthermore, it can be noted that the number of DNS queries in the normal traffic is very low compared to the

HTTP botnet traffic, in particular, the ones using DGA and/or malicious fast flux DNS, which is the case for virtually all the existing ones. Indeed, the infected machines do constantly notify their C&C servers in order to update their active status. Also, in leveraging the fast flux techniques, the C&C servers are assigned to domain names with low TTL by the botmaster, which result in constant DNS lookups. Therefore, it can be concluded that the *total number of queries* is a useful indicator of compromise.

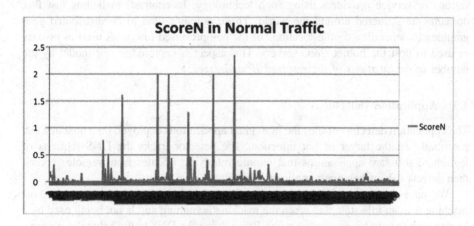

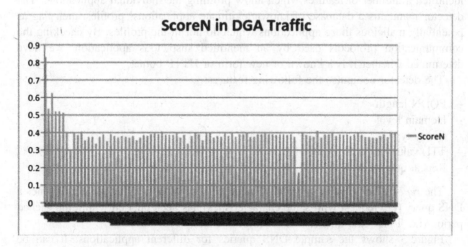

Fig. 2. Normalized ratio (ScoreN) of nonexistent domain over successful queries for normal and DGA traffic samples

The type of queries is also an interesting characteristic. In fact, normal activities have a variety of DNS query types while botnet traffic usually involves the same type of records. Therefore, counting the *total number of A and AAAA* records can be a useful indicator of compromise as well.

Another interesting characteristic is the number of distinct DNS servers found in the queries. Some bot-infected machines attempt to query different DNS servers. Normally, all DNS queries are redirected to the default DNS server set by the network administrator or by the host. Queries which are redirected to different DNS servers may suggest the presence of a malicious behavior.

Legitimate fast flux domains are typically co-located around the same geographic areas, for instance, they can be associated with the data centers operated by organizations or service providers using such technology. In contrast, malicious fast flux domains are scattered around the world. Those domains tend to be distributed geographically depending on the locations of the compromised machines used as proxies or used to host the botnet C&C servers. This aspect is captured in our model by the number *of geolocations of the resolved IP addresses*.

4.3   Application Detector

The application detector profiles the individual applications deployed on a host that can potentially be the target of bot infection. The detector tracks the DNS requests of legitimate software applications that require retrieving updates from remote servers, then detects the misbehaving application profiles.

We have studied the DNS interactions for individual applications when the host machine is in an idle state, i.e. when the machine is running and is not being used by a human user (e.g. to browse on the web). By studying the DNS traffic behavior, we have identified a number of features which allow profiling the individual applications. The detector maintains a database of known/legitimate applications' profiles, then flag as potentially malicious those applications which do not fit the profiles. By checking the communication protocols used by an identified suspicious application, we have determined whether it is a known or new form of HTTP botnet.

The detector computes the following features:

- FQDN length
- Domain level
- Query type
- TTL value
- Repeat query count

The *repeat query count*, one of the features in our model, is the number of times a DNS query (i.e. request with same characteristics) has been queried within the cached period (i.e. TTL – the time it was set to be cached).

Figure 3 shows the sample DNS queries for different applications. It can be observed that specific query pattern is issued at certain times for each application. The query pattern for Skype contains only CNAME queries whereas that for Avast involves only A requests. Likewise, we have used the *query type* as a feature in profiling the individual applications.

The TTL value appears to be a distinct characteristic of each application. By analyzing the sample data, we have noticed that the FQDNs of each application have almost the same TTL cache as shown in Figs. 3 and 4. For instance, all DNS queries of Avast shown in Fig. 3 have a TTL of 299 s, which may be due to the fact that these

7:59:34	192.168.50.14	8.8.8.8	IN	armmf.adobe.com.	CNAME	ssl.adobe.com.edgekey.net.	278
7:59:34	192.168.50.14	8.8.8.8	IN	ssl.adobe.com.edgekey.net.	CNAME	e4578.b.akamaiedge.net.	19922
10:05:00	192.168.50.14	8.8.8.8	IN	ardownload.adobe.com.	CNAME	ardownload.wip4.adobe.com.	10587
10:05:00	192.168.50.14	8.8.8.8	IN	ardownload.wip4.adobe.com.	CNAME	ardownload.adobe.com.edgesui	10
10:04:51	192.168.50.14	8.8.8.8	IN	ssl.adobe.com.edgekey.net.	CNAME	e4578.b.akamaiedge.net.	21460
10:04:51	192.168.50.14	8.8.8.8	IN	armmf.adobe.com.	CNAME	ssl.adobe.com.edgekey.net.	293

(a)   Sample of Skype CNAME Queries

7:39:30 AM	192.168.50.11	8.8.8.8	IN	auth.ff.avast.com.	A	77.234.41.21	299
7:40:43 AM	192.168.50.11	8.8.8.8	IN	vl.ff.avast.com.	A	77.234.41.59	299
7:40:43 AM	192.168.50.11	8.8.8.8	IN	vl.ff.avast.com.	A	77.234.41.53	299
7:40:43 AM	192.168.50.11	8.8.8.8	IN	vl.ff.avast.com.	A	77.234.41.74	299
7:50:00 AM	192.168.50.11	8.8.8.8	IN	su.ff.avast.com.	A	77.234.41.35	299
7:50:00 AM	192.168.50.11	8.8.8.8	IN	su.ff.avast.com.	A	77.234.41.26	299
7:50:00 AM	192.168.50.11	8.8.8.8	IN	su.ff.avast.com.	A	77.234.41.23	299
7:50:00 AM	192.168.50.11	8.8.8.8	IN	su.ff.avast.com.	A	77.234.41.34	299
7:50:00 AM	192.168.50.11	8.8.8.8	IN	su.ff.avast.com.	A	77.234.41.25	299
7:50:00 AM	192.168.50.11	8.8.8.8	IN	su.ff.avast.com.	A	77.234.41.24	299
9:41:17 AM	192.168.50.11	8.8.8.8	IN	ipm-provider.ff.avast.com.	A	77.234.41.88	299
9:41:17 AM	192.168.50.11	8.8.8.8	IN	ipm-provider.ff.avast.com.	A	77.234.41.92	299
9:41:17 AM	192.168.50.11	8.8.8.8	IN	ipm-provider.ff.avast.com.	A	77.234.41.93	299
11:01:23 AM	192.168.50.11	8.8.8.8	IN	vl.ff.avast.com.	A	77.234.41.55	299
11:01:23 AM	192.168.50.11	8.8.8.8	IN	vl.ff.avast.com.	A	77.234.41.56	299

(b)   Sample of Avast A Queries

Fig. 3. Sample of DNS queries for different applications

FQDNs are hosted on the same zone files. The TTL varies from one application to another, but each application has an almost stable number with a very small variation. Including the TTL value to our feature set helps characterizing such behavior.

The *domain level* considered in our feature model is an interesting discriminator between malicious domains and normal domains. As shown in Fig. 3, normal application queries are often structured as third-level domain, fourth-level domain or even more. In contrast, the FQDN queries are usually second-level domains (SLDs). For example, Table 1 shows the C&C servers using the second level domain.

4.4   Time Series Detector

As mentioned earlier, there is some regularity in the timing behavior of the HTTP bots. This is a side effect of the underlying architecture which uses pull-style communications. By analyzing the HTTP botnet traffic sample, we have noticed that almost every bot communicates with its C&C server on a scheduled time. As a result of this action, we have developed a detector that analyzes the DNS traffic flow based on short time interval between two queries. In this period of time, each query can be tracked and different statistical features can be extracted as follows:

- Total number of queries
- Time interval between successive queries (average, standard deviation, and variance)

Figure 5 depicts the average time interval computed over the normal and malicious traffic samples. It can be observed that there is a clear difference in the traffic patterns.

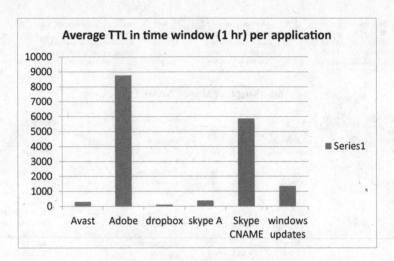

Series1 is the average TTL value

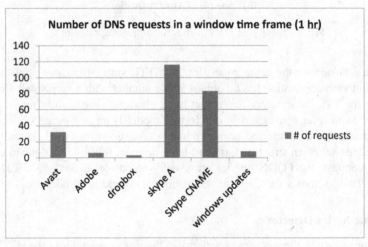

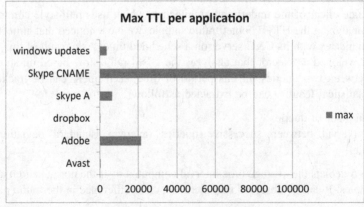

Fig. 4. Number of queries and TTL statistics for different applications over sample traffic

Table 1. Examples of C&C domain names found in HTTP botnet traffic sample

Domain name	Botnet name
mxxywhxoc.cc	Papras Trojan
dyybbsux.cc	Papras Trojan
jmexlakjdk.cc	Papras Trojan
kuhfkadnmaxr.cc	Papras Trojan
saxtostfsa.cc	Papras Trojan
qudjmojvow.cc	Papras Trojan
tqqpteoxlcih.cc	Papras Trojan
cmpzygrl.cc	Papras Trojan

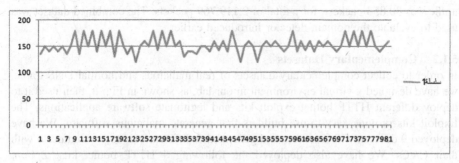

Graph showing average interval time in seconds of botnet DNS queries

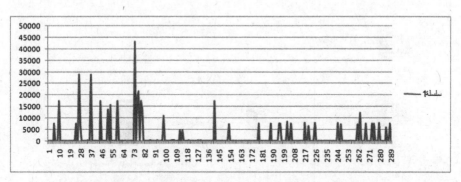

Graph showing average interval time in seconds of Normal DNS queries

Fig. 5. Average time interval over normal traffic vs. malicious traffic samples

5   Experimental Evaluation

5.1   Datasets

Since our proposed models can detect and classify different types of DNS activities, we have collected data from different public sources. However, not all the features considered in our models can be tested using the available public datasets. Therefore, we collected complementary datasets in our lab in order to achieve a full coverage of all the implemented detectors.

5.1.1 Public Datasets

We have acquired malicious traffic data from the Stratosphere IPS Project (https://stratosphereips.org/). This dataset was generated from a 8-days of operation of the Papras Trojan traffic that was running on a Windows XP machine. It contains a number of C&C calls and hard-coded DNS server (instead default DNS). It also contains only malicious traffic. Therefore, we have collected background normal traffic from our lab over three days and merged it with the malicious traffic from the Stratosphere IPS Project.

The size of the malicious dataset was 2,088,916 packets whereas that of the normal traffic was 30,853 packets, for a total of 2,119,769 packets. The combined dataset was used to evaluate the domain detector introduced earlier.

5.1.2 Complementary Datasets

In order to collect complementary datasets of real malicious and normal DNS traffic, we have designed a virtual environment in our lab, as shown in Fig. 6, then used it to deploy different HTTP botnet exploit kits and legitimate software applications. The Exploit kits provide easy-to-use builders that generate malicious software. We have deployed 9 different C&C servers and generated 9 different bots to communicate with their C&Cs. We have also deployed the following 9 HTTP botnet kits: *Zyklon, Blackout, Bluebot, Betabot, Duox, BlackEnergy, Citadel, Zeus*, and *Liyphera*.

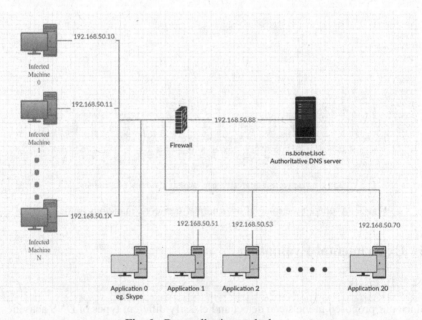

Fig. 6. Data collection testbed

The exploit kits include a bot builder package, which allows us to set certain settings such as the C&C host servers. To collect DNS requests from the deployed exploit kits, the domain name for each botnet was required. Using *bind9*, we have setup an Authoritative-Only DNS server for a domain name *botnet.isot*. The domain is operated locally, and we have assigned each C&C server to a sub domain of *botnet.isot*. Our purpose was to associate the infected machine (e.g. bots) to the domain names so that we can monitor the behavior of outgoing DNS lookups.

For instance, DNS A query of *zeus.botnet.isot* points to 192.168.50.101. For each of the deployed bots, we have assigned the domain names of their C&C servers, not their IP Addresses; otherwise no DNS traffic will be observed. Thus, our design will generate DNS queries according to the exploit kits networking design.

In order to test our proposed *application detector*, we have deployed 20 virtual machines, where each machine was running a specific application. Applications used during our data collection include Anti-Virus applications (MalwareByte, ByteFence, AVG), online chatting and instant messaging applications (Skype, Facebook Messenger), Internet Browsing Applications (Firefox, Chrome), and e-mail client applications (eM Client, Thunderbird), and other applications such as Adobe reader, Photoshop, and Dropbox. While each application was running, we captured their DNS traffic only. Among all the 20 applications that were deployed, only 16 of them generated the DNS traffic. These machines were deployed for 7 days. After collection, we eliminated background traffic such as Microsoft updates. We used a tool called PassiveDNS to parse the collected pcap files passively, and then used our own python-based tool to normalize and label the data according to the corresponding application. The collected applications data consisted of 56,190 DNS packets.

In order to evaluate the time series detector, we have deployed 9 different botnets to generate real botnet DNS traffic. The botnets ran for 5 days, and generated a total of 264,005 malicious DNS records. We also generated real normal DNS traffic in our experiment. The normal DNS capture ran for 3 days from one single machine while the botnet traffic came from 9 different infected machines. The total number of normal DNS traffic was 18,476 DNS records, yielding a dataset of 282,481 DNS packets in total.

5.2   Evaluation Results

As mentioned earlier, we studied 3 different classifiers, namely, Random Forests, J48 decision tree, and Naïve Bayes. We used an open source machine learning library for the Python programming language, which is called Scikit-learn. Each of the detectors ran using each of the aforementioned classifiers separately against the datasets described earlier. We ran each algorithm using a 10-fold cross validation, where in each run, the algorithm was trained on 90% of the data and 10% of the data was left for testing purpose. The results obtained are described in the sequel.

5.2.1   Domain Detector Evaluation
Table 2 shows the performance obtained for the domain detector. Random Forest shows promising results of 99.3% accuracy with 0.2% false positive rate.

Table 2. Domain detector evaluation results

Algorithm	Detection rate (%)	False positive rate (%)	Accuracy (%)
Gaussian Naïve Bayes	94.1	0.0	95.8
Random forest	99.2	0.2	99.3
Decision tree	99.2	0.3	99.3

The Gaussian Naïve Bayes (NB) achieved a lower performance compared to that of other classifiers. For instance, it has achieved a detection rate lower than that of the Random Forests by 4%. The Decision tree also showed a relatively better performance compared to the Gaussian NB, but not as good as that of the Random Forests.

5.2.2 Application Detector Evaluation

In the evaluation of the application detector, the traffic from known applications is flagged as normal whereas the traffic from unknown applications is considered malicious. In addition to the custom dataset collected in our lab which consists of HTTP botnets and known applications, we have also used the public malicious DGA traffic from stratosphereips.org.

It should be noted that the web browsing DNS traffic were excluded in our analysis because browsing traffic are generated from browsing, not from an active running application. Our detection is limited to any application running on the host machine, except web browsing. We did not considered the browsing data because such data is generated by human activities (non-automated). We make a distinction between data generated by a web browser application on its own such as getting updates (which is considered in our dataset) from data generated by a user browsing the web using such application. Table 3 summarizes the performance results that were obtained.

Table 3. Application detector evaluation results

Algorithm	Detection rate (%)	False positive rate (%)	Accuracy (%)
Gaussian Naïve Bayes	6.18	2.44	50.35
Random forests	94.85	3.90	95.44
Decision tree	95.50	6.37	94.58

The obtained results consist of a detection rate of 94% and a false positive rate of 6.37% when using the decision tree algorithm. The random forests achieved an even better performance, yielding a detection rate of 95% and a FPR of 3.90%.

5.2.3 Time Series Detector

Table 4 depicts the evaluation results obtained for the time series detector. The Decision tree and Random Forests show promising results on average, achieving over 99% accuracy with very low false positive rates at 0.8% and 0.4%, respectively. The Gaussian Naïve Bayes performed relatively poorly.

Table 4. Application Detector Evaluation Results

Algorithm	Accuracy (%)	Detection rate (%)	False positive rate (%)
Random forests	99.5	99.5	0.4
Decision tree	99.3	99.5	0.8
Gaussian Naïve Bayes	68.1	99.9	85.9

6 Conclusion

The HTTP botnet is much easier to develop and deploy compared to P2P and IRC botnets. Furthermore, due to the prevalence of HTTP communications, HTTP bots can evade the detection by using common HTTP ports, which are typically unfiltered by most firewalls. As a result, the detection of this type of botnet can be very challenging. In this paper, three different detection models have been designed, which perform relatively well on their own in detecting various types of HTTP botnets. However, each of these detectors operate using different time windows, ranging from short to longer time windows. Therefore, they can be considered as complementary detectors instead of competing ones. We have studied three different classifiers for each of the proposed detectors. Experimental results have shown that the Random Forests yielded the best performance, with the Decision tree coming as a close second. The Gaussian Naïve Bayes performed poorly.

As future work, we plan to investigate how the proposed detectors can be integrated effectively in a multi-detector framework so that the detection accuracy is maximized. We also plan to investigate how these detectors operate when confronted with new forms of HTTP botnets unseen at the training time.

References

1. Antonakakis, M., Perdisci, R., Dagon D., Lee W., Feamster, N.: Building a dynamic reputation system for DNS. In: The Proceedings of 19th USENIX Security Symposium (USENIX Security 2010) (2010)
2. Bilge, L., Sen, S., Balzarotti, D., Kirda, E., Kruegel, C.: Exposure: a passive DNS analysis service to detect and report malicious domains. ACM Trans. Inf. Syst. Secur. (TISSEC) **16**(4), 14 (2014)
3. Cai, T., Zou, F.: Detecting HTTP botnet with clustering network traffic. In: Proceedings of the 8th Conference Wireless Communications, Networking and Mobile Computing, pp. 1–7, September 2012
4. Chaware, S.P., Bhingarkar, S.: A survey of HTTP botnet detection. Int. Res. J. Eng. Technol. (IRJET) **3**(1), 713–714 (2016)
5. da Luz, P.M.: Botnet detection using passive DNS. Master thesis, Department of Computing Science Radboud University Nijmegen (2013/2014)
6. Fedynyshyn, G., Chuah, M.C., Tan, G.: Detection and classification of different botnet C&C channels. In: Calero, J.M.A., Yang, L.T., Mármol, F.G., García Villalba, L.J., Li, A.X., Wang, Y. (eds.) ATC 2011. LNCS, vol. 6906, pp. 228–242. Springer, Heidelberg (2011). doi:10.1007/978-3-642-23496-5_17

7. Garasia, S.S., Rana, D.P., Mehta, R.G.: HTTP botnet detection using frequent pattern set mining. Int. J. Eng. Sci. Adv. Technol. **2**(3), 619–624 (2012)

8. Haddadi, F., Morgan, J., Filho, E.G., Zincir-Heywood, A.N.: Botnet behaviour analysis using IP Flows with HTTP filters using classifiers. In: 2014 28th International Conference on Advanced Information Networking and Applications Workshops, pp. 7–12 (2014)

9. Khillari, A., Augustine, A.: HTTP-based botnet detection technique using Apriori algorithm with actual time duration. Int. J. Comput. Eng. Appl. **XI**(III), 13–18 (2017)

10. Piscitello, D.: Monitor DNS Traffic & You Just Might Catch A RAT. Dark Reading, UBM Technology, 6 December 2014. http://www.darkreading.com/attacks-breaches/monitor-dns-traffic-and-you-just-might-catch-a-rat/a/d-id/1269593. Accessed 27 June 2017

11. Nazario, J., Holz, T.: As the net churns: fast-flux botnet observations. In: 3rd International Conference on Malicious and Unwanted Software, MALWARE 2008. IEEE, 7–8 October 2008. doi:10.1109/MALWARE.2008.4690854

12. Sood, A.K., Zeadally, S., Enbody, R.J.: An empirical study of HTTP-based financial botnets. IEEE Trans. Dependable Secure Comput. **13**, 236–251 (2016). doi:10.1109/TDSC.2014.2382590

13. Tyagi, R., Paul, T., Manoj, B.S., Thanudas, B.: A novel HTTP botnet traffic detection method. In: IEEE INDICON (2015)

14. Tyagi, A.K., Nayeem, S.: Detecting HTTP botnet using Artificial Immune System (AIS). Int. J. Appl. Inf. Syst. (IJAIS) **2**(6) (2012). ISSN: 2249-0868. Foundation of Computer Science FCS, New York, USA

15. Kirubavathi Venkatesh, G., Anitha Nadarajan, R.: HTTP botnet detection using adaptive learning rate multilayer feed-forward neural network. In: Askoxylakis, I., Pöhls, H.C., Posegga, J. (eds.) WISTP 2012. LNCS, vol. 7322, pp. 38–48. Springer, Heidelberg (2012). doi:10.1007/978-3-642-30955-7_5

16. Weimer, F.: Passive DNS replication. In: Proceedings of 1st Conference on Computer Security Incident, Singapore (2005)

17. Weymes, B.: DNS anomaly detection: defend against sophisticated malware, 28 May 2013. https://www.helpnetsecurity.com/2013/05/28/dns-anomaly-detection-defend-against-sophisticated-malware/. Accessed 28 June 2017

18. Zhao, D., Traore, I., Sayed, B., Lu, W., Saad, S., Ghorbani, A., Garant, D.: Botnet detection based on traffic behavior analysis and flow intervals. Elsevier J. Comput. Secur. **39**, 2–16 (2013)

19. Zhao, D., Traore, I.: P2P botnet detection through malicious fast flux network identification. In: 7th International Conference on P2P, Parallel, Grid, Cloud, and Internet Computing - 3PGCIC 2012, 12–14 November 2012, Victoria, BC, Canada (2012)

Detecting Broad Length Algorithmically Generated Domains

Aashna Ahluwalia[1], Issa Traore[1(✉)], Karim Ganame[2],
and Nainesh Agarwal[3]

[1] ECE Department, University of Victoria, Victoria, BC, Canada
aashnaa@uvic.ca, itraore@ece.uvic.ca
[2] StreamScan, 2300 Rue Sherbrooke E, Montreal, QC, Canada
ganame@streamscan.io
[3] BC Provincial Government, Victoria, Canada
nainesh.agarwal@gov.bc.ca

Abstract. Domain generation algorithm (DGA) represents a safe haven for modern botnets, as it enables them to escape detection. Due to the fact that DGA domains are generated randomly, they tend to be unusually long, which can be leveraged toward detecting them. Shorter DGA domains, in contrast, are more difficult to detect, as most legitimate domains are relatively short. We introduce in this paper, a new detection model that uses information theoretic features, and leverage the notion of domain length threshold to detect dynamically and transparently DGA domains regardless of their lengths. Experimental evaluation of the approach using public datasets yields detection rate (DR) of 98.96% and false positive rate (FPR) of 2.1%, when using random forests classification technique.

Keywords: HTTP botnet · Botnet detection · Machine learning · Passive DNS · DGA domains · Malicious fast flux DNS · Domain length

1 Introduction

Botnets are considered to be one of the biggest online threats today [11]. Cyber criminals are controlling malware infected networks through command–and–control servers (C&C). It is quite challenging to capture bot behaviour due to its dynamic nature and fluxing IP addresses [12].

To evade blacklisting, modern botnets, such as HTTP botnets, are taking advantage of various Domain Generation Algorithms (DGAs). The DGAs embedded in the malware generate on a regular basis large amounts of pseudo-random domain names in a short period of time. The domains are generated based on seeds known only by the bots and the C&C servers, while the bot-master will typically register and activate only one or a handful of these domains. Reverse engineering such large volumes of non-existent algorithmically generated domain names is extremely time-consuming, resource intensive with low success rates, making detection harder.

A key characteristic of Algorithmically Generated Domains (AGD) is their length, which is unusually greater than Human Generated Domains (HGD). As a result, most

© Springer International Publishing AG 2017
I. Traore et al. (Eds.): ISDDC 2017, LNCS 10618, pp. 19–34, 2017.
https://doi.org/10.1007/978-3-319-69155-8_2

existing DGA detection schemes have been centered around length detection [4, 10]. However, several recent DGA strains have been using shorter domains lengths, which are indistinguishable in length from legitimate domains, making their detection much harder.

We study in this work the impact of length on DGA domains detection performance, and propose a simple adaptive model, which uses different feature models based on length threshold value. Our approach involves studying significant features from domain names that can help correctly distinguish between AGDs and HGDs. The features are extracted based on lexical and linguistic characteristics of the domain names. Information theoretic measures of domain characteristics are computed and used to detect broad range of DGAs regardless of the domain length. The extracted features are classified using machine learning. We investigated two different classification techniques, namely, Random Forests and Decision Tree. Experimental evaluation on public DGA datasets and (legitimate) Alexa top domains, yields for random forests, the best performing of both algorithms, detection rate (DR) of 98.96% and false positive rate (FPR) of 2.1%.

The remaining sections are structured as follows. Section 2 is a review of related works. Section 3 introduces our proposed approach and models. Section 4 presents the experiments conducted to study the impact of length on performance, and evaluates our proposed detection scheme. Section 5 makes concluding remarks and discusses future work.

2   Related Works

Several works have been published in the literature on DGA detection. We review and discuss a sample of closely related work in the following.

Antonakakis *et al.* [1] developed Pleiades, a DGA-detection system that uses few important statistical features to translate DNS NXDomains subsets to feature vectors. Such features include splitting domain name into various levels and distribution of n-grams. Few structural features like number of domain levels, length of domains and number of unique top-level domains are calculated. They also discuss character entropy calculation across various domain levels as a feature. The approach was evaluated experimentally using a dataset consisting of 30,000 DGA domains from the malware families Conficker, Murofet, Bobax and Sinowal. Also, 20,000 normal domain names from Alexa were used for training and testing of the DGA Classifier. The Hidden Markov Model (HMM) was used for classification and the results obtained were fairly good, with TPR around 91% and FPR of 3%.

Ma *et al.* [2] introduced a lightweight approach to classify URLs using lexical as well as host-based features. They consider lexical features of the URL such as length, number of dots, special characters in the URL path, etc., and label them as tokens. These tokens are collected and preserved for different categories like hostname, URL path and Top-level-domains (TLD). The extracted features are processed using machine learning classification. Three different classifiers were studied including Naïve Bayes, Logistic regression and Support Vector machine (SVM). Experimental evaluation was conducted across 20,000 to 30,000 URLs drawn from different sources, achieving prediction accuracy of 95–99%.

Wang and Shirley proposed in [9] an approach to detect malicious domains using word segmentation to derive tokens from domain names. The proposed feature space includes the number of characters, digits, and hyphens. Each set of features were calculated for 291,623 domains from a dataset collected over cellular network. Experimentally they were able to compile a list of 30 most referenced words and created a probability model for the words based on the Google N corpus by Norvig [5]. This is an interesting approach as it helps understand what words in the malicious domain can attract users. Hence this system can be used to monitor and analyse new words being used by malicious domains. Classification was done using logistic regression models, providing more meaningful associations between the features and domain maliciousness, thus improving prediction accuracy.

Schiavoni *et al.* [7] proposed the Phoenix model, which attempts to discover previously unknown DGAs and helps tracking DGA-based command–and–control centers over time, using linguistic features like meaningful character ratio and n-gram normality score. The Phoenix model was evaluated on 1,153,516 domains and resulted in prediction accuracy of about 94.8%.

McGrath and Gupta highlighted in [3] that Phishing URLs and domains possess different characteristics than normal domains and URLs. They found, for instance, that phishing domains used fewer vowels and fewer unique characters compared to normal ones. They proposed a detection model for malicious domains focused on comparison based on domain lengths (excluding Top-level-domains) and character frequencies of English language alphabets. The proposed model was studied experimentally using a dataset consisting of over 9 million unique URLs and 2.7 million unique effective second-level domain names. The focus of the work was essentially on identifying the characteristics of phishing. No concrete detection model was proposed. However, the characteristics can serve as useful basis for constructing adequate feature space for DGA domains detection.

Yadav *et al.* [8] have developed their detection methodology by studying patterns of lexical characteristics of domain names. Their study involves analysing distribution of alphanumeric characters to distinguish between normal and malicious domains. They believe unigram or single characters are not enough, hence bigrams are taken into account. They employ statistical measures like KL-divergence, Jaccard index and Levenshtein edit distance for classifying a group of domains. These domains included a set of legitimate domain names obtained via a crawl of IPv4 address space as well as DNS traffic from a Tier-1 ISP in Asia. They used malicious dataset consisting of domain names generated by recent botnets and domains generated by a tool, that produces English pronounceable words not present in the dictionary. The main contribution of their work is to have shown empirically that in detecting AGDs, metrics such as Jaccard index performs best, followed by Edit distance metrics, and then KL divergence.

Mowbray and Hagen [4] designed a procedure to detect unusual length distribution of second-level domains (2LDs). Features used by their approach are counts of individual character, character n-grams, dots, hyphens, digits, uppercase, lowercase and length. The paper also addresses the need to identify newer DGAs than just using machine learning to classify based on pre-existing malicious samples. By running the proposed model on DNS query dataset collected over 5 days at an enterprise network, they were able to detect 19 different Domain Generation Algorithms, including nine new ones.

Sharifnya and Abadi [6] developed a reputation system to classify hosts as malicious or non malicious. They built a system that can be used for real-time analysis of hosts producing large number of suspicious domain names or numerous failed DNS queries. These characteristics help build a suspicious matrix and assign a reputation score. Hosts with higher negative score are considered malicious. Evaluation using DNS query data indicate improving detection and false positive rates, over time.

While length was considered in one way or another in the existing literature, there has not been a systematic focus on how to alleviate its impact on DGA domains detection accuracy. Our work tackles this challenge.

3 Proposed Approach and Models

3.1 Approach Overview

Every domain name hierarchy is composed of a Top level domain (TLD) and a Second level domain (SLD) directly below it. TLD is the part of the domain name located to the right of the dot ("."). The most common TLDs are .com, .net, .org, .gov, .biz, .info and .ws. A domain name is a sequence of labels separated by dots. For example, in the domain www.isot.ece.uvic.ca, .ca is the TLD, *uvic* is the second-level domain (SLD) of the .ca TLD, while *isot* is a third-level domain (3LD).

The essence of domain names, originally, include memorability and friendliness. As such, the overwhelming majority of legitimate domain names convey specific information, which makes sense to humans, and makes it easy for them to grasp or remember the underlying concept. In contrast, AGDs are generated for the sole purpose of evading detection. As they are used for the consumption of bots, which are automated processes, the aforementioned (human) expectations are irrelevant. As such the conveyance of any meaningful information, beyond hosts referencing, is unnecessary. As a result, not only typical AGDs lack friendliness, the amount of information involved tend to be minimal. Our approach consists of measuring the amount of information carried by the name, and then treating the lack of meaningful information as suspicious. We measure the amount of information conveyed by the domain by analyzing character n-grams and computing the corresponding entropy. At the same, we leverage basic lexical and linguistic characteristics of the domain names which have proven effective at detecting DGAs, and are also a by-product of the underlying random structure. One such characteristic which has proven effective, while at some time being elusive is the domain length. We study the impact of length on detection accuracy, and leverage such knowledge to develop a simple detection model that uses the notion of length threshold to alleviate its impact on accuracy.

3.2 Basic Features Model

A common characteristic of early AGDs was their length. According to Weymes [10], in general, legitimate domain names are below 12 characters long, while AGDs are often much longer. In this perspective, the *Length* can be considered as a key feature in identifying DGA domains. However, as shown in Table 1, some of the recent malware have started generated shorter DGA domain names, which makes it difficult to distinguish them from legitimate domains (see Table 2 for samples).

Table 1. Sample DGA domain names with corresponding malware

Short DGA domains (length 5–7)	Long DGA domains (length 12–30)
jaorw.com - Cryptolocker	lhxmfkhppoww.com - Tinba
conxyb.cc - Zeus	uocwkscmkwwmkomc.org - Ramdo
klvupgfm.biz - Conficker	gmacsmsgecquasam.org - Ramdo
azrvtgf.net - Cryptolocker	mcgakswwegmeuwma.org -Ramdo
jltkyg.com - Cryptolocker	stabletiredflowerwardisappointed.com - Matsnu
pbfxmi.biz - Cryptolocker	herequiresassembledcircumstances.com - Rovnix
bfuqnb.info - Zeus	thatunanimoushiswarcorrespondence.com- Rovnix
dvlnrl.ws - Zeus	nzzhyhemzswcyrwpzjztdmbyptktk.ru - GameOver Zeus
vkdjisc.com - Conficker	uvgxmjeiucrkeqcmaeuokzganjjbvo.ru - GameOver Zeus
uhbqolxf.org - Conficker	eminpvkskrdygqphyhhypfahm.ru - GameOver Zeus

Table 2. Sample legitimate domain names from Alexa.com

Legitimate Domain Names
google.com
baidu.com
wikipedia.org
stackoverflow.com
taobao.com
sina.com.cn
bing.com
yandex.ru
hao123.com
instagram.com
9gag.com
americanexpress.com
adnetworkperformance.com

Likewise, the primary primitive feature in our model is the **Length** for a given domain. This is calculated by counting all the characters in the domain name excluding the TLD. Additional primitive features that capture linguistic and structural characteristics of the domain name, considered in our model include the following:

- **Vowels:** This feature is calculated by counting the number of vowels in the second level domain name (SLD) only.
- **Consonants:** Similarly, as above, this is the count of the consonants present in the second level domain name.
- **Digits:** The count of digits in the second level domain name.

Figure 1 illustrates the distribution of the basic features from a dataset consisting of 20,000 domain names, with 10,000 DGA and 10,000 normal domain names. The distributions indicate strong capability of these basic features to discriminate legitimate domains from malicious DGA domains. Therefore, using the aforementioned basic features model, and simple statistical techniques, we can achieve encouraging detection capability.

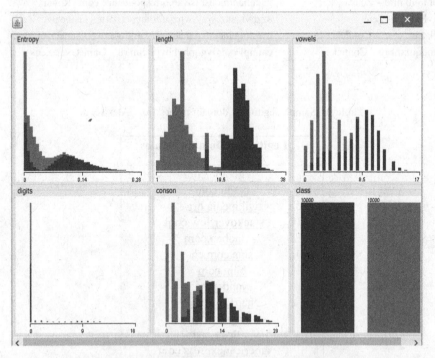

Fig. 1. Basic features distributions based on 50:50 mix of legitimate and DGA data; the blue represents the legitimate domains subset while the red is the DGA subset. (Color figure online)

3.3 Domain Name N-gram Entropy

The aforementioned basic features capture the idiosyncrasies of DGA domains names. But as mentioned earlier, an important characteristic of DGA domains is the lack of meaningful information involved. The amount of information can be calculated by the entropy.

By analyzing sample domain names, we found out that the entropy can be sensitive to the domain length. It is effective mainly for longer domains, and tend to struggle for shorter ones. Such sensitivity can be alleviated, by analyzing domain n-gram frequency subject to the length, in other words, the conditional probability with respect to the domain length.

Therefore, our feature model involves 6 features: the aforementioned 4 primitive features, and two advanced features consisting of the domain n-gram entropy and conditional probability. Analysis of different kinds of n-grams on sample data showed that n = 3 yields better results. So, we analyze and use trigrams in our feature model.

We compute the domain trigram entropy using word segmentation. First, we extract the SLD of domain d, and for each SLD we compute the entropy of the domain based on the trigram frequency. We derive trigram frequencies from the Google n-corpus. Google n-corpus is a large database created to help machine learning initiatives across the world [5]. It has English language words and their respective n-gram counts, such as two, three, four or five-letter word sequences.

Let $trigram(d)$ denote the set of all trigrams involved in SLD of domain d, and $Trigram(n\text{-}corpus)$ be the set of all trigrams involved in the n-corpus.

Given trigram $t_r \in trigram(d)$, let $count(t_r, n\text{-corpus})$ denote its occurrence count based on the (Google) n-corpus.

The occurrence probability for trigram t_r for domain d is calculated as follows:

$$P(t_r) = \frac{count(t_r, n\text{-corpus})}{\sum_{x_r \in Trigram(n\text{-}corpus)} count(x_r, n\text{-corpus})} \tag{1}$$

The entropy of domain d, denoted $H(d)$ is computed as follows:

$$H(d) = - \sum_{t_r \in trigram(d)} P(t_r) \log(P(t_r)) \tag{2}$$

A trigram may occur more than once, say n times in a domain name. Then probability of occurrence of the trigram in the domain is considered $n \times f$, where f is the frequency of occurrence of the trigram.

3.4 Domain Name N-gram Conditional Probability

As mentioned earlier, we noticed that the entropy values for domain length around some threshold value of l are very close for DGAs and legitimate domain names. This makes it difficult to distinguish between them. Hence, conditional probability is a parameter that takes into consideration the domain length.

The conditional probability $P(Y|X)$ quantifies the outcome of a random variable Y given that the value of another random variable X is known.

Let l be the domain length threshold. Let L denote the list of domains from the training datasets having length lesser of equal to l:

$$L = \{d : D | d.length \leq l\} \tag{3}$$

We consider separate domain subsets for positive and negative samples (i.e. DGA and normal). But as the process is the same in both cases; we will describe only one case.

For a given domain d ($d \in L$), let $trigram(d)$ be the set of corresponding trigrams. Let $Trigram(L)$ denote the set of all trigrams in L: $Trigram(L) = \bigcup_{d \in L} trigram(d)$.

Given a trigram t_r in $Trigram(L)$, let $count(t_r, L)$ denote the total occurrence number of t_r in $Trigram(L)$. The conditional probability of trigram t_r with respect to length l is calculated as follows:

$$P(t_r | l) = \frac{count(t_r, L)}{|Trigram(L)|} \tag{4}$$

where $|Trigram(L)|$ denote the size (or cardinality) of $Trigram(L)$.

The conditional probability of domain d with respect to length l is calculated as follows:

$$P(d|l) = \sum_{t_r \epsilon trigram(d)} P(t_r | l) \tag{5}$$

3.5 DGA Domains Detection Model

Our detection model consists of extracting the aforementioned features and classifying them using machine learning. We investigated two different classification techniques in our detection approach. Specifically, the following classification techniques were considered:

- J48 decision tree
- Random Forests algorithm.

We used the Weka machine learning tools to simulate the aforementioned classifiers. Weka is a collection of machine learning algorithms for data mining tasks. It contains tools for data pre-processing, classification, regression, clustering, association rules, and visualization.

We studied the impact of using each of the features separately and by grouping them in different subsets. The combination of all the features yield the best performance. However, a naïve combination, where all the features are grouped and used equally in a straightforward way is sensitive to the length of the domains, and yield reduced performance for shorter domains. We refer to this feature model as the "naïve model". We propose a simple alternate model, which uses different feature model based on whether the domain is greater or smaller than some length threshold value l. We refer to this model as the "split model", and it can be summarized as follows:

If (domain.length < l) then use (vowels, consonants, digits, conditional probability)

Else use (vowels, consonants, digits, conditional probability, entropy)

Our experiments show that the "split model" is less sensitive to the domain length, and yields much improved performance compared to the "naïve model".

4 Experiments

4.1 Datasets

We used in this work a global dataset of 100,000 legitimate domains consisting of legitimate domain names from alexa.com, and a dataset of 100,000 DGA domains, giving a complete dataset of 200,000 domain names.

4.2 Domain Length Impact Study

In order to assess the impact of the domain length on detection performance, we run several experiments using different length threshold values. We run these experiments over different feature subsets.

Given a feature subset, we vary the length threshold denoted l, and measure the detection performance for decision tree and random forests classifiers, respectively.

We conducted the experiments using a subset Δ of our global dataset consisting of 40,000, with a mix of 50% DGAs and 50% legitimate domains. In each run of the experiment for length threshold l, the subset $\Delta(l) = \{d \in \Delta | d.length \leq l\}$ (of the domains of length smaller than or equal to l) is used for training and testing.

We run each of the aforementioned experiments using 10-fold cross validation. We split the input dataset $\Delta(l)$ into 10 subsets of data. In each validation run, we train the machine learning classifier on all but one of the subsets, and then evaluate the model on the subset that was not used for training.

The first experiment was run varying length threshold l on dataset $\Delta(l)$, using as feature the domain trigram entropy only. Tables 3 and 4 show the performance obtained for J48 decision tree and random forests, respectively.

Table 3. Performance of J48 decision tree on domain trigram entropy only-model, when varying length threshold (experiment 1)

Length	Detection rate (%)	FP rate (%)
6	82.7	17.3
7	87	13
8	89.55	10.5
9	91.55	8.5
10	93.05	7

Table 4. Performance of Random Forests on domain trigram entropy only-model, when varying length threshold (experiment 1)

Length	Detection rate (%)	FP rate (%)
6	78.1	21.9
7	81.65	18.4
8	84.35	15.7
9	88.95	11.1
10	90.55	9.5

It can be noted in both cases that the performance improves as the domain length increases.

The second experiment was run under the same condition as previously, but this time using the domain trigram conditional probability as only feature. Tables 5 and 6 show the performance obtained for J48 decision tree and random forests, respectively.

Table 5. Performance of J48 decision tree on domain trigram conditional probability only-model, when varying length threshold (experiment 2)

Length	Detection rate (%)	FP rate (%)
6	85.15	14.9
7	90.05	10
8	91.8	8.2
9	92.45	7.6
10	94	6

Table 6. Performance of Random Forests on domain trigram conditional probability only-model, when varying length threshold (experiment 2)

Length	Detection rate (%)	FP rate (%)
6	85.15	14.9
7	90	10
8	91.35	8.7
9	92	8
10	94.25	5.8

We can notice that like in the previous experiment as the length threshold increases the accuracy of the detector improves. However, it can also be noted that the use of conditional probability alone achieves improved performance compared to using entropy alone.

The third experiment was run by varying length threshold l on dataset $\Delta(l)$, using our basic feature model (i.e. number of digits, number of consonants, and number of vowels) and the domain trigram entropy, excluding the domain trigram conditional probability. Tables 7 and 8 show the performance obtained for J48 decision tree and random forests, respectively.

Table 7. Performance of J48 decision tree on basic features and domain trigram entropy, excluding domain trigram conditional probability, when varying length threshold (experiment 3)

Length	Detection rate (%)	FP rate (%)
6	87.42	13.4
7	89.19	10.9
8	92.381	7.8
9	93.5	6.5
10	94.043	5.9

Table 8. Performance of Random Forests on basic features and domain trigram entropy, excluding domain trigram conditional probability, when varying length threshold (experiment 3)

Length	Detection rate (%)	FP rate (%)
6	82.98	17.7
7	87.52	12.6
8	91.09	9
9	92.75	7.3
10	93.88	6.2

The combined model achieves some improvement for the decision tree, but the opposite occurs for random forests. So it can be said no clear cut improvement is achieved by excluding the conditional probability.

The fourth experiment was run under the same condition as above, but this time using our basic feature model (i.e. number of digits, number of consonants, and number of vowels) and the domain trigram conditional probability, excluding the domain trigram entropy. Tables 9 and 10 show the performance obtained for J48 decision tree and random forests, respectively.

Table 9. Performance of J48 decision tree on basic features and domain trigram conditional probability, excluding domain trigram entropy, when varying length threshold (experiment 4)

Length	Detection rate (%)	FP rate (%)
6	89	11
7	90.9	9.1
8	93.2	6.8
9	93.1	6.9
10	95.6	4.5

Table 10. Performance of Random Forests on basic features and domain trigram conditional probability, excluding domain trigram entropy, when varying length threshold (experiment 4)

Length	Detection rate (%)	FP rate (%)
6	88.35	11.7
7	90.2	9.8
8	92.8	7.2
9	93.3	6.7
10	94.45	5.6

We can notice a notable improvement when using conditional probability and the basic features over when using entropy and the basic features model. There is also slight improvement when using conditional probability and the basic features over when using conditional probability only.

The fifth experiment was run using all features (i.e. basic features + entropy + conditional probability). We refer to this model as the "naive" model, as it combines the features without any particular transformation or restrictions. Tables 11 and 12 show the performance obtained for J48 decision tree and random forests, respectively. There is a slight improvement in performance over the previous experiments. This is also highlighted by Fig. 2, which depicts the ROC curves outlining the performances for the different experiments. The combined "naive" model achieves better performance over the other models involving a subset of the features, with Random Forests coming as best performing algorithm.

Table 11. Performance of J48 decision tree on all features combined (basic features, domain trigram conditional probability, and domain trigram entropy), when varying length threshold (experiment 5)

Length	Detection rate (%)	FP rate (%)
6	89.1	10.9
7	91.95	8.1
8	93.7	6.3
9	93.9	6.1
10	94.9	5.1

Table 12. Performance of random forests on all features combined (basic features, domain trigram conditional probability, and domain trigram entropy), when varying length threshold (experiment 5)

Length	Detection rate (%)	FP rate (%)
6	88.05	12
7	90.55	9.5
8	93.9	6.1
9	94.25	5.8
10	95.55	4.5

4.3 Split Model Study

Our split model relies on the consideration that the domain entropy does not contribute much for short domain length. So for short domains, the basic features and the domain trigram probability is used as feature model, while for longer domain names, all the features are used. The split is controlled by a length threshold. We studied different values by varying the length threshold using the same dataset of 40,000 domains as in the previous subsection. Tables 13, 14, 15 and 16 show the performance obtained when

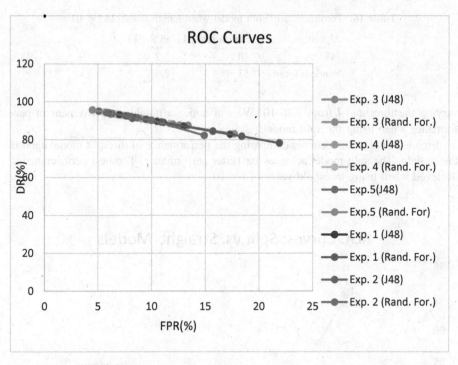

Fig. 2. ROC curves illustrating the performances obtained by varying the length thresholds with different features models.

Table 13. Performance of split model when length threshold l = 7

Algorithm	Detection rate (%)	FPR (%)
J48	95.59	4.45
Random forest	96.68	3.4

Table 14. Performance of split model when length threshold l = 8

Algorithm	Detection rate (%)	FPR (%)
J48	95.59	4.2
Random forest	96.81	3.2

Table 15. Performance of split model when length threshold l = 9

Algorithm	Detection rate (%)	FPR (%)
J48	96.82	3.3
Random forest	97.21	2.9

Table 16. Performance of split model when length threshold l = 10

Algorithm	Detection rate (%)	FPR (%)
J48	97.10	3.2
Random forest	97.53	2.6

varying the threshold l from 7 to 10. We can notice a notable improvement in performance when using the split model.

Figure 3 depict ROC curves comparing the performance of the split model against the straight. The split model achieves far better performance. The best performance is achieved when using threshold value of l = 10.

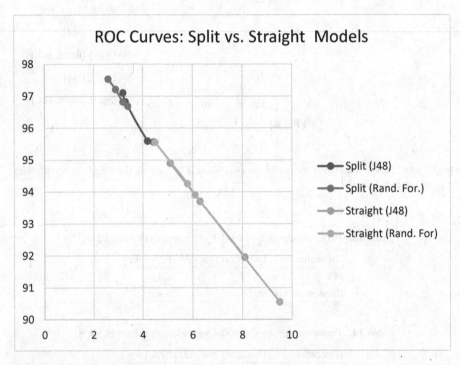

Fig. 3. ROC curves comparing the performances of the split model against the combined or straight model obtained when varying the length threshold values.

We run the split model using threshold l = 10 on a larger dataset consisting of 200,000 domain names, with 50% legitimate domains and 50% DGA domains. We run the experiment using 5-fold cross validation. Table 17 outlines the average performance obtained, which confirms and even slightly improves the performance shown in Table 16, which was obtained on a smaller dataset.

Table 17. Performance of split model on large dataset (200,00 domains) and threshold l = 10

Algorithm	Detection rate (%)	FPR (%)
J48	97.33	2.95
Random forest	98.96	2.10

Tables 18 and 19 show the performance of the algorithms on the two upper and lower partitions of the dataset (i.e. domains of length smaller than 10, and domains of length greater or equal 10).

Table 18. Performance of split model on large dataset – subset of domains of length < 10

Algorithm	Detection rate (%)	FPR (%)
J48	95.72	4.4
Random forest	99.24	0.7

Table 19. Performance of split model on large dataset – subset of domains of length ≥ 10

Algorithm	Detection rate (%)	FPR (%)
J48	98.94	1.5
Random forest	98.69	1.4

The Random forests algorithm achieves the best performance, and it performs almost similarly on shorter and longer domains. So the split model allows smooth transition, in quasi transparent way.

5 Conclusion

Modern botnets, such as HTTP botnets, heavily use AGDs as one of the preferred methods to evade detection. DGA-based malware try to contact C&C servers more than thousands of times in a day. The DGA domains are short-lived and difficult to blacklist. Hence it is very important to recognise the unique characteristics of DGA domains as part of any comprehensive strategy to detect botnets. Reverse engineering the Domain Generation Algorithm is a very tedious and difficult task, hence it is important to detect the generated domains themselves in a timely and efficient manner.

As a result of experimentation, we can say that *Length* is an extremely important factor in determining if the domain is normal or DGA-based. In this work, we can see that for domains with length below some threshold value, the characteristics of normal and DGA domains are very similar and as such, are difficult to distinguish. We developed in this work a simple model that uses information theoretic metric and length threshold value as pivot to transparently and dynamically detect DGA domains of various lengths, whether short or long. Two different machine learning classification techniques, namely decision tree and random forests, yielded very encouraging detection performances.

While detecting automatically generated domains is our main focus in this work, identifying the malware family to which the DGAs belong would be beneficial.

Future work will consist of expanding our feature space and algorithms to identify and categorize the specific algorithms used in generating the AGDs. Future work will also include testing the ability of the model for detecting novel, unseen form of AGD. This will be conducted by training the model on one dataset and testing it on another, totally different dataset. Novelty detection is important as one of the characteristics of malware such as botnets is evolution to escape detection.

References

1. Antonakakis, M., Perdisci, R., Nadji, Y., Vasiloglou, N., Abu-Nimeh, S., Lee, W., Dagon, D.: From throw-away traffic to bots: detecting the rise of DGA-based malware. In: 21st Usenix Security Symposium, 8–10 August 2012 (2012)
2. Ma, J., Saul, L.K., Savage, S., Voelker, G.M.: Beyond blacklists: learning to detect malicious web sites from suspicious URLs. In: Proceedings of the 15th ACM SIGKDD International Conference on Knowledge Discovery and Data Mining, Paris, France, 28 June–01 July 2009, pp. 1245–1254 (2009)
3. McGrath, D.K., Gupta, M.: Behind phishing: an examination of phisher modi operandi. In: Proceedings of 1st USENIX Workshop on Large-Scale Exploits and Emergent Threats, San Francisco, CA, USA, 15 April 2008 (2008)
4. Mowbray, M., Hagen, J.: Finding domain-generation algorithms by looking at length distributions. In: 2014 IEEE International Symposium Software Reliability Engineering Workshops (ISSREW), Naples, Italy, 3–6 November 2014 (2014)
5. Norvig, P.: Natural language corpus data. In: Beautiful Data, pp. 219–242, June 2009. Chapter 14
6. Sharifnya, R., Abadi, M.: A novel reputation system to detect DGA-based botnets. In: 2013 3rd International eConference on Computer and Knowledge Engineering (ICCKE), pp. 417–423 (2013)
7. Schiavoni, S., Maggi, F., Cavallaro, L., Zanero, S.: Phoenix: DGA-based botnet tracking and intelligence. In: Dietrich, S. (ed.) DIMVA 2014. LNCS, vol. 8550, pp. 192–211. Springer, Cham (2014). doi:10.1007/978-3-319-08509-8_11
8. Yadav, S., Reddy, A.K.K., Reddy, A.L.N., Ranjan, S.: Detecting algorithmically generated malicious domain names. In: Proceedings of the 10th ACM SIGCOMM Conference on Internet Measurement (IMC 2010), pp. 48–61. ACM, New York (2010)
9. Wang, W., Shirley, K.: Breaking Bad: detecting malicious domains using word segmentation. In: Proceedings of the 9th Workshop on Web 2.0 Security and Privacy (W2SP) (2015)
10. Weymes, B.: DNS anomaly detection: defend against sophisticated malware, 28 May 2013. Web, 28 June 2017. https://www.helpnetsecurity.com/2013/05/28/dns-anomaly-detection-defend-against-sophisticated-malware/
11. Zhao, D., Traore, I., Sayed, B., Lu, W., Saad, S., Ghorbani, A., Garant, D.: Botnet detection based on traffic behavior analysis and flow intervals. Elsevier J. Comput. Secur. **39**, 2–16 (2013)
12. Zhao, D., Traore, I.: P2P botnet detection through malicious fast flux network identification. In: 7th International Conference on P2P, Parallel, Grid, Cloud, and Internet Computing - 3PGCIC 2012, Victoria, BC, Canada, 12–14 November 2012 (2012)

Secure Cloud Computing: Multithreaded Fully Homomorphic Encryption for Legal Metrology

Alexander Oppermann[1], Artem Yurchenko[1], Marko Esche[1(✉)],
and Jean-Pierre Seifert[2]

[1] Department 8.5 Metrological IT, Physikalisch-Technische Bundesanstalt (PTB),
Berlin, Germany
{alexander.oppermann,artem.yurchenko,marko.esche}@ptb.de
[2] Security in Telecommunications, Technische Universität Berlin, Berlin, Germany
jpseifert@sec.t-labs.tu-berlin.de

Abstract. A significant disadvantage of fully homomorphic encryption is the long periods of time needed to process encrypted data, due to its complex and CPU-intensive arithmetic techniques. In this paper, the fully homomorphic encryption library LibScarab is extended by integer arithmetics, comparisons, decisions and multithreading to secure data processing. Furthermore, it enhances 32 and 64-bit arithmetic operations, improving them by a higher factor. This extension is integrated into a cloud computing architecture in the field of Legal Metrology. The resulting parallelized algorithm solved the time constraint issues for smart meter gateway tariffs. Several tests were performed, fulfilling the tariff specifications of the German Federal Office for Information Security (BSI). It was concluded that this extension of the fully homomorphic encryption library meets the requirements of real world applications.

Keywords: Cloud computing · Parallel computing · Fully homomorphic encryption (FHE) · Applied cryptography · Secure computing · Smart meter gateway · Legal metrology

1 Introduction

In Europe, certain measuring instruments are subject to legal control when they are used in business transactions or for public purposes. Among these regulated measuring instruments are diverse devices such as gas and water meters, fuel pumps, weighing instruments, taximeters, heat meters and electricity meters. All of these are subject to the Measuring Instruments Directive (MID) 2014/32/EU [1]. For electricity meters in particular, the Directive 2009/72/EC [2] prescribes the introduction of intelligent measuring systems from 2012 onwards. In Germany, these intelligent measuring systems consist of relatively simple cumulative meters that send their data to a smart meter gateway (SMGW), which acts as a security and communication interface for simple meters as well as a data storage unit. The gateway serves the dual purpose of assuring the privacy of

© Springer International Publishing AG 2017
I. Traore et al. (Eds.): ISDDC 2017, LNCS 10618, pp. 35–54, 2017.
https://doi.org/10.1007/978-3-319-69155-8_3

customers' data and preventing external manipulations. Thus, the main application scenario for fully homomorphic encryption (FHE) becomes the cumulative addition of many individual measuring results without any intermediate decrypt operations.

Nowadays, most measuring instruments still consist of one hardware unit that contains all parts necessary for the instrument's operation such as sensor, data processing unit, storage, communication unit and display. Due to the needs of the globalized market and increased customer demands, it is expected that these measuring instruments will be reduced to a sensor and a communication unit in the near future. The rest of the instrument, i.e. processing unit, storage and a possible secure display, will be most likely moved to the cloud [3].

This scenario poses several challenges in the field of Legal Metrology. In contrast to the common IT security area, Legal Metrology does not assume the existence of a trustworthy system administrator role. Instead, all parties (including the manufacturer, the user of the instruments and their customers) are considered as potential attackers. Therefore, the instrument itself is regarded to be the only trustworthy component which all other parties can rely on. Furthermore, industry is concerned about potential security breaches that leak data to competitors or attackers and thus demands privacy by design.

Virtualization of a measuring instrument in the cloud poses new challenges in protecting measurement data and their distributed processing. In this scenario, classical protective mechanisms for cloud computing solutions with their respective roles [4] do not fit the requirements of Legal Metrology. This means virtualization solely does not satisfy the requirements of Legal Metrology, e.g. security, integrity and authenticity of measurement data cannot be guaranteed sufficiently by this technique. Therefore, the authors propose an approach to secure the processing within a cloud computing environment via fully homomorphic encryption [3], which allows processing of encrypted data without decrypting them first.

Since the first realization of FHE in 2009 by Gentry [5], new algorithms, patterns and optimizations of the original approach have been presented [6–8] and have led to the development of a handful of open source libraries.

Most prominent is the first reference implementation HElib [9] which is very versatile but complex to handle. On the other side of the spectrum, there are very lightweight solutions like FHEW [10] and LibScarab (see Table 1). In this paper, only those libraries and schemes are considered that implement a fully homomorphic approach, i.e. where multiplication and addition in the encrypted domain are feasible.

The LSIM (LibScarab extended for Integer arithmetics and Multithreading) is based on the LibScarab implementation [11] and extends it for integer arithmetics. It uses zero comparisons, parallelization and massive multithreading of arithmetic operations to specifically suit the needs of tariff applications in Legal Metrology. Nevertheless, LSIM should be widely applicable in other areas as well where fast integer and fixed-point arithmetics are required. The limitations of each library are investigated and compared to the proposed LSIM approach and put into the context of tariffing models for electricity power meters and their dedicated SMGW.

The remainder of this paper is organized as follows: Sect. 2 describes the related work and gives an overview of the available algorithms. The use cases and targeted functionality of this work are discussed in Sect. 3. Afterwards, Sect. 4 gives details about the used library and the authors' contributions. Section 5 comprises performance tests. The summary and planned future work are provided in Sect. 6.

2 Related Work

Before describing the features of the LSIM implementation, an overview is given over the most prominent representative algorithms from the wide field of fully homomorphic encryption schemes. Each of them is briefly characterized with respect to their implementation, their advantages and disadvantages as well as their suitability for the envisioned application scenarios.

Table 1. Overview of fully homomorphic libraries

Library	Language	Encryption scheme	Key handling
HElib	C++	BGV	Asymmetric
SEAL	C++	Fan & Vercauteren	Asymmetric
LibScarab	C	Smart-Vercauteren	Asymmetric
FHEW	C	LWE	Symmetric
HE	R	Fan & Vercauteren	Asymmetric

Since in FHE schemes, all arithmetic operations, especially multiplications, add noise to the encrypted data, a concept called bootstrapping was introduced by Gentry [5] in order to reduce the noise and allow unlimited number of successive arithmetic operations. This is achieved by "recrypting" the cipher-text in the encrypted domain without giving up security. One receives a new noise-reduced cipher-text for the same clear-text. The libraries given in Table 1 are shortly summarized and describe the related work.

HELib. The software library HELib [9] is a C++ implementation of the homomorphic encryption scheme of Brakerski-Gentry-Vaikuntanathan (BGV) [12]. It provides Smart-Vercauteren [8] cipher text packing techniques and Gentry-Halevi-Smart optimizations. In 2015, the library was extended to include bootstrapping, which allows cipher text refreshes in the encrypted domain. This library is very flexible and configurable but at the same time quite complex to handle for non-experts. Furthermore, it provides low-level routines like *set, add, multiply, shift,* etc. The library is highly optimized for single instruction multiple data (SIMD) operations, which is unrewarding for our application scenarios, since the library cannot compare numbers in the encrypted domain. While testing this library with small numbers for the security parameters, the memory usage for 6 multiplications on 7-bit integers amounted to over 6 GBytes. The library is still under active development.

SEAL. The Simple Encrypted Arithmetic Library (SEAL) [13] is being developed by the Microsoft Research Group and originally implemented the YASHE scheme. In the most recent version, the scheme was switched to Fan and Vercauteren [7]. In the tested version 2.1 of the library it supported only leveled homomorphism, i.e. by using modulus switching, one can only perform a predefined amount of multiplications. Since a flexible approach is needed for the targeted application scenarios, it would be counter-productive to limit the amount of operations by the library beforehand. The library itself is well documented and relatively easy to use, but is restricted to a Microsoft Windows environment. In addition, it does not support bootstrapping and comparisons in the encrypted domain.

LibScarab. LibScarab is a C implementation of the Smart-Vercauteren scheme [6] created by Perl et al. [11]. It supports bootstrapping, XOR as well as AND operations on single bits. The library is easy to use along with a clear and compact structure. The library is clearly structured and easy to extend. The authors had to port the library to the latest FLINT 2.5.2, GMP 6.1.1 and MPFR 3.1.5 libraries since LibScarab was last updated in 2013 and does not support multi-threading out of the box. A recrypt operation is executed automatically after every arithmetic operation.

FHEW. The "Fastest Homomorphic Encryption in the West" (FHEW) [10] is a C implementation of the Learning With Errors (LWE) scheme, which makes use of the "Fastest Fourier Transformation in the West" (FFTW) library [14]. FHEW uses a symmetric key, i.e. the same key is used for encryption and decryption. It also offers bitwise encryption and NAND-Gates. Because of the symmetric key procedures this library is unsuitable for the envisioned application scenarios (see Subsect. 3.3). This library was last updated in 2015.

Homomorphic Encryption (HE). The Homomorphic Encryption (HE) [15] is a package for the statistic language R and implements a scheme from Fan and Vercauteren [7]. The R package itself is a wrapper for the arithmetic functions written in C/C++. While easy and intuitive to use, the library itself lacks bootstrapping and therewith the possibility for a cipher-text-refresh, which prevents running several multiplications consecutively. Thus, it is not practical with respect to the application scenarios.

3   Use Cases and Targeted Functionality

Classical security approaches use encryption to ensure privacy and signatures for verifying the authenticity of messages. These attempts aim for securing the communication between two endpoints. In the cloud computing context, the attention shifted to secure computation (see Fig. 1). Classical encryption is *static*, thus messages have to be decrypted first before being able to be processed. Similar conditions apply for classical signature schemes. They are designed for *static* messages. In order to verify remote computation, a proof is needed for correct and trustworthy results. Verifiable Computing demands that the evaluation of an interactive proof [16] needs to be more compact than the actual computation.

FHE offers an elegant way to ensure privacy by design since it prevents cleartext information leaks. While externalizing confidential processes to the cloud, industry places little trust in external service providers. The authors chose FHE over a homomorphic signature scheme not only to help solving this conflict, but it also offers a more powerful, practical and flexible approach to secure remote computing. Furthermore, there are several approaches that combine homomorphic encryption with verifiable computation [17,18], so that it is still feasible at a later time to integrate verifiable computation with this line of research.

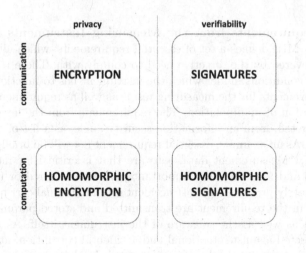

Fig. 1. Overview of different security techniques and their area of application

Even though homomorphic encryption usually aims at ensuring data privacy [5], it may be used in other areas and for other purposes as well. For example, if an attacker is unaware of the actual values of the data currently being processed, intentional manipulation is no longer possible. Instead, only random changes to data and likewise random manipulation of the executed algorithm are the only aims an attacker may achieve. If homomorphic encryption is carefully combined with testing a running algorithm via precalculated test data, even such random effects may be detected. Subsequently, the scheme detailed here [3] may be used to achieve a certain degree of robustness towards algorithm and data manipulation, too.

In this section, a number of common tariff models, which constitute a representative set of algorithms used in measuring instruments, are examined and requirements for the homomorphic encryption scheme detailed in Sect. 4 will be derived.

3.1 Legal Metrology and Tariffing

As indicated in the introduction, Legal Metrology covers all areas of measurements where lawmakers consider the outcome of a measurement to be crucial for consumer protection. In the following paragraphs, the principal concept of Legal Metrology will be examined in more detail as well as the different tariffing scenarios. Tariffing generally refers to the process of price calculation based on one or more determined measurement values consisting of a physical quantity together with the appropriate SI unit (Système international d'unités [19]). Here the term will be used in the context of smart meters for electrical energy. Although the concept may easily be applied to other areas of Legal Metrology as well.

Essential Requirements from the Measuring Instruments Directive. Annex I of the MID defines a set of essential requirements, which all measuring instruments covered by the directive need to comply with. These requirements cover physical conditions, under which the instrument has to function correctly, accuracy requirements for the measuring result as well as requirements concerning the prevention of manipulation. The requirements from the latter category may be interpreted, from an information security angle, as a list of assets to be protected [20]. As an example, essential requirement 8.4 will be briefly examined here. It states, "Measurement data, software that is critical for measurement characteristics and metrologically important parameters stored or transmitted shall be adequately protected against accidental or intentional corruption." The assets defined in the requirement are transmitted and stored parameters, measurement data as well as the software of the instrument itself. As all of these are to be protected against intentional and accidental corruption, at least their integrity and authenticity need to be guaranteed. In the context of this paper, the main focus will be on the integrity and privacy of the measurement data. Availability of the software is not required by the MID as no false measurement data can be generated if the instrument is out of order.

The Roles of Manufacturer, Notified Body, User and Market Surveillance. In the MID, certain roles are defined for players in the field of Legal Metrology. Firstly, the manufacturer of an instrument is responsible for putting instruments on the market and into use that comply fully with the directive.

To assure conformity with the MID, the manufacturer submits a prototype of the instrument to a so-called Notified Body for conformity assessment. The *Physikalisch-Technische Bundesanstalt* (PTB), Germany's national metrology institute is one such Notified Body.

Should the prototype be in conformance with the requirements, the Notified Body issues a certificate accordingly. The manufacturer will then sell an instrument with the same properties as the prototype to the user together with a declaration of conformity. A market surveillance authority is subsequently tasked with supervising the use of the instrument. In regular intervals, the authority will also reverify the instrument to ensure that it still performs within the parameters set by the ID and the certificate issued by the Notified Body. In this context, only the market surveillance authority and the Notified Body will be considered to be trustworthy as they are under constant supervision by the respective EU member states. All other parties (manufacturer, user of the instrument and the user's customer) can be seen as potential attackers. This fact will be described in Sect. 3.2.

3.2   Measuring Instruments and Trustworthy Components

In the context of the intelligent measuring system, all parties need to authenticate themselves before initiating a communication connection. To this end, the SMGW as well as partners communicating with it over the wide area network (WAN) are in possession of Hardware Security Modules (HSM), which are in charge of key handling, signature verification and white listing of communication partners.

A HSM is an essential security measure in order to enable secure key handling and exchange of keys between associated clients and devices within the public key infrastructure (PKI). It also acts as a trust anchor to guarantee the integrity and authenticity of a root Certificate Authority (CA) and its sub CAs. The HSM can be used to sign and secure TLS-certificates, OpenSSL certificates for end-to-end cryptography and signature certificates to sign measurement data and thus prove their integrity as well as authenticity [21]. The HSM performs various checks with the certificates before being able to continue with the respective procedure, i.e. it checks the signature of the certificate, the lifetime span (maximum of 7 years) of the issued certificates, checks revocations lists and the issuer of the certificate, reviews the mode of usage such as key usage validation and extended key usage validation.

In Legal Metrology, the concept of a trustworthy system administrator does not exist. Therefore, all parties must be considered untrustworthy, i.e. the HSM is the only trust anchor for security concepts, which is considered as completely unbiased and thus can be accepted by all parties involved. In a cloud environment, the HSM needs to be replaced by a suitable software alternative.

3.3   Application Scenarios

To derive well defined application scenarios, the legal framework for smart metering will here be examined briefly. Afterwards, algorithmic requirements will be derived based on the legal requirements.

Tariff Models According to TR03109-1. While the measuring of commodities such as electrical energy, gas, water and heat are all regulated in the MID, national law may prescribe additional constraints if the measurements, for instance, touch upon informational privacy or other aspects subject to national legislation. In Germany, due to the implementation of the aforementioned Directive 2009/72/EC, the federal bureau for information security *Bundesamt für Sicherheit in der Informationstechnik* (BSI) has published a technical requirement document (TR) [21] with an associated protection profile [22]. While the first mainly covers compatibility requirements and secure communication protocols for the SMGW, the latter is only focused on the SMGW's integrated HSM. Apart from defining communication protocols and the general environment of an intelligent measuring system, the TR also lists all approved tariff application scenarios (TAF) that may be used in an intelligent measuring system. These are of utmost importance for the SMGW, as it is usually in charge of connecting meter and time data (time stamping) and is also responsible for price calculation.

Out of the 12 TAFs defined in the TR, four will be examined and implemented in a secure cloud solution in this paper (see Table 2). The four scenarios have been selected as they constitute a representative application of tariffing that may also be found in other measuring systems.

Table 2. Overview of the implemented tariff application scennarios (TAF)

TAF 1	Tariffs with low data usage, where energy is always billed with the same price and collected data are only sent at the end of the billing period requiring no external trigger
TAF 2	Time-dependent tariffs, where energy is billed with different tariffs according to the time at which a certain amount of energy is consumed. The switching between tariffs is time-dependent but the switching points are static
TAF 3	Power-dependent tariffs, where the price does not depend on the total energy consumed but on the current power consumption (energy per time interval) The switching into different price categories is therefore done according to the value of the current measurement result
TAF 4	Consumption-dependent tariffs, where a new price is used when a certain energy budget has been consumed. The budgets are statically predefined and the condition for assigning new measurement values to the next price category has to be checked regularly

Required Logical and Arithmetic Operations. The implemented algorithm described in Sect. 4 aims at realizing the SMGW's tariffing functionality in a way that can be run on any system with suitable computation capacity without having to realize additional protective means. While SMGWs are very unlikely to be realized in the cloud any time soon due to the hardware requirements of the TR, the approach may easily be applied to many other measuring systems that all perform similar price calculations as listed below:

- addition, subtraction, multiplication, division,
- comparison,
- input-dependent source selection,
- input-dependent destination selection.

The addition operation is, of course, needed to add new energy values to an existing tariff register. Subtraction, division and negative numbers are likewise needed to calculate the current energy flow (the power) based on consecutive readings of an cumulative meter. The multiplication operation is required when a tariff and an energy amount are combined to form a price to be paid. Comparisons of input values are needed to realize input- and time-dependent switching statements.

Required Time for Processing. Two separate tasks performed by the SMGW need to be distinguished: One is the accumulation of data coming continuously from the electricity meters. The other one is the monthly reading of the resulting registers. Data coming from smart meters will be accumulated within the SMGW to which the meters are connected. According to the current design of the SMGW, a maximum of 32 m can be connected to the gateway simultaneously. Each individual meter sends a new measurement value every 15 min. In order for the gateway to efficiently cope with the arriving amount of data, every single request for data accumulation subsequently needs to be processed in under $\frac{15 \times 60\,s}{32} = 28\,s$. Parallelization of the accumulation process is not feasible and wanted since there are inter-dependencies between measurements which may have an effect on the chosen register for subsequent values. The monthly retrieval of accumulated register values from the SMGW is not time-critical as the reading only works on static data that does not change during reading. The retrieval can thus happen in a separate process.

4   Algorithm Description and Extensions

This section comprises the algorithm description and the extensions of LibScarab that were needed, in order to implement the application scenarios TAF 1–4 explained in detail in Subsect. 3.3. Furthermore, a brief description and an overview of implementation details of the addition, multiplication and division operations as well as simple decision and comparisons in the FHE environment are given in Subsect. 4.2.

4.1 Choosing and Extending the Library

Fully homomorphic encryption schemes support two operations: addition and multiplication. Depending on the implemented scheme, also a sign change is possible, which enables subtraction. A lot of simple algorithms are based on these three operations and thus can be implemented. But nevertheless, no solution exists for comparing two numbers in the encrypted domain, which makes it impossible to make a decision in the encrypted domain and consequently to implement a division algorithm for example.

One possible way to implement a division algorithm is to represent numbers as fractions by saving nominator and denominator separately in order to bypass division. But this approach does not solve the problem of comparisons in the encrypted domain. It also seems impossible to render an unencrypted result from an encrypted operation without giving up security and privacy. This means that all algorithms should be either completely deterministic or there should be enough computing power to calculate all possible results in parallel.

A final decision should always be made in the unencrypted domain for the targeted algorithms. Since they neither have a completely deterministic structure nor is the decryption of the data in an insecure environment an option, a different approach was pursued replacing integers with binary numbers.

The LibScarab library is a good choice for the prototype, since it provides all necessary tools without adding too much complexity. In addition, it is easily configurable yet simple to modify and to extend. On top of that it is very fast. A "recrypt" procedure is executed after each operation. Thus, there is no further need for noise control to fulfill the requirement of unlimited multiplications as mentioned in Sect. 3. As already pointed out in Sect. 2, the library did not support multi-threading out of the box, since it was built on old versions of the libraries FLINT, GMP and MPFR. Therefore, it was ported to newer versions in order to comply with the requirements.

4.2 Implementation of Arithmetic Operators

Using binary numbers only two operations are left; the modulo-2-addition which corresponds to an XOR-gate and a modulo-2-multiplication that corresponds to an AND-gate. Another operation is the (unencrypted) binary complement of the encrypted number which corresponds to toggling bits in the encrypted domain. With these two operations (see Eqs. 1 and 2) it is possible to derive all the boolean functions and, as a consequence, to provide arithmetic and logical operations on encrypted integers, which are represented as arrays of encrypted bits. The addition, subtraction and multiplication operations for integers had to be reimplemented according to the chosen binary word sizes (e.g. 32-bit and 64-bit length).

$$A \lor B = \neg(\neg A \land \neg B) \tag{1}$$

$$((1 \oplus A) = \neg A). \tag{2}$$

Zero-Test of Encrypted Integers. This binary approach yields the opportunity to implement a zero-test as a simple bitwise $\vee$ on all bits of the represented number. The result of this operation should be complemented to return an encrypted 1 in case the examined number was 0. This corresponds to a logical NOR operation with 32-bit inputs. The encrypted result can be directly used as an input for further encrypted arithmetic and logical operations. To verify the computed result it has to be decrypted in the end.

Comparison of Encrypted Integers. A simple implementation of a comparator consists of the subtraction of both input parameters $(A - B)$ and of the sign-evaluation of the result. This operation delivers two possible results $A < B$ or $A \geq B$. The latter needs to be checked with the help of the zero-test, so that it can be distinguished between $A > B$ and $A = B$. If this clarification is not needed, this approach can be reduced to the calculation of borrow-bits only, since the result of the subtraction itself is not important.

Simple Decisions on Encrypted Integers. It is significant to highlight that the result of a decision should remain in the encrypted domain. Therefore, it is not possible to externally influence the program flow. Nevertheless, simple algorithmic constructs are feasible based on the result of the comparison or zero-test operator. These are *source* and *destination selections*. The source selection, on the one hand, is represented by the following C-construct, which is similar to an if-then-else-construct with the constraint that only data flow can be controlled:

$$Y = (condition)?A : B \tag{3}$$

To implement this decision a 2:1-multiplexer is required, which can be described as:

$$Y = \neg C \cdot A + C \cdot B \tag{4}$$

where C is the output of the zero-test, the comparison operator or any other possible boolean equation.

The destination selection, on the other hand, consists of a demultiplexer and binary adders. The selection is triggered by a boolean equation (e.g. comparison or zero-test). After the output selection operation, the selected output or destination contains the input number and all the other outputs are set to an encrypted 0. All outputs will be added to the corresponding registers. All registers are modified, but only one will be increased by the input value of the demultiplexer. All the others will be increased by an encrypted 0. It is important to mention that the addition of an encrypted zero always produces a different encrypted version of the same number. Hence it is not possible to say which of the registers are actually changed by a FHE-operation.

Addition of Encrypted Integers. The implementation of arithmetic circuits is done with special regard to multithreading. A particular challenge was to find a solution with a small amount of gates and a small circuit depth at the same time. An analogue problem is known in the field of digital design as Area-Speed-Tradeoff, since a lower circuit depth usually results in a higher number of gates used. Each additional gate needs computing time, so that fast digital circuits have often poor performance in the area of the homomorphic operations. Especially for multiplication and division some advanced algorithms exist, but due to the massive use of multiplexers or lookup-tables these solutions are not reasonable with respect to the execution time.

Three different versions of an adder were implemented and compared. A Carry Look Ahead Adder (CLA) [23] with block size of 4 and 8 bit, also known as "fast adder" proved to be the slowest adder within the constraints of this paper. The Carry Select Adder (CSA) [23] rendered mid-range performance. The modified Ripple Carry Adder (RCA) [23] revealed the shortest execution time, since the operations of the first half adder was executed completely in parallel. The same adder could be used to implement subtraction, but this would contain an array of XOR-gates to form the complement. Considering performance the subtraction was outsourced to a separate routine, in order to save time during addition operations.

Multiplication of Encrypted Integers. Fast multiplications using higher radix solutions [23,24] require a massive use of multiplexers or/and operand recoding which are costly in size as well as time consuming.

In case of conventional binary multiplications, two problems can be identified: (1) the generation of the partial products, (2) their summation. While the generation of partial products can be carried out completely (bitwise) in parallel, the summation can only be partially parallelized. A tree structure of conventional word adders provides insufficient performance. For this reason, a multi-level bit-wise tree adder is used here (see Fig. 2).

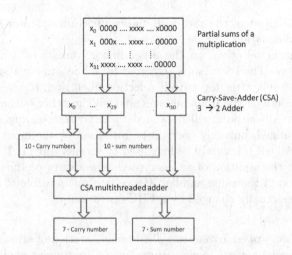

Fig. 2. Tree structure of the optimized adder part

The main principle of a tree adder is that a full adder is used to add three bits. At the output, one sum bit and one carry bit are generated. The resulting number, consisting of carry bits, is shifted one place to the left. Due to the fact that there is no carry propagation in the case of the 32 partial products of the multiplication of two 32 bit numbers, 30 (x_0 to x_{29}) of them can be processed by bit-wise full adders in a bit-parallel manner in the first stage. The resulting 20 numbers are supplemented by x_{30} to deliver 21 numbers and are processed in the next stage. After several iterations, there are only 2 numbers left which are added together by a conventional adder.

The difficulty here is the bitwise addition of the shifted partial products with respect to the significant bit position, which requires manual optimization and proper planning of the multi-threaded operations.

Division of Encrypted Integers. The division operation is the most difficult one to parallelize because of inter-step dependencies. One possible improvement leading to a reduced number of iterations is the use of high-radix number systems to perform the division. Unfortunately, the complexity of each iteration is also increased in this case. Advanced higher radix algorithms like Sweeney-Robertson-Tocher (SRT) division uses lookup-tables and/or a lot of multiplexers [23,24]. These are very expensive in case of a FHE software implementation, so that a simpler solution was investigated.

The simplest way to implement the division is the well-known paper and pencil method adapted to the binary number system also known as restoring-division [23]. The divisor is subtracted from the shifted dividend, in case of a negative remainder the divisor is added back to the remainder and the result will be shifted. The restoring operation implicates one extra addition or use of a multiplexer in each iteration. In contrast to the restoring division the non-restoring-algorithm requires only one addition or subtraction in each iteration. The underlying concept can be easily derived from the restoring algorithm. In case of a negative remainder after one subtraction the divisor (D) should be added back to the remainder (R) and the result (S) shifted to the left, i.e.

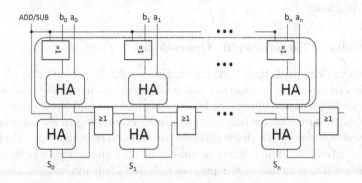

Fig. 3. Multi-threaded combined adder and subtracter

$S = 2 \cdot (R+D)$. In the next iteration D will be subtracted again: $2 \cdot R + 2 \cdot D - D = 2 \cdot R + D$, which is equal to the simple shift of the negative remainder of the first iteration and replacing of the subtraction by an addition in the next iteration. Addition and subtraction are performed by the same boolean circuit (see Fig. 3). The sign-bit of the result is used to select the operation (addition/subtraction) for the next iteration.

5   Experimental Comparison

This section describes the experimental comparisons that were conducted on a Linux server with an Intel Xeon CPU E5-2620 v3 @2.40 GHz, 24 cores and 64 GB of RAM. In the first subsection, key generation, recrypt operation and single arithmetic operations of FHE are compared, after improving and extending LibScarab as described in Sect. 4. The second subsections comprises results of the application scenarios TAF 1–4 that were already outlined in Subsect. 3.1. The speedup and efficiency are calculated for both single operations as well as for the tariff applications.

The relative performance gain achieved by parallelization (speedup) can be measured and is defined in [25] as a metric. This can be written as:

$$S(n) = \frac{T_s(n)}{T_p(n)} \tag{5}$$

where T_s is the execution time of the best sequential algorithm for solving the problem and T_p marks the execution time of the parallelized algorithm using n processing units.

The efficiency is also defined by [25] as a metric that measures the fraction of time in which a processing unit is usefully employed. This can be asserted as:

$$E(n) = \frac{S(n)}{n} \tag{6}$$

where S is the speedup for the algorithm (see Eq. (5)) and n marks the number of processing units.

5.1   Results of Homomorphic Operations

Key Generation and Recrypt Operations. While parallelizing the basic arithmetic operations, e.g. addition and multiplication, it was determined that the speedup factor is not significant for creating a monic and irreducible polynomial $F(x)$ with a resultant p being prime (see KeyGen() [6]) in a multi-threaded environment compared to a single threaded one, i.e. no relevant time gain for key generation is realized. The authors assume that performance gain is lost due to the randomized generation of the polynomials and their evaluation, because of the great spread of the results and the necessary synchronization of the threads. Thus, the times stated in Table 3 for key generation and recrypt operation are

Table 3. Overview of key geometry and performance gain

Key geometry	Key size (kB)	Keygen (s)	Speedup	Recrypt (ms)	Speedup
384/16/05	1.8/30	1.1	15.5	34	7.7
384/32/16	1.8/60	1.17	11.9	90	3.4
384/64/16	1.8/120	1.24	12	181	3.7
2048/64/16	9.6/626	516	6.1	670	2
4096/64/16	18/1250	5204	2.7	1660	1.9

single threaded. Nevertheless, in comparison to Brenner's reference implementation [11] and the stated times for key generation for 384-bit key length a speed up of 15.5 could be yielded, i.e. instead of 17 s it only took 1.1 s to generate a key. The main factors are optimizations in the implementation, modernized libraries as already explained in Sect. 2 and faster hardware than in 2012. The recrypt operation achieved a speed up factor of 7.7 for 384-bit key length, i.e. a recrypt costs only 34ms instead of 263ms. The amount of disk space for public and private keys do not distinguish from Brenner's data.

Arithmetic Operations. By parallelizing the arithmetic operations the greatest benefit was earned within multiplication by a factor of 7.29. In Fig. 4 one can see the asymptotic characteristic of the optimization for the time usage. While executing a single thread utilization took 124 s for a single multiplication, a 48 threads utilization only took 17 s for a single multiplication. Considering memory usage, the optimum is reached by utilizing 16 threads with 19 s for a single multiplication with a calculated efficiency gain of 41% (see Eq. 6) and a speedup of 6.53. The least significant benefit from parallelization was realized for the addition operation. It is already the fastest operation in the encrypted domain needing only two seconds for one addition for a single thread while it could be pushed down to one second for a single addition utilizing 48 threads.

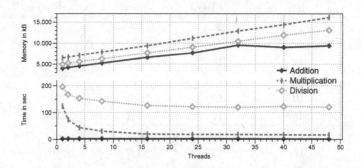

Fig. 4. Plot of single 32 Bit-FHE-operations (Add, Mult, Div) on a Server with an Intel Xeon CPU E5-2620 v3 @ 2.40 GHz and 64 GB RAM.

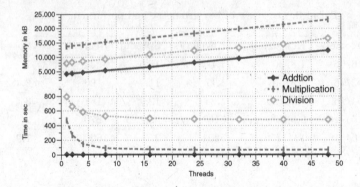

Fig. 5. Plot of single 64 Bit-FHE-operations (Add, Mult, Div) on a Server with an Intel Xeon CPU E5-2620 v3 @ 2.40 GHz and 64 GB RAM.

The efficiency optimum is reached here by using only two threads with a 50% efficiency and a speedup of 1 needing two seconds.

The division is traditionally a very complex arithmetic operation which often has its own compartment on modern CPUs in order to optimize its performance. Bearing this in mind for the software implementation in the encrypted domain, the benefit through parallelizing the division operation was achieved by a factor of 1.6. This means that a single thread for one division took 196 s while this was reduced to 121 s utilizing 48 threads. The optimum for this operation is reached using 16 threads with a speedup of 1.6 with a 10% efficiency. Similar results could be yielded for 64 bit arithmetic operations as seen in Fig. 5. Obviously, more memory was needed for the single arithmetic operations due to the nature of the bigger operands. Again, the multiplication benefited the most by a factor of 6.8, needing almost 8 min (470 s) for a single threaded multiplication compared to 69 s using 48 threads (Tables 4 and 5).

Table 4. Overview of 32 bit operation results

	n	t (sec)	S(n)	E(n) in %
Add	1	2	-	-
	2	2	1	50
	48	1	2	4
Mult	1	124	-	-
	16	19	6.5	41
	48	17	7.3	15
Div	1	196	-	-
	16	126	1.6	10
	48	121	1.6	3

Table 5. Overview of 64 bit operation results

	n	t (sec)	S(n)	E(n) in %
Add	1	5	-	-
	4	4	1.3	31
	48	3	1.7	3
Mult	1	470	-	-
	16	75	6.3	39
	48	69	6.8	14
Div	1	796	-	-
	16	497	1.6	10
	48	467	1.7	3

The optimum is reached using 16 threads with a speedup of 6.3 and a efficiency gain of 39% needing 75 s.

Additions in the 64 bit space are optimized by a factor of 1.6, i.e. needing 5 s for one addition using one thread compared to 48 threads lasting 3 s. The optimum is reached for 4 threads with a speedup of 1.3 and a 31% efficiency. Again addition is the fastest operation.

For the division the same factor of 1.6 could be reached as for the 32 bit operands. Speaking in absolute numbers it is still a huge difference from roughly 13 min (796 s) for a single threaded division compared to about 8 min (479 s) using 48 threads. The optimum is reached using 16 threads with a speedup of 1.6 and 10% efficiency needing 8.5 min (497 s).

5.2 Results of Application Scenarios

In contrast to the tests performed in Subsect. 5.1 where only arithmetic operations are measured, these results cover the combination of arithmetic operations and comparisons applied to the application scenarios described in detail in Subsect. 3.3. A recrypt is included after each arithmetic operation to reduce the noise.

The calculations for the application scenarios are split into accumulating the measurement data (see Fig. 6) and summing them up on demand (see Fig. 7), e.g. at the end of the month. The latter includes the more complex arithmetic operations and comparisons in the encrypted domain.

While TAF 1 and 4 performed very similar in accumulating measurement data (see Fig. 6) in respect to time and utilizing threads, the gain is 1.3 needing about 5 s for a single thread to only 3.8 s utilizing 48 threads. The optimum is reached using only 4 threads with a speedup of 1.3 and about 30% efficiency needing 4.2 and 4.3 s.

TAF 2 gained a factor of 1.7 needing single threaded 9.3 s and for 48 threads 5.6 s. The optimum is reached using two threads with a speedup of 1.8 and a 91% efficiency needing 5.4 s to accomplish this task.

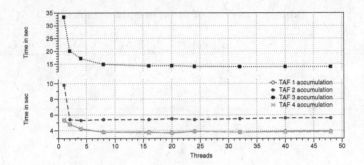

Fig. 6. Plot of accumulating measurement data on a Server with an Intel Xeon CPU E5-2620 v3 @ 2.40 GHz and 64GB RAM.

TAF 3 is the only scenario where a lot of comparisons and decisions were performed additionally, thus the time difference. A gain of factor 2.4 was yielded for a single thread needing 33.4 s compared to 48 threads consuming only 14 s. The optimum is reached using 8 threads with a speedup of 2.2 and 28% efficiency needing 14.9 s to finish. For all TAFs, parallelization helped to push execution time below the required boundary of 28 s.

For the monthly "read out" of the summed up measurement data the application scenarios (see Fig. 7) differ more than for the accumulation process. TAF 1, low data usage, is the fasted and simplest one gaining factor 7 for a single thread using 123.3 s compared to 48 threads consuming only 17.6 s. The optimum is reached using 16 threads with a speedup of 6.3 and a 39% efficiency needing 19.6 s to finish.

TAF 2, time-dependent tariff, records a gain of 6.7 for a single thread using 250.6 s compared to 37.3 s utilizing 48 threads. The optimum is reached using 16 threads with a speedup of 6 and a 38% efficiency needing 41 s.

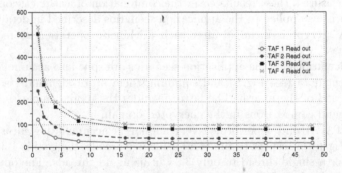

Fig. 7. Plot of "read out" of the measurement data. Final calculation for different application scenarios on a Server with an Intel Xeon CPU E5-2620 v3 @ 2.40 GHz and 64GB RAM.

The TAF 3, power-dependent tariff and TAF 4, consumption-dependent tariff, are more complex thus take around 9 min (503.3 s/533 s) for a single thread and for 48 threads using around 1.5 min (78,6 s/95 s). The performance gains are factor 6.4 and 5.6, respectively. The optimum is reached for both using 16 threads with a speedup 5.8 and 5.2 as well as a 36% and a 32% efficiency needing 86 s and 103 s to finish.

6 Summary

In this paper, an extension to the fully homomorphic encryption library Lib-Scarab has been presented. After a brief comparison of the existing encryption schemes, this extension (LSIM) and its properties were described and evaluated. LSIM comprises fast integer arithmetic, logic operations and multithreading. The resulting gain can be as high as a factor of 7.3 for multiplications of 32 bit numbers, with smaller gains for addition, subtraction and division. The key generation and recryption were also optimized by a factor of 15.5 and 7.7, respectively. In the context of Legal Metrology, LSIM was applied to different tariff application scenarios, achieving a gain of 7 for TAF 1, presumably the most common tariff. For all TAFs, parallelization helped to push execution time below the required boundary of 28 s. Therefore fully homomorphic encryption could be used nowadays for real-world application scenarios. The proposed solution provides the required functionality for its application in the current regulated sector.

Future work will focus on porting LSIM to CUDA/OpenCL and carrying out tests on graphic cards for massive multithreading and parallelization. Furthermore, since OpenMP was utilized for this prototype, it will be interesting for further investigations to find out if Posix Threads (pthreads) or a GMP-library optimization will improve parallelization with respect to computing time. Additionally, ongoing challenges should be studied, such as the computing times in comparison with those realized by a secure hardware solution for FHE.

References

1. European Parliament and Council. Directive 2014/32/EU of the European Parliament and of the Council. Official Journal of the European Union (2014)
2. European Parliament and Council. Directive 2009/72/EC of the European Parliament and of the Council. Official Journal of the European Union (2009)
3. Oppermann, A., Seifert, J.-P., Thiel, F.: Secure cloud reference architectures for measuring instruments under legal control. In: CLOSER, vol. 1, pp. 289–294 (2016)
4. Liu, F., Tong, J., Mao, J., Bohn, R., Messina, J., Badger, L., Leaf, D.: NIST cloud computing reference architecture. NIST Special Publication (2011)
5. Gentry, C., et al.: Fully homomorphic encryption using ideal lattices. In: STOC, vol. 9, pp. 169–178 (2009)
6. Smart, N.P., Vercauteren, F.: Fully homomorphic encryption with relatively small key and ciphertext sizes. In: Nguyen, P.Q., Pointcheval, D. (eds.) PKC 2010. LNCS, vol. 6056, pp. 420–443. Springer, Heidelberg (2010). doi:10.1007/978-3-642-13013-7_25

7. Fan, J., Vercauteren, F.: Somewhat practical fully homomorphic encryption. IACR Cryptology ePrint Archive 2012:144 (2012)
8. Smart, N.P., Vercauteren, F.: Fully homomorphic SIMD operations. Des. Codes Crypt. **71**, 1–25 (2014)
9. Halevi, S., Shoup, V.: Algorithms in HElib. In: Garay, J.A., Gennaro, R. (eds.) CRYPTO 2014. LNCS, vol. 8616, pp. 554–571. Springer, Heidelberg (2014). doi:10.1007/978-3-662-44371-2_31
10. Ducas, L., Micciancio, D.: FHEW: bootstrapping homomorphic encryption in less than a second. In: Oswald, E., Fischlin, M. (eds.) EUROCRYPT 2015. LNCS, vol. 9056, pp. 617–640. Springer, Heidelberg (2015). doi:10.1007/978-3-662-46800-5_24
11. Perl, H., Brenner, M., Smith, M.: Poster: an implementation of the fully homomorphic smart-vercauteren crypto-system. In: Proceedings of the 18th ACM Conference on Computer and Communications Security, pp. 837–840. ACM (2011)
12. Brakerski, Z., Gentry, C., Vaikuntanathan, V.: (Leveled) fully homomorphic encryption without bootstrapping. ACM Trans. Comput. Theory (TOCT) **6**(3), 13 (2014)
13. Laine, K., Player, R.: Simple encrypted arithmetic library-seal (v2. 0). Technical report, Microsoft Research, September 2016
14. Frigo, M., Johnson, S.G.: The fastest fourier transform in the west. Technical report, DTIC Document (1997)
15. Aslett, L.J.M., Esperança, P.M., Holmes, C.C.: A review of homomorphic encryption and software tools for encrypted statistical machine learning. Technical report, University of Oxford (2015)
16. Kilian, J.: A note on efficient zero-knowledge proofs and arguments. In: Proceedings of the Twenty-Fourth Annual ACM Symposium on Theory of Computing, pp. 723–732. ACM (1992)
17. Gennaro, R., Gentry, C., Parno, B.: Non-interactive verifiable computing: outsourcing computation to untrusted workers. In: Rabin, T. (ed.) CRYPTO 2010. LNCS, vol. 6223, pp. 465–482. Springer, Heidelberg (2010). doi:10.1007/978-3-642-14623-7_25
18. Chung, K.-M., Kalai, Y., Vadhan, S.: Improved delegation of computation using fully homomorphic encryption. In: Rabin, T. (ed.) CRYPTO 2010. LNCS, vol. 6223, pp. 483–501. Springer, Heidelberg (2010). doi:10.1007/978-3-642-14623-7_26
19. BIPM. Système international d'unités, The International System of Units (SI), 8th edn. Technical report, Bureau International des Poides et Mesures (BIPM) (2006)
20. Esche, M., Thiel, F.: Software risk assessment for measuring instruments in legal metrology. In: 2015 Federated Conference on Computer Science and Information Systems (FedCSIS), pp. 1113–1123. IEEE (2015)
21. BSI. Anforderungen an die Interoperabilität der Kommunikationseinheit eines intelligenten Messsystems (BSI TR-03109-1). Technical report, Bundesamt für Sicherheit in der Informationstechnik (BSI), Bonn (2013)
22. BSI. Schutzprofil für die Kommunikationseinheit eines intelligenten Messsystems für Stoff- und Energiemengen (Smart Meter Gateway PP). Technical report, Bundesamt für Sicherheit in der Informationstechnik (BSI), Bonn (2014)
23. Koren, I.: Computer Arithmetics Algorithms. A.K. Peters, Ltd. (2002). ISBN 1568811608
24. Lu, M.: Modular structure of large multiplier. In: Arithmetic and Logic in Computer Systems, 1st edn., pp. 120–122. Wiley (2004)
25. Grama, A., Gupta, A., Karypis, G., Kumar, V.: Introduction to Parallel Computing, 2nd edn. Pearson Education, London (2003)

Detecting Command and Control Channel of Botnets in Cloud

Wei Lu[1(✉)], Mark Miller[2], and Ling Xue[3]

[1] Department of Computer Science, Keene State College, USNH, Durham, USA
wlu@keene.edu
[2] Amadeus-Hospitality, Portsmouth, NH, USA
[3] UBit Labs, Amherst, MA, USA

Abstract. The rapid rise of cloud computing technology marks the next wave of enterprise information technology, catering up a market demand of a digitized economy to deliver traditional utilities such as electricity, gas, water. It, however, also paves a secure and cheap way of forming a so-called botnet in the cloud. A botnet consists of a network compromised machines controlled by an attacker (a.k.a. botmaster). Traditionally botnets have been integrated with computers, and have been the primary cause of many malicious Internet attacks. However, with emerging technologies such as cloud computing have presented new challenges in simulating what a modern botnet could look like, and how effective they can be executed with the easily accessible resources provided by such technologies. In this paper we implement a novel cloud based botnet and then propose a new method for detecting it. It is our belief that each cloud based botnet has a unique level of entropy in their networking exchanges, and thus determining the randomness of the communications between the command and control server and the bots could be applied to discriminate bot behaviors from normal cloud users. The proposed approach is evaluated in a closed networking environment and the preliminary experimental evaluation results are promising and show significant potentials of using entropy to detect command and control channel of botnets in the cloud.

1 Introduction

Over the past thirty years, we have witnessed a strong convergence of human activities with computing and online communication, increasing dramatically the opportunities for new businesses. It, however, has also paved the way for a large number of criminal activities to thrive. While these crimes are being committed in the 'cyberspacial' domain, they are nevertheless having strong implications in the real world in which one of the biggest threats has recently been botnets, mainly responsible for criminal activities such as key-logging passwords, unauthorized recovery of personal account information, emitting spam emails or phishing scams, as reported in a recent Symantec research report [1]. A botnet refers to a group of infected computers (bots) that interact to accomplish some distributed work for illegal purposes. The bots are controlled by an attacker, also known as botmaster, through various command and control (C&C) channels. These channels can operate on different communication protocols such as

© Springer International Publishing AG 2017
I. Traore et al. (Eds.): ISDDC 2017, LNCS 10618, pp. 55–62, 2017.
https://doi.org/10.1007/978-3-319-69155-8_4

Hypertext Transfer Protocol (HTTP), Internet Relay Chat (IRC) and use various botnet topologies, e.g. client-server centralized or peer-to-peer distributed (P2P). In Fig. 1 we illustrate a typical life-cycle of a botnet and its attack behaviors.

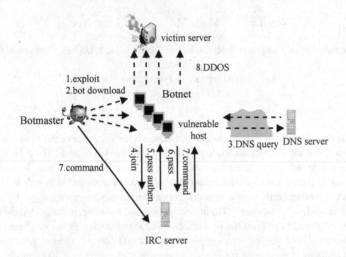

Fig. 1. Typical life-cycle of an IRC botnet and its attack behaviors

Cloud computing is a tool that most internet users utilize without even realizing it. Companies, such as Google and Amazon, allow us to use their servers. These services allow companies and individuals access to powerful computers at a low cost. They are accessible anywhere with an internet connection. The rapid rise of cloud computing technology marks the next wave of enterprise information technology, catering up a market demand of a digitized economy to deliver traditional utilities such as electricity, gas, water, to name a few. The tremendous benefits of cloud computing technologies are being leveraged by companies of all sizes, leading lots of novel concepts and implementations, such as Software as a Service, Platform as a Service, Storage as a Service, and Infrastructure as a Service. It, however, also offers a secure and cheap way of forming a botnet in the cloud, i.e. Botnet as a Service (BaaS).

Bot masters seek out vulnerable computers all over the world-wide-web to infect. In [2] Rajab et al. determined that some botnets had a size of over 100,000 bots, with thousands of bots active at any time. Typically, bot masters prey on computers with outdated operating systems, systems that have unpatched security vulnerabilities, or those without antivirus or malware detection software. Once infected, these vulnerable systems become bots, and are now part of a botnet in the cloud. Unbeknownst to the owner, their computer may be performing illegal actions, such as Distributed Denial-of-Service (DDoS) attacks, spamming, and/or sending sensitive information to criminals [3]. Often times, bot masters are unable to choose their targets and vulnerable machines can be infected easily. For instance, an unsuspecting Alice may wirelessly connect her laptop to an unprotected coffee shop network. Unknowingly, Bob's infected computer, which is also connected to the coffee shop's network, spreads the botnet malware to Alice's computer. Even though the bot master has infected another machine, and subsequently added another machine to his botnet arsenal, it may not be of much use to him. Alice's computer may infrequently be connected to the internet, or her computer may be too outdated to help carry-out the bot master's commands. Traditionally, bot acquisition is a challenge. In order to infect a bot, botmasters target systems with outdated antiviruses or utilize zero-day-attacks to avoid detection of their malware. Secondly, infected machines are unpredictable. They go offline, can vary greatly in system resources, and have a wide variety of internet speeds.

In a fashion of BaaS, both issues of the traditional botnets could be easily addressed. The bot runs on a virtual machine in the cloud, which it is much more reliable, and grants us a full control to the behaviors of a bot. By utilizing many accounts and providers, building a powerful botnet in a cloud becomes much easier compared to the traditional botnet in which social media is widely used to setting up a command and control channel. For example in BaaS, each bot periodically checks the social media page in which two commands are embedded, i.e. *STOP* and *ATTACK*. When the command *STOP* is sent, the bot will do nothing, and continue listening for a new command. The *ATTACK* command usually contains an IP address, a port number, and the duration for attacking. Once bots receive the command, they can commence immediately a DDoS attack on the specified target.

In this paper, we propose a new method for detecting cloud-based botnets. Our method includes determining the randomness of the communications between the command and control server host in a very popular social media website and the bots. It is our belief that each botnet should have a unique level of entropy in their network exchanges. The proposed approach was then evaluated using a cloud based botnet within a closed networking environment. The main contributions of the paper include (1) we propose a novel approach to form a botnet in a cloud in which bots run on virtual machines and command and control channel is set up through a HTTP based social media website, addressing the challenge of acquiring bots in BaaS; (2) an entropy based approach is used to determine randomness of communication, forming a unique pattern of botnets during their information exchanges over the network. The rest of the paper is organized as follows. Section 2 is a brief introduction to the related works on existing botnet detection approaches. In Sect. 3, we present the method of simulating a botnet in the cloud. Section 4 presents the detection approach for identifying command and control channel of botnets in the cloud and shows a preliminary evaluation result within a closed network environment. Section 5 makes some concluding remarks.

2 Related Work

Some typical examples of traditional botnets are the early Sinit [4], Nugache [5], Phatbot with WASTE command [6], and the recent Peacomm (Storm worm) [7]. Compared to such traditional botnets based on the centralized C&C channel, a distributed P2P botnet is much harder to destroy due to a more distributed communication channel through selected servers. Previous attempts aiming at detecting botnets were mainly based on honeypots [8–13], traffic-application classification [14–17] and

passive-anomaly analysis [18–21], with limited success. The ineffectiveness of these
solutions relates directly to the quickly evolving strategies employed by botmasters.
For instances, recent studies in 2013 have already shown that the TOR network has
been employed by botmasters for creating stealthiness and untraceability, leading being
more difficult to be taken down considering the anonymous C&C servers provided by
TOR hidden services [22]. Moreover studies in [23, 24] have also shown that cloud
could be applied to build a large botcloud, for the purpose of DDoS flooding and click
fraud attacks.

3   Cloud Based Botnet

Cloud computing has recently been used to form a botnet due to its capacity of bot
acquisition, bot availability, and overall botnet power. There are many cloud computing providers, such as Google, Amazon, and Microsoft. Companies and individuals
alike choose to use cloud computing because it provides a lot of computing power and
is quite inexpensive when compared to the cost of a traditional server setup. Some
cloud providers boast an uptime of at least 99%, which provides great reliability for the
botnet. Many providers also offer business class or better internet to even their free
users, which gave potential attackers ample bandwidth.

For the purpose of research and proof of concepts, a simple prototype botnet is
simulated in the cloud. Figure 2 illustrates the proposed botnet topology in which two
cloud computer virtual instances are used as bots. The bot malware is manually loaded.
As a means of command and control channel, we used a very popular social website. In
order to communicate with the bot, we edit the social media profile and then simply
type the command into the biography section of the profile. In such a case every five
minutes, the bot will scrape our profile and check one of two commands, either *STOP*
or *ATTACK*. Contained within the attack command received from the C&C server is
the target server's information. The attack command is formatted as such: *TargetIP*,
DestinationPort, *Duration*. The attack command orders the bots to flood the target
webserver with UDP packets, and thus creating a DDoS attack.

Immediately after the attack is finished, the bot will check the C&C for a new
command. If the command received is stopped, the botnet will sit idle, and will check
for a new command every five minutes. In the following we introduce how to operate
this botnet step by step in more details:

At first the botmaster uploads a command to the social media profile. This serves as
a means of command and control communication channel. The command is in the
format of *IPAddress*, *Port*, *Duration*. Before the command is uploaded, it is converted
from plaintext into base64 code.

The bots run on web server instances hosted by a popular cloud service provider.
The bots can easily run on another cloud infrastructure, or on personal computers or
web servers. A bot is created by loading the software onto the instance, and then the bot
is ready to go. To create more bots, the original instance is cloned.

Bots check the social media C&C channel every 5 min. They do this by scraping
the website's html. The bot will receive either two commands, either !stop@, or
something similar to *!MTkyLjE2OC4xLjEsODAsNjAw@*.

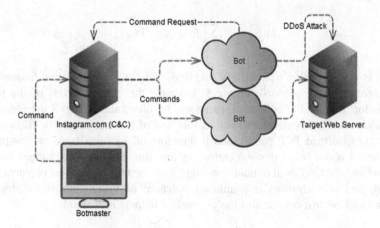

Fig. 2. A cloud based botnet topology

The exclamation marks the beginning of the command, and the *at* symbol marks the end of the command. If the command is stop, the bot does nothing, and checks the C&C again in five minutes. If the bot receives any other command it will

(1) Decode the given string between the ! and @ symbols.
(2) Determine if the command is authentic by:
    a. Making sure it has an IP address that is valid i.e.: 192.168.1.1
    b. Make sure it has a port number between 1 and 65535.
    c. Make sure it has a valid duration (Less than ten minutes) given in seconds.
(3) It then will attack the target by doing the following:
    a. Creating a UDP Packet with a payload size of 65000 bytes (Random characters)
    b. Sending the UDP packet to target IP Address and port.

After the attack has been carried out for the proper duration (i.e. 600 s) it checks the C&C for a new command. This check is performed 5 s after the completion of the previous command.

4 Detection of the Cloud Based Botnet

The proposed detection approach is based on entropy. Entropy is the level of uncertainty of certain information and it is used to detect HTTP based botnets. During the preliminary experiment, we monitored the traffic in the cloud. As expected, every five minutes, the bots request a new command from the C&C web server. Such an information exchange behavior could be captured. We then collected five instances of packet captures over five minutes from one bot throughout the whole day. Since the command and control channel is done by HTTP, only TCP packets of these exchanges are investigated. The entropy of these five captures is calculated with the following equation:

$$H(S) = -\sum_{i=0}^{n} P(s_i) \log_2(P(s_i))$$

where S is a TCP packet's payload of length n, and $P(s_i)$ is the relative frequency of each character in the payload. Figure 3 illustrates the entropy levels of the packet payloads for the 5 traffic collection instances. As illustrated in Fig. 3 the entropy of each packet received is consistent across four out of five captures. The fifth capture received a malformed TCP packet, and is therefore off by one. Based on this preliminary result it is our belief that the entropy of any future network exchanges between the botnet and the C&C will remain consistent with the first four packet captures as we analyzed, and thus showing a significant potential of using entropy for detecting command and control communication channel of botnets in a cloud.

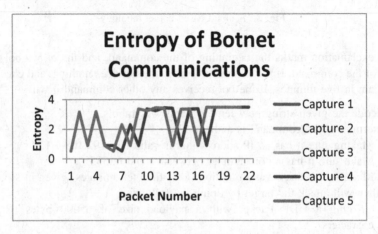

Fig. 3. Entropy levels of botnet command and control communication exchange

5   Conclusions

We propose in this paper a new method for detecting cloud based botnets. Our method includes determining the randomness of the communications between the command & control server and the bots. The proposed approach was evaluated using a cloud based botnet within a closed networking environment and preliminary results conclude our belief that each botnet command and communication channel should have a unique level of entropy in their network exchanges. In the near future we will improve the current cloud based botnets. In particular we will speed up the packet creation process by having every packet to contain the same 65000 bytes and creating worker threads to create new strings of random bytes to use. Moreover we will encrypt communications between C&C and the bots in the cloud based botnets. In terms of experimental evaluation we will extend the traffic collection to a longer time period and then automate the task of identifying a consistent and unique entropy fingerprint for botnet detection by comparing the entropy of network packet sequences to a database of previously discovered botnet traffic.

References

1. Symantec. http://www.symantec.com/security_response/publications/threatreport.jsp. Accessed 1 June 2017
2. Rajab, M., Zarfoss, J., Monrose, F., Terzis, A.: My botnet is bigger than yours (maybe, better than yours): why size estimates remain challenging. In: Proceedings of the 1st Workshop on Hot Topics in Understanding Botnets (HotBots 2007), 10 April 2007 (2007)
3. Uses of botnets, The Honeynet Project. https://www.honeynet.org/node/52
4. Sinit. http://www.symantec.com/security_response/writeup.jsp?docid=2003-100910-5701-99. Accessed 1 Apr 2017
5. Nugache. http://www.symantec.com/security_response/writeup.jsp?docid=2006-043016-0900-99. Accessed 1 Apr 2017
6. Phatbot. http://www.symantec.com/security_response/attacksignatures/detail.jsp?asid=20658. Accessed 1 Apr 2017
7. Peacomm. http://www.symantec.com/security_response/writeup.jsp?docid=2007-011917-1403-99. Accessed 1 Apr 2017
8. Rajab, M.A., Zarfoss, J., Monrose, F., Terzis, A.: A multifaceted approach to understanding the botnet phenomenon. In: Proceedings of the 6th ACM SIGCOMM Conference on Internet Measurement, pp. 41–52 (2006)
9. Baecher, P., Koetter, M., Holz, T., Dornseif, M., Freiling, F.: The nepenthes platform: an efficient approach to collect malware. In: Zamboni, D., Kruegel, C. (eds.) RAID 2006. LNCS, vol. 4219, pp. 165–184. Springer, Heidelberg (2006). doi:10.1007/11856214_9
10. Yegneswaran, V., Barford, P., Paxson, V.: Using honeynets for internet situational awareness. In: Proceedings of the 4th Workshop on Hot Topics in Networks, College Park, MD (2005)
11. Li, Z., Goyal, A., Chen, Y.: Honeynet-based botnet scan traffic analysis. In: Lee, W., Wang, C., Dagon, D. (eds.) Botnet Detection. ADIS, vol. 36, pp. 25–44. Springer, Heidelberg (2008). doi:10.1007/11555827_19. ISBN 978-0-387-68766-7
12. Freiling, F.C., Holz, T., Wicherski, G.: Botnet tracking: exploring a root-cause methodology to prevent distributed denial-of-service attacks. In: de Capitani di Vimercati, S., Syverson, P., Gollmann, D. (eds.) ESORICS 2005. LNCS, vol. 3679, pp. 319–335. Springer, Heidelberg (2005). doi:10.1007/11555827_19
13. Holz, T., Steiner, M., Dahl, F., Biersack, E., Freiling, F.: Measurements and mitigation of peer-to-peer-based botnets: a case study on storm worm. In: Proceedings of the 1st Usenix Workshop on Large-Scale Exploits and Emergent Threats, San Francisco, California (2008)
14. Strayer, T., Walsh, R., Livadas, C., Lapsley, D.: Detecting botnets with tight command and control. In: Proceedings 2006 31st IEEE Conference on Local Computer Networks, pp. 195–202 (2006)
15. Strayer, W.T., Lapsely, D., Walsh, R., Livadas, C.: Botnet detection based on network behavior. In: Lee, W., Wang, C., Dagon, D. (eds.) Botnet Detection. ADIS, vol. 36, pp. 1–24. Springer, Heidelberg (2008). doi:10.1007/978-0-387-68768-1_1
16. Livadas, C., Walsh, R., Lapsley, D., Strayer, T.: Using machine learning techniques to identify botnet traffic. In: Proceedings 2006 31st IEEE Conference on Local Computer Networks, pp. 967–974, November 2006
17. Goebel, J., Holz, T.: Rishi: identify bot contaminated hosts by IRC nickname evaluation. In: Proceedings of USENIX HotBots 2007 (2007)
18. Karasaridis, A., Rexroad, B., Hoeflin, D.: Wide-scale botnet detection and characterization. In: Proceedings of the 1st Conference on 1st Workshop on Hot Topics in Understanding Botnets, Cambridge, MA (2007)

19. Binkley, J.R., Singh, S.: An algorithm for anomaly-based botnet detection. In: USENIX SRUTI: 2nd Workshop on Steps to Reducing Unwanted Traffic on the Internet (2006)
20. Gu, G.F., Zhang, J.J., Lee, W.K.: BotSniffer: detecting botnet command and control channels in network traffic. In: Proceedings of the 15th Annual Network and Distributed System Security Symposium, San Diego, CA, February 2008
21. Gu, G.F., Perdisci, R., Zhang, J.J., Lee, W.K.: BotMiner: clustering analysis of network traffic for protocol- and structure-independent botnet detection. In: Proceedings of the 17th USENIX Security Symposium (Security 2008), San Jose, CA (2008)
22. Klijnsma, Y.: Large botnet cause of recent Tor network overload. http://blog.fox-it.com/2013/09/05/largebotnet-cause-of-recent-tor-network-overload/. Fox-It, 5 September 2013
23. Clark, K.P., Warnier, M., Brazier, F.M.T.: Botclouds - the future of cloud-based botnets? In: Leymann, F., Ivanov, I., van Sinderen, M.J., Shishkov, B.B. (eds.) Proceedings of the 1st International Conference on Cloud Computing and Services Science (CLOSER 2011), pp. 597–603. Science and Technology Publications (2011)
24. Torkashvan, M., Haghighi, H.: CBC2 a cloud-based botnet command and control. Ind. J. Sci. Technol. **8**, 1–15 (2015)

An Experimental Framework for Investigating Security and Privacy of IoT Devices

Ali Tekeoglu[1(✉)] and Ali Şaman Tosun[2]

[1] Network Computer Security Department, SUNY Polytechnic Institute,
100 Seymour Ave., Utica, NY 13502, USA
ali.tekeoglu@sunyit.edu

[2] Computer Science Department, The University of Texas at San Antonio,
One UTSA Circle, San Antonio, TX 78249, USA
ali.tosun@utsa.edu

Abstract. With the rapid growth of Internet-of-Things (IoT) devices, security and privacy issues emerged as a potential roadblock for widespread adoption. Preliminary research indicates that many types of IoT devices have serious vulnerabilities. It is not easy to investigate security and privacy issues since each type of device is different and manual experiments need to be conducted on the device. In this paper, we propose a framework for investigation of security and privacy issues of IoT devices. The framework consists of four components, a testbed, set of topics to be investigated, a set of experiments for each topic investigated and a final report. Fundamental approach used in the framework is to capture layer 2 and layer 3 packets and to analyze the packets for various features. Proposed framework is low cost and is based on off-the-shelf hardware and open source software. Using the framework, we can investigate security and privacy issues of many IoT devices including HDMI sticks, IP cameras, activity trackers, smartwatches and drones. A large set of topics can be investigated on IoT devices using the framework including vulnerability issues, protocol security, firmware updates, authentication issues and privacy violations. Sample experimental results show the promise of the proposed framework. We believe this framework will serve as the foundation for a general automated framework to investigate security and privacy issues of most IoT devices.

Keywords: IoT devices · Security · Privacy · Framework · IoT testbed

1 Introduction

Internet-of-Things (IoT) is the network of physical objects or "things" embedded with electronics, software, sensors, and network connectivity, which enables these objects to collect and exchange data. In addition to the smartphones and tablets, IoTs include large number of novel consumer devices including HDMI sticks, IP cameras, smartwatches, connected light bulbs, smart thermostats, fitness trackers, smart locks, connected sprinkler systems, garage connectivity kits, window

© Springer International Publishing AG 2017
I. Traore et al. (Eds.): ISDDC 2017, LNCS 10618, pp. 63–83, 2017.
https://doi.org/10.1007/978-3-319-69155-8_5

and door sensors, smart light switch, home security systems, smart ovens, smart baby monitors, smart slow cooker and blood pressure monitors. There will probably be many more connected products introduced in the near future.

Many analysts indicate tremendous growth for IoT devices in the future. Gartner research forecasts that 4.9 billion connected things will be in use in 2015, and will reach 25 billion by 2020. Cisco's Internet of Things Group (IOTG) predicts there will be over 50 billion connected devices by 2020. IDC predicts that wearables (subcategory of IoT devices), will reach a total of 45.7 million units in 2015 and it will reach 126.1 million units in 2019 resulting in a five-year CAGR of 45.1%. Google's Chromecast HDMI stick that converts a TV with an HDMI stick into a smart TV has sold over 20 million copies in 2 years on the market. Even based on the most conservative predictions we will have tens of billions of IoT devices.

One of the driving forces behind IoTs is the cost factor. A Google Chromecast device costs about $35, a typical IP camera sells for $60 and many older versions of fitness trackers cost about $50. Smart thermometer that connects to a smartphone costs about $20. We will soon witness an era where connected devices will have a very small premium over older systems.

With the deployment of so many different IoT devices over a short period of time, many security and privacy issues were discovered in these devices. For many manufacturers time to market is more important than having a fully tested device with rigorous security and privacy features. Security firm Symantec investigated 50 connected home devices and found various security and privacy issues. 20% of mobile apps for IoT devices did not use SSL. Mutual authentication between the server and the client was not used by any of the devices. Symantec identified 10 security issues in 15 web portals used to control IoT devices. HP investigated 10 IoT devices and discovered that 70% of devices used unencrypted network service, 80% failed to require passwords of sufficient complexity and length in addition to other security and privacy issues. These studies indicate serious issues in security and privacy of these devices.

A framework is necessary to simplify the investigation of security and privacy of IoT devices. This framework has to be general and extensible and produce a report with minimal manual work. For example, an HDMI stick is plugged in to a network and a set of experiments are evaluated to produce a report on privacy and security issues on the device. To investigate security of several HDMI sticks you need to perform the same experiments on each one and examine the results. To investigate the security of several IP cameras, you need to perform the same experiments on each one and examine the results. The framework captures the common things in evaluation and experiments to simplify the process to produce results with minimal work.

In this paper, we propose a framework to investigate the security and privacy issues of IoT devices. The framework consists of a testbed, a set of topics, a set of experiments for each topic investigated and a final report. Testbed is used to capture and analyze the packets exchanged. Topics determine the security and privacy issues investigated. For each topic, experiments are designed to investigate the topic in detail. Report includes potential security and privacy issues as well as suggestions to improve the security and privacy. Major capabilities of the framework are as follows;

- Captures layer 2 and layer 3 packets sent/received by WiFi or Bluetooth connected IoT devices.
- Uses off-the-shelf hardware and open source software resulting in a low-cost configuration.
- Can be used to investigate a wide range of security and privacy issues known on IoT devices.
- Can be extended to cover all WiFi and Bluetooth connected IoT devices.
- Enables both passive and active investigation of security and privacy.

The rest of the paper is organized as follows: In Sect. 2, we describe various IoT devices that can benefit from proposed framework. Section 3 discusses the related work. Proposed framework is explained in detail in Sect. 4. Experimental results and findings are presented in Sect. 5. We conclude with Sect. 6.

2   IoT Devices

IoT devices include a large number of consumer devices including HDMI sticks, IP cameras, Smartwatches, Activity Trackers, Smartlocks. Most communicate using WiFi or bluetooth. Next, we briefly explain some of the devices that can be analyzed using the proposed testbed.

Multimedia IoT devices vary with respect to their form-factor. Set-top boxes include Apple TV, Amazon FireTV, Roku 1-2-3, Netgear's NeoTV series, GoogleTV enabled boxes from Sony, Asus, Vizio and Hisense. These devices are usually in the size of a wireless home router and they have built-in wireless network card, Bluetooth, USB/HDMI/Ethernet ports, internal storage, microphone etc. HDMI dongles are larger than a regular USB stick. They include Google's Chromecast, Netgear's NeoMediacast [1], and Roku's Streaming Stick and Amazon FireTV Stick [2]. These small form factor devices are both a cost effective solution to add smart-TV functionality to an older TV set (with an HDMI port) and easy to set up and use. Integrated Smart-TVs include LG's 2nd generation 3D GoogleTV [3]. The cost of smart TVs is quite high compared to set-top boxes and HDMI dongles, while almost similar functionality is provided.

Most common HDMI sticks are Chromecast from Google, FireTV Stick from Amazon and Roku Streaming Stick from Roku. Chromecast is a thumb-sized media streaming device that plugs into the HDMI port on TVs. It can be controlled with an app on a smartphone or a tablet to send video to a larger screen, which is typically a TV. Chromecast has dimensions of $72\,mm \times 35\,mm \times 12\,mm$, weighs $34\,g$ and costs \$35. As the brain of Chromecast, Marvell 88DE3005-A1 (Armada 1500-mini) [4] system-on-chip is used. Amazon's Fire TV Stick connects to a TV's HDMI port. It's an easy way to watch movies on Netflix, Amazon Instant Video, HBO NOW, and Hulu Plus, plus games and music. Fire TV stick has 4 times the storage and 2 times the memory of Chromecast in addition to a dual-core processor and 1 GB of memory. FireTV stick does not have a USB port, developers connect the device over the WiFi in the local network. The Roku Streaming stick is designed to play a variety of streaming content directly from the Internet.

There are many different types of IP cameras on the market. Most have similar underlying hardware. We have NetCam and Dropcam as representative devices of this category. NetCam is a cloud based wireless IP camera by Belkin. NetCam comes embedded with a VGA 1/4 in. CMOS sensor. The focal length of the lens is 3.1 mm. Horizontal view angle is 64°, Vertical view angle is 48° while diagonal view angle is 80°. NetCam uses MJPEG and JPEG for still images. Resolution of the images could be 160×120, 320×240 or 640×480. Dropcam is an easy to set-up and use, cloud based wireless IP camera by Nest. It is designed for indoor use and mostly used for home, business monitoring. With Cloud Video Recording (CVR), Dropcam constantly uploads the captured video stream to a remote cloud server owned by Nest. Dropcam uses H.264 encoding with 720p quality for images. Multimedia stream is captured with 1280×720 image size at 30 frames/sec.

There are many smartwatches with various capabilities on the market including Apple Watch, Samsung Gear Live, Motorola Moto 360, ASUS Zenwatch, Sony Smartwatch and LG G watch. Most have 4 GB storage and 0.5 GB ram. Typical resolution is 320×320. They use a stripped down OS such as Android Wear or WatchOS. Most have WiFi and Bluetooth connectivity. A few including Sony smartwatch has GPS and some support wireless and magnetic charging.

Activity Trackers on the market are from Fitbit, Jawbone, Garmin, TomTom, Mio and Runtastic. They work with a smartphone app and display daily metrics such as number of steps and sleep time. They synch with the smartphone using Bluetooth. Some are just a wrist band and others include smart watch functionality. They typically don't have GPS. Display is OLED or LCD in most cases. They support mobile OSs including Android and iOS. Typical battery life is 4–10 days. Most of them have sleep tracking functionality and have a hearth rate monitor.

Smart locks gained popularity recently. Although they are expensive they offer desirable high tech features. August smart lock uses Bluetooth and can open the lock as you approach the door using your smart phone. It also works with a key if your phone runs out of battery. Second generation uses voice commands and Siri on iPhone can be used to open the lock. Kwikset Kevo lets you grant ekeys to guests and tradesman. It has Bluetooth proximity sensing and opens the lock without the need to pull the phone out of pocket. Yale keyless connected lets you open the door using a key fob or a pin. Schlage Sense requires entering an access code on your phone to open the lock. Lockitron Bolt works with both Bluetooth and WiFi and lets you unlock the lock remotely. Mul-T-Lock ENTR uses biometric authentication using a fingerprint ID.

3 Related Work

In this section, the related work on security and privacy of IoT devices is briefly mentioned. Preliminary results on security and privacy issues of Chromecast device is discussed in [5,6]. Many HDMI sticks run a stripped-down version of Android OS. Although there has been a flurry of research on Android security recently, most of the research focuses on full-fledged Android OS and application security. More than 1000 Android malware samples were investigated in [7] and most of the malware were repackaged versions of legitimate applications with malicious payloads. Different approaches were used to investigate security of Android applications. Taintdroid [8] monitors behavior of Android applications to detect misuse of private information and Kirin [9] is a security service for lightweight certification to mitigate malware at install time. Static analysis was used on more than 1,000 Android applications for security [10] and widespread misuse of private information and advertising networks is detected. Readers are referred to [11] for an overview of Android Security Framework. All of the above research focuses on a complete Android OS and to our knowledge no work exists for stripped-down android OS used on Chromecast device.

A serious vulnerability in Foscam wireless IP cameras that are connected to the Internet was discovered [12]. Exploiting this weakness, attackers could hijack the camera and alter the firmware. Another vulnerability that enables remote attackers to access the live-stream was disclosed for Trendnet IP cameras [13]. A more recent hack of a popular IP camera was revealed in DefCon'22 conference [14]. In their investigation, researchers took apart Dropcam IP camera in order to get access to the root shell by attaching cables to the PCB board under the hood over the UART pins, modified and re-flashed the firmware with malicious code. Analyis of security and privacy issues of NetCam shows that NetCam does not encrypt the images sent to the cloud and encrypted images can be reconstructed with some effort [15].

Security of activity trackers has received a lot of attention recently and many problems were reported on security and privacy issues. Center for Secure Design [16] explains how secure design of an activity tracker should be done using a fictional device WearFit. This fictional device uses the operating principles of activity trackers on the market and this work serves as secure design guidelines to activity trackers. A comparative analysis of fitness tracker security and privacy is investigated in [17]. They investigated widely used activity trackers and associated smartphone apps and discovered several issues with studied activity tackers. Symantec analysis of self-tracking devices [18] has found security risks in a large number of self-tracking devices and applications. One of the significant findings was that all of the devices examined are vulnerable to location tracking.

Smartwatches are another IoT category with large volume of sales and a device is offered by almost any IoT related company. A research study [19] conducted by Hewlett-Packard has found that 100% of popular device models contain severe vulnerabilities. This study combined manual testing along with the use of digital tools. This study revealed that insufficient user authentication and authorization are common issues within smartwatches and 70% of devices have problems with firmware updates.

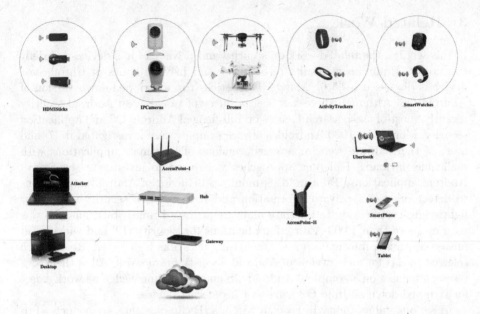

Fig. 1. Testbed network setup

4   Framework

The proposed framework provides a platform for investigating security and privacy issues of IoT devices. Since there are many different IoT devices on the market, we focus on issues that are common to the majority of the devices. Our approach is based on capture and analysis of layer 2 and layer 3 packets sent/received by the IoT devices. A lot of information is available in the transmitted packets. Proposed framework works by connecting an IoT device to a testbed and letting it run as usual. We also use active methods to test attack resilience. Proposed framework is extendible and other types of devices can be added to the framework for analysis.

The proposed framework consists of four parts; (i) a testbed, (ii) set of topics to be investigated (iii) set of experiments for each topic investigated and (iv) a report.

4.1   Testbed

Testbed is designed to facilitate investigation of a wide range of topics on security and privacy of IoT devices. Primary goal is to build a low cost testbed using publicly available open source software and low cost off-the-shelf hardware. Proposed testbed is designed to investigate security and privacy issues in IoT devices that use WiFi or Bluetooth by capturing transmitted packets. As seen in Fig. 1, we have several different categories of IoT devices in the testbed. HDMI sticks have integrated WiFi and are communicating with a local mobile app for control as well as remote server for content. They are connected to home WiFi network, which we denote as AccessPoint-1 in Fig. 1. IP Cameras also came with an integrated WiFi and connect to home WiFi network. They stream the multimedia content continuously to cloud servers. Drones have 2 different WiFi interfaces integrated to them. 2.4 GHz interface is used to stream live video to a mobile app on the ground, while 5 GHz signal is connected for receiving control packets.

Activity trackers and Smartwatches are using Bluetooth most frequently. Bluetooth consumes less power however the range and bandwidth is limited compared to WiFi. Since Smartwatches and Activity trackers are designed to communicate to a smartphone or tablet, they are usually close enough to utilize Bluetooth connection. In our testbed we have used Ubertooth [20] to capture Bluetooth communication packets. Project Ubertooth is an open source wireless development platform suitable for Bluetooth experimentation. Ubertooth ships with a capable BLE (Bluetooth Smart) sniffer and can also sniff data from Basic Rate (BR) Bluetooth Classic connections. Ubertooth is a custom board connected to a laptop. It monitors close-by Bluetooth channels and captured packets are sent to the laptop over USB port. We used Wireshark and Kismet to dissect captured packets.

Controlling mobile apps are installed on an Android smartphone and an Android Tablet as seen in Fig. 1. These devices are connected to a different WiFi device, depicted as AccessPoint-II in our testbed, since we wanted the communication between MobileApps and IoT devices to be forced into Layer-3. If controlling mobile apps and IoT devices were all connected to the same access-point, they utilize Layer-2 to communicate locally, thus packets can not be captured.

Our testbed involved 5 groups of IoT devices; HDMI sticks, IP cameras, Drones, Activity-Trackers and Smart-Watches. Among these devices first 3 utilized WiFi and the last 2 communicated over Bluetooth. We have used Google's Chromecast, Amazon's FireTVStick and Roku's Streaming Stick in the HDMI sticks category. IP cameras installed in the test-bed included NetCam by Belkin and Dropcam by Nest. 3D Robotics' IRIS+ drone was integrated in the test-bed. We have examined DJI's Phantom drone and made sure testbed could capture it's communications too. As Activity-Trackers, Jawbone and Fitbit devices were used. Android based Smartwatch from Samsung is utilized in our Testbed as seen in Fig. 1. Readers are referred to [21] for details of the testbed. An earlier version of the testbed is used in [5] and [6] to investigate security and privacy issues of Chromecast HDMI stick.

4.2 Topics Investigated

Second component of the framework is a set of topics on security and privacy issues that can be investigated using the testbed. Each topic is investigated using a set of experiments to find information on the issues investigated. We next list the major topics in our framework and briefly explain them.

1. *Vulnerability and Nmap Scans:* Vulnerability scanners such as OpenVAS, Nessus and Nexpose are designed to assess computers, networks and appli-

cations for weaknesses. However, They are not designed for IoT devices and have limited support. Nmap scan discovers the device and reveals the open ports, accepted protocols, fingerprints the OS and the kernel.

2. *Firmware Update:* IoT devices are relatively new and firmware update is a way of adding features to these devices. However, some IoT devices may sit on store shelves for months before they are sold and used. IoT devices should update the firmware before first use and update periodically to add features and fix security and performance issues. If network communication is not secure, IoT devices download the firmware over cleartext without any encryption and authentication. This can lead to various types of attacks including installation of malicious firmware and unrequested firmware upgrades.

3. *Protocol Security:* Network Time Protocol (NTP), DIAL, STUN and mDNS are some of the protocols used by IoT devices. NTP is a networking protocol for clock synchronization between computers. IoT devices use NTP protocol as well. Older versions of NTP protocol are vulnerable and should be avoided. Some IoT devices including HDMI sticks connect to the cloud and use specific protocols such as STUN and DIAL. There is limited work on the security of these protocols.

4. *Password Security:* Some IoT devices use passwords for authenticating the user. Many IoT devices allow the user to choose weak passwords. Most IoT devices don't have a mechanism to prevent brute-force password guessing and are vulnerable. Passwords should also be periodically updated and captchas should be used to prevent automated attacks on IoT devices.

5. *Attack Resilience:* IoT devices are vulnerable against various type of attacks including Man-in-the-middle (Mitm) and DoS attacks. Mitm attacks can lead to major security and privacy issues. Potential DoS attacks range from SYN flood attacks to more advanced attacks. DoS resilience of IoT devices should be investigated since they have limited resources and are vulnerable to these attacks.

6. *Mobile App Security:* Almost every IoT device comes with a mobile app installed on a smartphone. Vulnerabilities in these mobile apps can lead to problems on the IoT devices. For example, data read from an activity tracker can be modified on the phone before being submitted to the cloud. Falsified activity data can be inserted using the smartphone app. Thus, mobile apps should be tested for potential vulnerabilities.

7. *Cloud Security:* State-of-the-art IoT devices are cloud based, and are in constant communication with the cloud. Typically, there is a server running in the cloud that controls/orchestrates the device, and we the security of services running on the cloud should be investigated. For example, web interface on the cloud can lead to potential attacks on the server.

8. *Network Traffic Analysis:* Many IoT devices are in constant communication with the cloud even if they are not actively used. Monitoring of idle network traffic and connections kept-alive reveal a lot about the IoT devices. DNS queries during idle varies by the device and the query pattern and the servers

queried reveals the existence of a device behind a network since many IoT devices query hard-coded DNS servers regularly.

9. *Privacy:* Privacy is a major issue for IoT devices since a lot of sensitive data is collected by the IoT devices. For example, activity trackers keep track of when you are active, your location and when you sleep. What is sent to the servers needs to be investigated along with the privacy policy of the device. Some IoT devices may share the data with third parties to used for marketing purposes. Information sent to the servers should be encrypted and authenticated.

10. *Proper use of Security Protocols:* Cipher suites is are combinations of authentication, encryption, message authentication code (MAC) and key exchange algorithms used to negotiate the security settings for a network connection using the Transport Layer Security (TLS)/Secure Sockets Layer (SSL) network protocol. Latest version of SSL/TLS should be used for security. Since IoT devices have limited hardware resources they may prefer weaker cipher suites. Weaker cipher suites should be avoided. Certificate and Key strength used by the IoT devices should be high.

11. *Device Specific Topics:* There are device specific issues unique to a group of IoT devices such as IP cameras, HDMI sticks or activity trackers. For example, reconstruction of images sent by an IP camera may be possible if proper security measures are not deployed. When data is cast from a tablet to an HDMI stick, data and the link should be secured properly. Activity tracker data stored on a smartphone should be secured properly.

4.3   Experiments on Topics Investigated

Third component of the framework is a set of experiments on each topic that is investigated. This set of experiments collects the data that is used to creation of the final report.

We mostly use open source software for the experiments due to the advantages they offer. Software used for experiments include Wiresark in Desktop and Laptop, Kismet in Laptop, Kali Linux in Attacker box, Open-Wrt on the wireless access points.

- *Wireshark:* is used to capture and dissect the network packets that are captured.
- *Kismet:* is used to capture and dissect wireless and bluetooth packets.
- *Open-WRT:* installed on wireless access points. We used the iptables's TEE module to send a copy of the packets
- *Kali Linux:* utilized in the attacker machine. It comes with vast amount of pentesting tools.
- *OpenVAS, Nessus, Nexpose:* are used as vulnerability scanners.
- *binwalk:* is used to analyze and investigate the firmware of IoT devices.
- *Scapy:* is used to manipulate packets to test attack resilience of IoT devices.

We next briefly discuss the major experiments for each topic.

1. *Vulnerability and Nmap Scans:* OpenVAS (Open Vulnerability Assessment System) [22] is an open source vulnerability scanner that is updated daily from several security advisories. We run the most rigorous test against IoT devices to scan them for known vulnerabilities. OpenVAS rates vulnerabilities on a scale of 1 (low) to 10 (high). We do an Nmap scan on IoT devices to find open ports and find accepted protocols.

2. *Firmware Update:* We first check if the IoT device updates the firmware when it is first set up. This is necessary since they may be sitting on store shelves for months and new firmware may be released during that time. We check if the IoT device has a regular firmware update mechanism built in. If there is one, we check if the firmware update is authenticated and whether it is sent in cleartext. If firmware is sent in cleartext, *binwalk* software can be used to identify the file headers that exist in the firmware file. It may also possible to decompile the firmware, update it and stitch it together to form a malicious firmware if cleartext transmission and no authentication is used.

3. *Protocol Security:* Older versions of protocols typically have bugs and vulnerabilities that are fixed in later versions. For this topic, we check the version of NTP protocol used, version of Dial protocol used, version of mDNS protocol used and version of STUN protocol used.

4. *Password Security:* Some IoT devices require passwords for authenticating the user. We check the length and strength of the password required by IoT device, We check if they have any schemes to prevent automated brute-force password cracking attacks, we also check if they require the user to change any default passwords that are used to access the device when it is first set up. We investigate if there is a password reset/recovery scheme implemented.

5. *Attack Resilience:* We perform various types of Denial-of-service attacks on the IoT devices and examine how they respond to the attacks. We expect increased response time but no system crashes. We also perform Man-in-the-middle attacks and investigate the results.

6. *Mobile App Security:* We investigate whether the mobile app uses proper authentication and encryption for the connections between the IoT and the mobile device and the mobile device and the cloud. We also use decompiling tools to reverse engineer the mobile app to modify it.

7. *Cloud Security:* We investigate the security of the web interface at the cloud server against OWASP top 10 most critical web application security risks. We use tools such as *sqlmap* for sql injection attack vulnerabilities at the server since servers run some form of database.

8. *Network Traffic Analysis:* We investigate the network traffic during normal operation and during idle. We examine servers connected, connections, DNS queries and NTP servers connected. Many IoT devices have a connection open to the server all the time and generate traffic even during idle.

9. *Privacy:* We investigate the privacy policy of the IoT device. If no encryption is used, we capture and analyze the data sent to the cloud. We investigate whether the data stored on a mobile device is properly secured. We also

check if the data is sent to other sites from the mobile or IoT for data analytics purposes.

10. *Proper use of Security Protocols:* We first check if SSL/TLS is used to secure communication. If SSL/TLS is used, we check if the latest version is used and examine the cipher suites that the IoT devices uses and compare them against Cipher Suite Black List [23]. We also check certificate and key strength used by the protocols.

11. *Device Specific Topics:* For IP cameras, we check if the transmitted images can be reconstructed if no encryption mechanism is used. For HDMI stick, we investigate whether casting process from a tablet or a mobile to the HDMI stick is secured properly. For activity trackers, we check if the data stored on a smartphone is secured properly.

4.4 Report

Report has a brief description of the IoT device being investigated and results of the security and privacy experiments conducted on the device. Report is organized by topics and lists potential problems with the device as well as mitigation schemes. For example, for Roku streaming stick, Vulnerability and Nmap scans topic lists one vulnerability with 2.6 (low severity) on TCP timestamp implementation. For chromecast HDMI stick, NTP experiment lists version 3 being used where latest stable release is 4.2.8 at ntp.org official site. This report can be evaluated by the IoT design staff to improve the security and privacy of the IoT device.

5 Results and Findings

In our experiments, we installed Chromecast, FireTV, Roku, Dropcam and Net-Cam Android applications on our Nexus-7, Android 4.4.4 tablet. The Chrome browser running on desktop computer has GoogleCast plug-in version 14.805.0.6 for TabCasting experiments. IoT devices automatically check for updates every time they boot up. We have found several interesting points that might be either improved or extended for better privacy of these devices. Following are experiments that have been done on the test-bed to examine the network packets exchanged under different scenarios.

5.1 Vulnerability and Nmap Scans

OpenVAS (Open Vulnerability Assessment System) [22] is an open source vulnerability scanner that is updated daily from several security advisories. We run the most rigorous test against Chromecast, Roku and FireTVstick to scan them for known vulnerabilities.

OpenVAS scan against Roku revealed one vulnerability with 2.6 (Low Severity). This vulnerability was about TCP Timestamps being implemented in Roku networking stack, therefore allowing to compute the uptime by a remote attacker.

Scan also listed a service running at TCP port 8060 as a web server. Besides, the HTTP server's type and version running on port 8060 was discovered as UPnP/1.0 MiniUPnPd/1.4.

Chromecast is scanned with the same rigorous vulnerability scan test and listed 3 different vulnerabilities with 5.0 (Medium), 4.3 (Medium) and 2.6 (Low) severity levels. First and most important vulnerability, Infinite HTTP Request on TCP port 8008, was found which makes it possible to kill the web server by sending an invalid Infinite HTTP Request that never ends. An attacker might exploit this vulnerability to make the web server on port 8008 crash continually by consuming all available memory or even execute arbitrary code on the system. Even though OpenVAS found this serious vulnerability, it noted that it was unable to crash the web server running on Chromecast's port 8008. Second vulnerability discovered with 4.3 (medium) severity level was about the presence of 6 weak SSL Ciphers presented by the web server running on port 8009. The last and least severe vulnerability was the implementation of TCP Timestamps which would reveal uptime.

The same vulnerability scan test on FireTVstick returned more serious problems. The first vulnerability listed had the top severity score of 10 (High). The server running on FireTVstick's TCP port 49986 found to be vulnerable against Format String Attack on URI. This means an attacker might use this flaw to crash the server or execute arbitrary code. Second vulnerability listed was also about the server running on the same port, and had a high severity level of 7.5. This problem was called CERN httpd CGI name heap overflow vulnerability. Abusing this flaw, an attacker possibly disrupt, kill or run malicious code on the server. Third listed vulnerability with severity level 5.0 (Medium) was the Infinite HTTP Request flaw, which is same as the Chromecast's problem mentioned above. The last vulnerability had severity level 4.3 (medium) and was about Cross Site Scripting.

We also did several different Nmap scans on the 3 HDMI sticks. Nmap TCP SYN scan listed 2 open ports in Chromecast; 8008 and 8009. Port 8008 is listening for http connections and port 8009 is listed as "ajp13" (Apache JServ Protocol version 1.3) service. Nmap TCP SYN scan on Roku listed the TCP port 8060 as open a "http-proxy" service waiting for connections. Same Nmap scan on FireTVstick listed TCP port 8008 as open with a "http" service listening for incoming connections.

IP cameras; NetCam and Dropcam are scanned with OpenVAS. Several problems with NetCam such as open ports, default/weak credentials were found. The most severe vulnerability found by the scanners was the "HTTP Brute Force Logins with Default Credentials". Scanners found out that the HTTP server running on the TCP port 80 was using default login credentials **admin:admin**. The next less severe vulnerability listed by the scanners was "TCP Timestamps: RFC1323 is implemented" which means an attacker can compute the uptime leading to other attacks. The remaining vulnerabilities such as were listed as having 0 severity.

DropCam did not reveal any serious vulnerabilities. It had the same 0 severity vulnerabilities as NetCam.

5.2 Firmware Update

New functionality is frequently pushed to IoT devices via firmware updates. We examined the long network traces and looked for clear-text firmware updates. Roku Streaming stick found to have this security issue. During the first time setup of Roku Streaming Stick, it connects to a remote host at "firmware.roku.com" and queries the latest firmware that is available to download. After getting the DNS response for "firmware.roku.com", Roku sends a HTTP HEAD request which actually asks the firmware server about the details of the latest firmware such as build date, file size etc. In case Roku decides that its current firmware is out of date, it sends a HTTP GET request and downloads the firmware.

We have extracted the firmware bytes from the Wireshark capture, and run the "binwalk" tool against the extracted binary. Binwalk was able to collect some interesting information about the firmware running on Roku. Such as the firmware containing a Linux OS kernel, the CPU architecture firmware compiled for is ARM, it is compressed with gzip format and the name of the kernel image in the firmware was "linux-2.6.35.14-grsec2.2.2", also the compile time for the image was "last modified: Wed Sep 24 12:38:44 2014".

We have seen that Chromecast has updated itself several times during our experiments, however in the network captures there were not any evidence that the updated binary was downloaded in clear-text as Roku did. Thus, we believe that it is downloaded from one of the servers in *.google.com that Chromecast communicates over TLSv1.2. Similary for the FireTVstick, there were not any clear-text binary download, which implies that the updates were downloaded over SSL/TLS channels.

5.3 Protocol Security

In [24], authors discuss the security issues of NTP protocol. As a solution to address the security problems in NTP protocol, authors proposed a new security model named *Autokey* which is implemented in NTP version 4.

Chromecast uses NTP protocol right after it is rebooted in order to get the current time through a NTP server. However, there are some known vulnerabilities in this protocol, specifically the version that is used by Chromecast and time servers it is connecting to. The most current stable version of NTP is listed as 4.2.8 at ntp.org official website [25]. Chromecast uses NTPv3 which was released in 1999 that has long been deprecated. Even though Chromecast uses an insecure version of NTP, this connections are infrequent. Figure 4a shows that NTP servers are connected only 5 times over a 65 h of idle period.

Amazon FireTVstick is also utilizing remote NTP servers for time synchronization during reboot and initialization. Similar to Chromecast, it is using NTP client version 3. Only difference from Chromecast is that, FireTVstick queries either 2.android.pool.ntp.org or ntp-g7g.amazon.com from the DNS server before connecting to update its internal clock.

Roku Streaming Stick take network time synchronization more seriously and did not rely on public NTP servers nor NTP protocol. Roku streaming stick DNS queries ntp.rokutime.com server and connects to it over encrypted TLSv1 stream to update its internal time.

Chromecast uses the STUN protocol, however, instead of using registered UDP port number 3478 for this protocol, Chromecast communicates over port 19302 with Google STUN server which is for Google Talk Voice and Video connections.

5.4 Password Security

Some IoT devices use passwords for authenticating the user. Many IoT devices allow the user to choose weak passwords. The strength of the password required is analyzed. Most IoT devices don't lock users after a number of failed login attempts, leading to brute-force attacks. dropcam.com/login requires passwords with at least 8 characters, upper and lower-case letter, numbers and symbols. netcam.belkin.com checks for weak passwords but does not enforce it. User can even have 123456 as a password. FireTV stick comes with Amazon account of the owner already set-up, thus it uses Amazon username and password. Amazon requires 6 characters minimum as a password. Chromecast and Roku mobile apps do not require login to use the device. Once the app is launched, it finds the local IoT sticks. However there is no authentication implemented.

5.5 Attack Resilience

NetCam IP camera and Belkin cloud server keeps a TCP connection alive always with regular [PSH-ACK] packet exchange. We wanted to attack this connection to trick the cloud that NetCam is going offline. By using a Python library for crafting & sending custom network packets called *Scapy* [26], we put together [RST] and [FIN] packets and send them to both NetCam and cloud server that's at the other end of the connection. This attack, renders the NetCam as unavailable in the list of cameras when a user logs into his/her account at netcam.belkin.com. Since keep-alive [PSH, ACK] packets are exchanged in a regular interval, if an attacker can synchronize sending crafted connection RST and FIN packets right after the keep-alive packets, a NetCam owner would see his NetCam as offline all the time.

5.6 Network Traffic Analysis

Chromecast maintains a couple of connections to Google servers when it is connected to the home wireless network, but not streaming video. One connection is for retrieving the images that are displayed on screen as a wallpaper. For this purpose, Chromecast connects to a Google server every 60 s to download the next image.

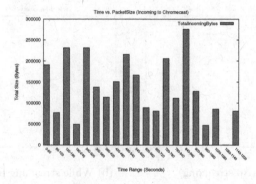

Fig. 2. Bar graph of incoming packets to chromecast at idle

These images are retrieved from several different Google servers. Chromecast queries the Google's DNS server at 8.8.8.8, which in turn responds with couple of different IP addresses of Google content servers that Chromecast can connect and download a new image to display as wallpaper. Chromecast opens a connection to the first address in the DNS response. After a successful TCP-Handshake they set-up a TLS v1.2 connection, with Chromecast offering Cipher Suites for authentication-bulk encryption-decryption-Hashing and signature. In case Chromecast would keep downloading the image from the IP address, it keeps the connection alive with a TCP Keep-Alive packet, which is sent 45 s after wallpaper image is downloaded from the server. 15 s after the TCP Keep-Alive, another image is requested from the same server or DNS is queried again to get another IP to keep downloading wallpaper images.

The bar-graph in Fig. 2 shows us the total amount of data incoming to Chromecast device per minute. This corresponds to the wallpaper images that are displayed on screen when the Chromecast is not used actively by another local remote control device. Although the packets are encrypted with TLS v1.2, someone listening the traffic from outside can differentiate which image is displayed on the screen from the total size of incoming packets every 60 s.

Data from a 3 days of network trace plotted in Fig. 3a shows that Chromecast, when running in idle, is connecting to many different IP addresses. Even though its connecting to 11 different domains as shown in Fig. 4a, every once in a while IP address corresponding to the same domain name changes for load balancing & availability reasons. This could be mistaken as a malware leaking information from internal network over-time.

Figure 4b, shows us the number of queries per domain name sent by Chromecast to DNS server during a streaming session of 2 h from YouTube. When Fig. 4a and b are compared, YouTube streaming session of only 2 h establishes connections to more domains as opposed to days of idle streaming.

To examine the total number of different IP address that Chromecast connects during the same 2 h YouTube streaming experiment; Fig. 3b is plotted. Chromecast connects to several Google content servers on different IPs for image

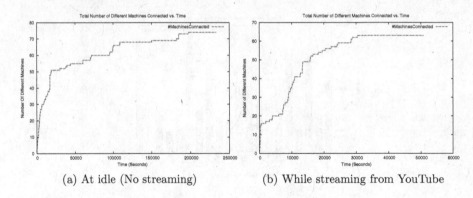

(a) At idle (No streaming)   (b) While streaming from YouTube

Fig. 3. Chromecast connecting to different IPs

download on idle as seen in Fig. 3a and for downloading different parts of stripped video as depicted in Fig. 3b while streaming from YouTube.

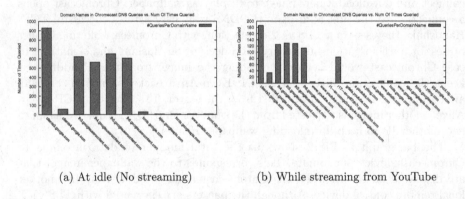

(a) At idle (No streaming)   (b) While streaming from YouTube

Fig. 4. Chromecast DNS queries

Chromecast always uses the Google DNS Server, 8.8.8.8. As show in Fig. 4a the requests at idle are for the following Address Mapping Records(A). For random wallpaper image download at idle, first Chromecast queries the Google DNS server for an Address Mapping Record(A) with the name lh3.googleusercontent.com, lh4.googleusercontent.com, lh5.googleusercontent. com or lh6.googleusercontent.com. Then, DNS server replies with couple of IP addresses which maps to the cannonical name (CNAME) googlehosted.l.googleusercontent.com. Also, Address Mapping Records(A) for clients3.google.com and clients4.google.com are queried from DNS server and it replies with usually 17 IP records for canonical name clients.l.google.com. Another DNS query Chromecast sends, asks for the IP address of tools.google.com, which the DNS server replies with 17 IP addresses mapped to the Canonical Name Record (CNAME) of tools.l.google.com. However, this query is not common, in our experiments it was queried once in every 3–4 h. Chromecast also queries the DNS server for pool.ntp.org address, however it was not frequent.

Roku has the minimal network traffic during idle. It has three characteristic communication patterns; 3 SSDP NOTIFY packets over UDP port 1900 every 20 min advertising its location in the network, ICMP Ping Requests every 5 s to local network gateway with a payload of 184 bytes consisting of English alphabet (minus last 3 characters) repeating 8 times and DNS querying the "giga.logs.roku.com" followed by a TLSv1 connection which uploads encrypted data end terminates the connection. There were also other infrequent DNS queries and connections to netflix domains.

Amazon FireTVstick also sends regular SSDP NOTIFY packets to the local network to advertise itself just like Roku and Chromecast. FiretTVstick, however, provides more information in the SSDP NOTIFY packet sequence. It sends 12 packets at a time compared to Roku's 3. Also, it sends the 12 packet every 15 min compared to 20 min in Roku. FireTV stick connects to many servers in amazon.com domain and also utilizes mDNS for advertising itself besides DIAL/SSDP packets similar to Chromecast, while Roku does not utilize mDNS.

5.7 Proper Use of Security Protocols

According to SSL/TLS protocol, after TCP handshake, client and server exchange Client Hello and Server Hello messages. A Client Hello message contains a list of Cipher Suites that client supports. Server responds with a Server Hello message in which it chooses one of the Cipher Suites from the client supported cipher suites list [27].

Chromecast always uses TLSv1.2 for communicating with TLS capable servers. Chromecast's Client Hello messages include 34 bytes of TLS Extension with an Extension Type (0×0010) that Wireshark listed as "Unknown". This extension tells the server that Chromecast supports "spdy/2, spdy/3, spdy/3.1 and http/1.1" over SSL encryption and it's unique to Chromecast.

We found that Chromecast offers two different cipher suite lists in its Client Hello messages. Lists either consisted of 18 or 62 cipher suites. About 99% of the Client Hello messages consisted of 18 cipher suites, where the tiny 1% offered 62 different cipher suites.

Out of the list of Cipher Suites supported by Chromecast, $TLS\_ECDHE\_ECDSA\_WITH\_AES\_128\_GCM\_SHA256$ was the most chosen by Google's Servers which was also listed as the first cipher suite in the Chromecast's list, 99.29% of the time. $TLS\_ECDHE\_RSA\_WITH\_AES\_128\_GCM\_SHA256$ and $TLS\_ECDHE\_RSA\_WITH\_AES\_256\_GCM\_SHA384$ were also chosen.

Amazon's FireTVstick always utilizes SSL with TLSv1.0 when communicating sensitive information with remote servers over the internet, compared to Chromecast's TLSv1.2. We captured the first 66 h of traffic when the FireTVstick was initially set up. Not all the Client Hello messages sent by FireTVstick has a "TLS Server Name" extension, only 71% had during the experiments.

FireTVstick `Client Hello` messages, offer one of 3 different lists to the servers during TLS handshake. This lists either have 35, 13 or 3 cipher suites. The list containing 35 cipher suites is used in 83% of the `Client Hello` messages during the initial 66 h experiment. Each of the other two lists are used about 8% of the time. The most popular cipher suite both FireTVstick and Amazon servers agrees upon 71% of the time was $TLS\_RSA\_WITH\_RC4\_128\_MD5$. Which is one of the top cipher suites in the HTTP version 2, Cipher Suite Black List [23].

Roku Streaming stick utilize SSL mainly with TLSv1.0 (67%) and also with TLSv1.2 for specific domain servers (33% of all `Client Hellos`). We captured the 64 h initial setup followed by idle traffic of Roku. TLSv1.2 is used for *.net-flix.com domains, and TLSv1.0 used for the reşt. In this experiment 75% of the `Client Hello` messages had "TLS Server Name" extension.

Roku `Client Hello` messages offered Cipher Suite lists of length either 46(%33), 19(41%) or 3(25%). Cipher Suite of length 46 is used with *.net-flix.com domain servers with TLSv1.2. Cipher suite list with only 2 cipher suites was used when TLSv1.0 handshaking with *.roku.com servers. List of 19 Cipher Suites is used during TLSv1.0 communication with "giga.logs.roku.com", *.mgo.com and *.mgo-images.com domain servers. Out of the Cipher Suites proposed by Roku Streaming Stick, the most chosen ones by the remote servers were $TLS\_DHE\_RSA\_WITH\_AES\_128\_CBC\_SHA$ (32%) followed by $TLS\_DHE\_RSA\_WITH\_AES\_256\_CBC\_SHA$ (28%), both of which are in the Cipher Suite Black List for HTTP/2 [23].

NetCam experiment that take 20 h of mixed idle and live stream-ing traffic showed that only ssl/tls traffic was between www.seedonk.com at TCP port 443. NetCam supports 46 different Cipher Suites; where $TLS\_ECDHE\_RSA\_WITH\_AES\_256\_CBC\_SHA$ is the first one in the list. Second cipher in the list is; $TLS\_ECDHE\_ECDSA\_WITH\_AES\_256\_CBC\_SHA$ and $TLS\_DHE\_RSA\_WITH\_AES\_256\_CBC\_SHA$ is the third one. From the list the 3rd one is chosen by the www.seedonk.com server at the other end of the TLSv1.0 connection. There are also 25 different elliptic curves sup-ported by NetCam. All the cipher suites used are in "TLS 1.2 Cipher Suite Black List" for HTTP/2 [23].

5.8 Device Specific Issues

- *Tablet Casting YouTube to Chromecast:* YouTube app in Android tablet has a cast to Chromecast button enabled. Once tapped, the tablet would stop show-ing the video in the small screen and start streaming the YouTube video to the Chromecast attached larger screen. Tablet device becomes a remote con-trol. In this setting the control packets such as play, stop, pause etc. are sent through clear-text over HTTP from tablet to YouTube servers. This would pose a security threat and provide feasibility for man-in-the-middle attacks and replay-attacks. The video control packets are sent from the mobile remote device to YouTube servers and video is streamed directly to the Chromecast. When looked closer to the control packets; they use HTTP POST, HTTP GET methods to control the video played on Chromecast attached screen. Several information that could be extracted from these packets that are going unencrypted such as; the google account username (if logged in to YouTube), which video is being watched at what time of the day, what kind of Operating System and which version is installed on the remote device (Android 4.2.2, iOS etc.), brand and model of remote device used (brand = Asus, model = Nexus) etc. Even if listened passively from outside home-network without any attacks, this information could be seen as a leak of privacy.

– *NetCam: Reconstructing unencrypted MJPEG stream:* We discovered that NetCam does not encrypt streams it sends to the cloud and we tried to reconstruct the streams. Our first attempt using Xplico [28] tool was unsuccessful. Since JPEG images are always sent in multiple TCP packets due to the size of a JPEG file, we looked for packets carrying the maximum amount of data in the TCP data payload section. *Maximum Transmission Unit (MTU)* for today's networks is 1500 bytes, thus we expected to find binary JPEG image data in TCP packets with sizes closer to MTU. Using a *Wireshark Display Filter*, we obtained the big enough packets (frame.len $\geq$ 1000) that has the source IP of NetCam that are not ssl or telnet packets.

These filter left us with packets that are destined to a specific IP address, which was in 64.62.206.0/24 range, at specific TCP port 4103. This is the same machine that NetCam have been keeping the connection alive at all times by periodic TCP [PSH, ACK] packet exchange through TCP port 4104. TCP 4103 port is registered as *Braille Protocol* (brlp-2) by IANA in the *User Ports Range* [29]. Several known port assignments databases [30], list the TCP 4103 port as used by NVR/CCTV/DVR software. This might possibly imply that our NetCam is sending the images (JPEG) and video (M-JPEG) to a Network Video Recorder software that is running on the cloud servers. We used that searches for the TCP packets that carry a payload containing special JPEG marker bytes; also known as *JPEG Magic Numbers* [31]. JPEG data is stored as a stream of blocks, and each block is identified by a marker value. For example, every JPEG file has a special format which includes a header file that has some markers for denoting the start of image, end of image, start of binary image data etc... The most important JPEG markers to recover the hidden images in the packets of the TCP flow were the JPEG *Start Of Image (SOI)* marker, **FF D8 FF** and *End Of Image (EOI)* marker, **FF D9**.

We wrote a Python script that first goes over the pcap trace, using a library named **dpkt** [32], to extract and append to a binary file. Script only extracts the TCP payload of a packet if it contains the local IP of NetCam as Source IP, 4103 as a Destination Port and if the TCP payload length is greater than 0. Then the second part of the script reads the extracted binary data 1 byte at a time to check for JPEG SOI marker bytes. Once marker is found, it appends the upcoming bytes to a separate JPEG file until the JPEG EOI marker is encountered and at that time current JPEG file is constructed. In our 20 h live and idle trace, this script reconstructed 253 JPEG images. The reason Xplico tool couldn't reconstruct the images is because the JPEG images were always preceded by 32 bytes that carry some encoded information about the connection including the NetCam's owner's username. By hiding the JPEG SOI marker behind some random or implicit data bytes, NetCam might have expected to secure the image stream however *security by obscurity* is no security at all. Since these images are reconstructed from the data going to a remote server, anyone in between sniffing the packets would be able to reconstruct them.

6   Conclusion

With the rapid increase in number of IoT devices, security and privacy of these devices needs to be addressed. In this paper, we propose a framework to evaluate the security and privacy issues of IoT devices. The framework is extensible and can be used for other types of IoT devices as they are released. The framework consists of a testbed to facilitate experiments, a set of topics investigated, a set of experiments for each topic investigated and a report to describe the findings. We applied the framework to IoT devices including HDMI sticks and IP Cameras. There are various security and privacy issues in these devices ranging from simple issues such as passwords to more complex issues such as insecure mobile app and web interface. Communication is not secured in some devices leading to many security and privacy issues. Proposed framework can easily be applied to other IoT devices just connecting them to the access point and executing the experiments. Our work indicates that more work needs to be done on security and privacy of IoT devices to convince the public to use them without hesitation.

References

1. Netgear Inc.: NeoMediacast HDMI Dongle (2016). http://www.netgear.com/images/pdf/NETGEAR-NTV300D-D-12202013-3.pdf
2. The Wall Street Journal: Amazon to Ship Video Streaming Device in April (2016). http://online.wsj.com/news/article_email/SB10001424052702303287804579445721946202990
3. LG Electronics: LG Smart-TV with Google-TV (2016). http://www.lg.com/us/lggoogletv/index.jsp
4. Marvell Inc.: Armada 1500-Mini (2016). http://www.marvell.com/digital-entertainment/armada-1500-mini/
5. Tekeoglu, A., Tosun, A.Ş.: Blackbox security evaluation of chromecast network communications. In: 2014 IEEE International Performance Computing and Communications Conference (IPCCC), pp. 1–2, December 2014
6. Tekeoglu, A., Tosun, A.Ş.: A closer look into privacy and security of chromecast multimedia cloud communications. In: International Workshop on Multimedia Cloud Communications, 2015 IEEE INFOCOM, pp. 121–126, April 2015
7. Zhou, Y., Jiang, X.: Dissecting Android Malware: characterization and evolution. In: IEEE Symposium on Security and Privacy (2012)
8. Enck, W., Gilbert, P., Chun, B.-G., Cox, L.P., Jung, J., McDaniel, P., Sheth, A.N.: TaintDroid: an information-flow tracking system for realtime privacy monitoring on smartphones. In: Proceedings of the 9th USENIX Conference on Operating Systems Design and Implementation, OSDI 2010. USENIX Association, Berkeley (2010)
9. Enck, W., Ongtang, M., McDaniel, P.: On lightweight mobile phone application certification. In: Proceedings of the 16th ACM Conference on Computer and Communications Security, pp. 235–245 (2009)

10. Enck, W., Octeau, D., McDaniel, P., Chaudhuri, S.: A study of Android application security. In: Proceedings of the 20th USENIX Conference on Security, SEC 2011. USENIX Association, Berkeley (2011)
11. Enck, W., Ongtang, M., McDaniel, P.: Understanding Android security. IEEE Secur. Priv. **7**(1), 50–57 (2009). doi:10.1109/MSP.2009.26
12. Shekyan, S., Harutyunyan, A.: To Watch or Be Watched: Turning Your Surveillance Camera Against You (2016). http://conference.hitb.org/hitbsecconf2013ams/shekyan-harutyunyan/
13. Trendnet Cameras - I always feel like somebody's watching me (2016). http://console-cowboys.blogspot.com/2012/01/trendnet-cameras-i-always-feel-like.html
14. Wardle, P., Moore, C.: Optical Surgery: Implanting a Dropcam. Synack Labs, Defcon 22 Hacking Conference, August 2014. https://www.synack.com/labs/projects/implanting-a-dropcam
15. Tekeoglu, A., Tosun, A.Ş.: Investigating security and privacy of a cloud-based wireless IP camera: NetCam. In: 5th International Workshop on Privacy, Security and Trust in Mobile and Wireless Systems (MobiPST), 2015 IEEE ICCCN, pp. 1–6, August 2015
16. West, J., Kohno, T., Lindsay, D., Sechman, J.: WearFit: security design analysis of a wearable fitness tacker. Technical report, IEEE Center for Secure Design (2016)
17. Hilts, A., Parsons, C., Knockel, J.: Every step you fake. Technical report, Open Effect Report (2016)
18. Barcena, M., Wueest, C., Lau, H.: How safe is your quantified self. Technical report, Symantec Security Response (2014)
19. Internet of things security study: Smartwatches. Technical report, Hewlett-Packard (2015)
20. Ubertooth, P.: Ubertooth. https://github.com/greatscottgadgets/ubertooth. Accessed Sept 2014
21. Tekeoglu, A., Tosun, A.Ş.: A testbed for privacy and security of IoT devices. In: IEEE International Workshop on Data Science for Internet of Things, MASS 2016, pp. 1–6, October 2016
22. Open Vulnerability Assessment System (2016). http://www.openvas.org
23. Belshe, M., Peon, R., Thomson, M.: Hypertext Transfer Protocol version 2, TLS 1.2 Cipher Suite Black List, 19 February 2015. https://http2.github.io/http2-spec/#BadCipherSuites
24. Mills, D.L.: A brief history of NTP time: memoirs of an internet timekeeper. SIGCOMM Comput. Commun. Rev. **33**, 9–21 (2003)
25. ntp.org: Network Time Protocol (2016). http://support.ntp.org
26. Biondi, P.: Scapy (2016). http://www.secdev.org/projects/scapy/
27. Dierks, T., Rescorla, E.: The Transport Layer Security (TLS) Protocol Version 1.2. RFC 5246 (Proposed Standard), Internet Engineering Task Force, August 2008. Updated by RFCs 5746, 5878, 6176
28. Costa, G., Franceschi, A.D.: Xplico: Open Source Network Forensic Analysis Tool (NFAT) (2016). http://www.xplico.org/
29. IANA: Service Name and Transport Protocol Port Number Registry, for TCP Port 4103 (2016). http://www.iana.org/assignments/service-names-port-numbers/service-names-port-numbers.xhtml?&page=78
30. Port 4103 Details (2016). http://www.speedguide.net/port.php?port=4103
31. JPEG (2016). http://en.wikipedia.org/wiki/JPEG
32. Python Packet Creation Library (2016). https://code.google.com/p/dpkt/

Dynamic Cipher for Enhanced Cryptography and Communication for Internet of Things

Paramjeet Cheema[(✉)] and Neeraj Julka

Asra College of Engineering and Technology, Bhwanigarh, Patiala, India
Paramcheema99@gmail.com, asraecef3@gmail.com

Abstract. Security represents a vital element for sanctioning the widespread adoption of Internet of Things technologies and applications. While not guarantees in terms of system-level confidentiality, credibility and privacy the relevant stakeholders are unlikely to adopt Internet of Things solutions on an oversized scale. In early-stage Internet of Things deployments (e.g., supported RFIDs only), security solutions have principally been devised in an advert hoc approach. This comes from the very fact that such deployments were sometimes vertically integrated, with all elements beneath the management of one body entity during this work we have a tendency to propose a brand new dynamic cipher to access quite one device at the same time during a network employing a single controller by creating use of Dynamic variable cipher security certificate protocol. This protocol uses key matrices thought during this protocol we have a tendency to create use of key matrices and store same key matrix the least bit the human action nodes. So once plain text is encrypted to cipher text at the causing facet, the sender transmits the cipher text while not the key that's to be won't to decode the message. To access more than one device simultaneously in a network using a single controller by making use of Dynamic variable cipher security certificate protocol.

Keywords: Internet of things · Security · Encryption · Dynamic cipher

1 Security in IoT

As with the advancement of IoT, the application of IoT/M2 M is affecting our daily lives. So it is very important to ensure the security of the IoT/M2 M system. As IP addresses are being used in order to develop IoT/M2 M systems, the system has become the target of various intruders and attacks. With time these attacks will grow complex and more sophisticated and it is necessary to stop such attacks by incorporating various security measures in the IoT/M2 M system. Also there are large number of endpoints in the IoT system, so the intruder can enter through any of the end-point in the system, thus making it more complex to establish security in the system. The potential attack can span from just minor stalking to damage to infrastructure or loss of life.

As seen, the threats to the IoT system may be similar to that of the conventional system but the damage that can be done is significantly different. That is why there are many efforts to analyze the threats and risks.

I. Traore et al. (Eds.): ISDDC 2017, LNCS 10618, pp. 84–94, 2017.
https://doi.org/10.1007/978-3-319-69155-8_6

One of the fundamental elements in securing an IoT infrastructure is around device identity and mechanisms to authenticate it. Many IOT devices may not have the required compute power, memory or storage to support the current authentication protocols. Today's strong encryption and authentication schemes are based on cryptographic suites such as Advanced Encryption Suite (AES) for confidential data transport, Rivest-Shamir-Adleman (RSA) for digital signatures and key transport and Diffie-Hellman (DH) for key negotiations and management. While the protocols are robust, they require high compute platform and a resource that may not exist in all IoT-attached devices. Authentication and authorization need to be done in an appropriate way in order to make our new IoT world threat free.

The authentication and authorization protocols need human intervention which is not possible in some cases due to limited access to IoT devices. Therefore these devices need initial configuration to be done to protect from tampering, thefts and any other form of attack throughout its life.

In order to overcome these issues new authentication and authorization need to be built using the experience of today's strong encryption algorithms.

2   Related Work

Most of the security for IoT depends on encryption. As new work process come up for sensors and elements connected to internet, devices might outlive the effectiveness of encryption method. The communication and data transport channels should also be secured to allow devices to send and receive data with no effect from outside. Various Algorithms and methods have been developed by researchers to provide security in IoT domain including.

(Skarmeta 2014) proposed a paper that provides various challenges that are present in this field and also provides description of some challenges that need to be overcome in coming years for full acceptance of IoT by the society. The paper also proposes a capability-based access control mechanism which is built on public key cryptography in order to eradicate or overcome these challenges. Its solution is based on token used to access the constrained application protocol (CoAP). It also uses an optimized implementation of Elliptical curve Digital Signature Algorithm (ECDSA) inside the smart entities.

(Xingmei 2013) proposed a paper that introduces various aspects like basic characteristics, network architecture, key technologies and Security problems of internet of things. The basic characteristics include overall perception, reliable transmission and intelligent processing. The network architecture is divided into layers via- sensing layer, transport layer and application layer. The Key technologies comprise of radio frequency identification (RFID), Sensor technology and network and embedded system technology. The paper also describes some method to provide security in internet of things.

(Lee et al. 2015) have published a paper on securing internet of things network. As we know that using the present internet, data owners can provide integrity and authentication when data is getting generated. But confidentiality is not implemented by the owners as it is implemented by the symmetric keys between ends. But in internet of things confidentiality cannot be implemented suitably using this method as there are many consumers. Also consumers differ in their ability to use only a specific a part of the cipher text as the nodes don't know about the context. In this paper they have shown work as how confidentiality can be done in IoT. They have proposed a way in which producer encrypts the data along with context. They have improved key policy attribute based encryption and cipher text policy attribute based encryption to allow consumers to decrypt data according to context.

(Lee et al. 2015) proposed an authentication scheme based on elliptical curve cryptosystem and opened in the internet of things. In internet of things secure communication should be designed between one node and the other. In this paper they have focussed on an efficient secure key establishment based on ECC. This proposed method can prevent attacks like eavesdropping, man in the middle, replay attacks.

(Leusse et al.) proposed a paper on internet of things. In this paper it has stated as in internet of things large number of items can be addressed through internet and thus various attacks can be done. Therefore, it has led to the conclusion that current internet cannot be used as the platform to IoT. In this paper the authors has also stated various requirements for resources that will make them to be used in IoT environment. Also the authors have proposed an architectural model of self managed security cell.

(Peretti et al. 2015) proposed a paper entitles "An end to end security framework for internet of things". The paper describes a framework called as BlinkToSCoAP. The name due to the integration of three lightweight technologies of DTLS, CoAP and 6LoWPAN over tinyOS.

(Hochleitner et al. 2012) proposes a paper in which they have given a method of making the end points trustworthy. One of the important end point of internet of thing environment are mobile phones. These end points help users to interact with their appliances known as "things" in IoT. This paper presents an approach that provides users with the underlying security information on mobile systems and helps them to establish trust in internet of things.

(Radomirovic et al. 2008) proposed a paper in which they provide a security model which allows to ponder about security and privacy of communication protocols in the internet of things. The model they provided is designed on few assumptions and on various observations on various threats that we may face in internet of things.

(Suo et al. 2012) proposed a paper in security of internet of things. In the past decade internet of things is finding its use in full throttle. The key features of IoT application are security and privacy. With such advancement in technology Internet of things is still facing various enormous challenges in its application. The paper proposed by the author puts emphasis on these key features i.e. security. The paper has discussed the status of the key technologies being used in implementation of internet of things. These technologies include encryption mechanism, communication security, protection of sensor data and various cryptographic algorithms.

(Wen 2012) proposed a paper that describes the security structure of sensor level, network layer and application layer in internet of things. The paper analyses the security feature of the sensor layer and then applies a protocol called as Dynamic variable Cyber security certificate, a new method for authentication mechanism among various nodes in sensor level. This certificate is based on the principle "one time one cipher" between communicating nodes. This technology or method uses time stamp technology band timeliness is guaranteed between two parties. Dynamic variable cipher certificate can be applied for communication among various nodes in IoT. The dynamic variable security certificate is an authentication protocol; based on request-reply mechanism.

Internet of thing is one of the latest technologies that are widely being accepted. We can make use of this technology in our day to day life and thus reducing human workload. With the help of this technology we can access any object to which an IP address can be assigned. One of the toughest challenges of this technology is its security. There have been many proposals in order to achieve secure transmission between the nodes. One of the proposed method is making use of "Dynamic variable Cipher Security Certificate" Protocol. We can make the use of same protocol and combine multiple cipher texts and transmits the cipher text to multiple devices in the network. The devices will make use of the specific part of the cipher text for its operation. Thus we can access multiple devices using a single controller that will generate a combined cipher text for all the devices.

3 Dynamic Variable Cipher Security Certificate

Dynamic variable cipher security certificate is a protocol that works on reply-request mechanism. In this protocol a key matrix is generated and same key matrix is stored at all communicating parties. The advance thing in using this protocol is that the sender does not need to send decryption key instead it sends the co-ordinate of the key matrix where this key is stored. As same key matrix is stored at all the nodes, the recipient will use the co-ordinate sent by the sender and will get the key from its key matrix using this co-ordinate. The authentication process of this protocol is shown between two parties A and B as client and server respectively (Fig. 1).

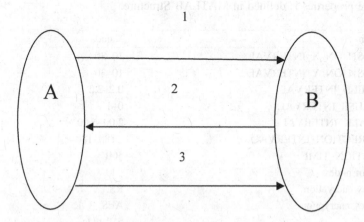

Fig. 1. Reply request mechanism of dynamic cipher certificate protocol

The process is as follows:

1. A B: Pos_x1_y1, E(Kab1: ID_A, cmd, Ta1)
2. B A: Pos_X2_Y2, E(Kab2: ID_B, Com_x_y, Ta1, Tb1)
3. A B: E(Kab3: Text, ID_A, Ta2, Tb1)

Where ID_A, ID_B means ID number of node A and node, Cmd means connection request, Pos_X_Y means coordinates of the key matrix, TA and TB means timestamp of node A and node B, E(Kab:m) means using password Kab to code message m, Text means message constant.

As seen from the above description, three steps exists, in the first step client node A send the encrypted information ID_a, a connection request Cmd, and a timestamp Ta1, and at the same time client A starts a timer and id it does not receive acknowledgment in allotted time then cancels the session.

If some information is received by server B, it will verify the ID_a from node A. If A validates it then B sends an encrypted information to A. The encrypted information consists of encrypted information ID_b, co-ordinates of key matrix Com_x_y, Timestamp Ta1, Timestamp Tb1 and at the same tie B starts a timer. If it does not receive any feedback from client A, it will cancel the session.

When some information is received at A, it will verify the encrypted information Ta1. If B is validity the A gets a communication password Kab according to co-ordinates of the key matrix. Then A generates a new time stamp ta2, combines with ta1 and sending message constant. Whole of this will be sent to B and up to this point a communicational channel is set between two parties.

4 Simulation Parameters

Following table describes the simulation parameters for IoT mobility in MATLAB, each node properties is defined in MATLAB Structure.

Parameter	Value
Node POSITION_X_INTERVAL	10–30
Node POSITION_Y_INTERVAL	10–30
Node SPEED_INTERVAL	0.2–2.2
Node PAUSE_INTERVAL	0–1
Node WALK_INTERVAL	2.00–6.00
Node DIRECTION_INTERVAL	−180–180
SIMULATION_TIME	500
Number of nodes	20
Public key encryption	RSA
Private key encryption	AES
Packet size	512 bytes

Node POSITION_X_INTERVAL: X position of the Node at any given moment, updates due to Random Way Point Model.

Node POSITION_Y_INTERVAL: Y position of the Node at any given moment, updates due to Random Way Point Model.

Node SPEED_INTERVAL: Speed Range of Each Node factor of 0.2 to 2.2× speed with respect to stationary nodes.

Node PAUSE_INTERVAL: For how long a node will stay stationary.

Node WALK_INTERVAL: For how long a node will stay moving.

Node DIRECTION_INTERVAL: In which direction the node will be moving.

SIMULATION_TIME: Overall Simulation Time of the Node.

Number of Nodes: Total number of nodes present in the Simulation (default: 20).

Public Key Encryption: Encryption Scheme used to Encrypt Messages using Public Key of the node and Decryption using the Private keys.

Private Key Encryption: Encryption Scheme used to encrypt Private Key of the Node using the Location of each node before sending any data.

Step 1: Receiver **R** Requests data from the node **S**, only receiver knows the exact location of itself.

Step 2: On receiving request from the **R** node the sender initiate public key Exchange using RSA algorithm and stores keys P_k as Private Key of the node R and P_u as the public key to encrypt the data.

Step 3: Node S then Request the Location L_{Rxy} of the node R.

Step 4: After receiving request from the node S the R sends its location L_{Rxy} to the node S.

Step 5: S then Encrypts the private key of the by using L_{Rxy} as Private Key using AES algorithm.

Step 6: For multiple recipients the same process in repeated and a matrix is formed in following manner and forwarded to recipients.

Step 7: After receiving the packet the recipient decrypts the private key using its location and then decrypts the data sent by the sender (Fig. 2).

Encrypted Data (RSA)	L_{Rxy} private key of the receiver 1 (AES)
	L_{Rxy} private key of the receiver 2 (AES)
	....
	L_{Rxy} private key of the receiver N (AES)

Fig. 2. Packet data format for dynamic cipher protocol

The nodes need to send data between each other. But if the nodes will send the data in plain text, any attacker or intruder can get that data and misuse it or even alter it. So in order to restrict an intruder to carry out any sort of attack on the data, the data is sent in a form that is not easily understandable by any third party person. We used AES algorithm to encrypt the private key of the authenticated user by estimating its exact location (Fig. 3).

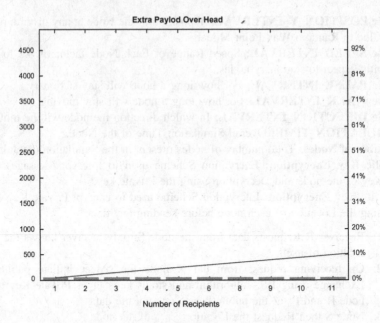

Fig. 3. Number of recipients and network overhead (payload)

As for each location a new private key is generated and attached to the packet, we require that there must not be a significant overhead as the Number of recipient grow (Fig. 4).

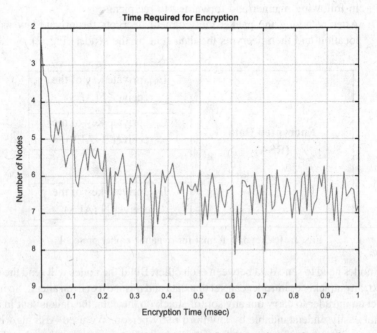

Fig. 4. Time required for encryption 512 bytes data packet used

The two main characteristics that identify and differentiate one encryption algorithm from another are its ability to secure the protected data against attacks and its speed and efficiency in doing so. This speed surmounts the symmetric encryption problem of managing secret keys. As on the other hand, this unique feature of public key encryption makes it mathematically less prone to attacks. However, asymmetric encryption techniques are slower than symmetric techniques, because they require more computational processing power. As it can be seen from above figure the encryption time does not increases too much when number of nodes increase as seen in above figure. So does the decryption process as seen below (Figs. 5 and 6).

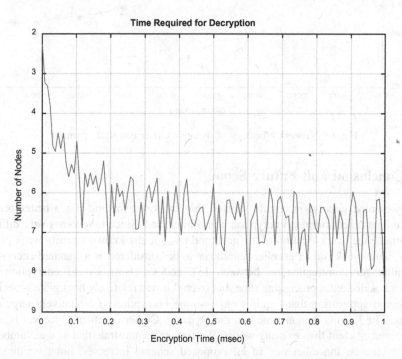

Fig. 5. Time required for decryption 512 bytes data packet used

The Results demonstrate that the Dynamic Cipher certificate Protocol is more secure and efficient than existing works. We further demonstrate that as the Number of node increases, the efficiency of all proposed scheme increases, but the efficiency gained by the more flexible and dynamic Cipher certificate Protocol schemes over the fixed scheme increases also. We also observe that the as the number of nodes increase the overall quality of service in encryption and decryption time is preserved.

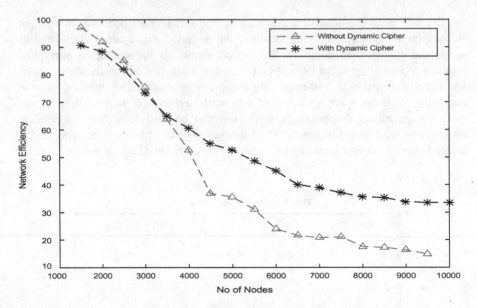

Fig. 6. Network efficiency of dynamic cipher certificate protocol

5   Conclusion and Future Scope

The presented simulation results showed that proposed method has a better performance than other common encryption algorithms used. Since it becomes very difficult to estimate the exact location of the node and has not any known security weak points so far, which makes it an excellent candidate to be considered as a standard encryption algorithm for communication between IoT nodes? Using hybrid encryption has although added extra processing time, but overall it was relatively negligible especially for certain application that requires more secure encryption to a relatively large data blocks. The Results demonstrate that the Dynamic Cipher certificate Protocol is more secure and efficient than existing works. We further demonstrate that as the Number of node increases, the efficiency of all proposed scheme increases, but the efficiency gained by the more flexible and dynamic Cipher certificate Protocol schemes over the fixed scheme increases also. We also observe that the as the number of nodes increase the overall quality of service in encryption and decryption time is preserved. In future we can work on dynamic block based encryption for IoT specific hardware to solve such issues. Also for future work, we aim at a deeper feasibility analysis of the discussed protocols in different settings and for different trust models.

References

Kopetz, H.: Internet of Things. Real-Time Systems, pp. 307–323. Springer, Heidelberg (2011). doi:10.1007/978-1-4419-8237-7

Feldhofer, M., Dominikus, S., Wolkerstorfer, J.: Strong Authentication for RFID Systems Using the AES Algorithm. In: Joye, M., Quisquater, J.-J. (eds.) CHES 2004. LNCS, vol. 3156, pp. 357–370. Springer, Heidelberg (2004). doi:10.1007/978-3-540-28632-5_26

Smith, D.R., Palmer, J.T.: Universal fixed messages and the Rivest-Shamir-Adleman cryptosystem. Mathematika 26(01), 44–52 (1979)

Jara, A.J., Lopez, P., Fernandez, D., Castillo, J.F., Zamora, M.A., Skarmeta, A.F.: Mobile digcovery: discovering and interacting with the world through the internet of things. Pers. Ubiquit. Comput. 18(2), 323–338 (2014)

Xingmei, X., Jing, Z., He, W.: Research on the basic characteristics, the key technologies, the network architecture and security problems of the internet of things. In: 2013 3rd International Conference on Computer Science and Network Technology (ICCSNT), pp. 825–828. IEEE (2013)

Lee, J., Oh, S., Jang, J.W.: A work in progress: context based encryption scheme for internet of things. Proc. Comput. Sci. 56, 271–275 (2015)

Lee, J.J., Hong, Y.-S., Lee, K.Y.: An authentication scheme based on elliptic curve cryptosystem and openID in the internet of things. In: Proceedings of the International Conference on Security and Management (SAM), p. 192. The Steering Committee of the World Congress in Computer Science, Computer Engineering and Applied Computing (WorldComp) (2015)

Peretti, G., Lakkundi, V., Zorzi, M.: BlinkToSCoAP: an end-to-end security framework for the internet of things. In: 2015 7th International Conference on Communication Systems and Networks (COMSNETS), pp. 1–6. IEEE (2015)

Hochleitner, C., Graf, C., Unger, D., Tscheligi, M.: Making devices trustworthy: security and trust feedback in the internet of things. In: Fourth International Workshop on Security and Privacy in Spontaneous Interaction and Mobile Phone Use (IWSSI/SPMU), Newcastle, UK (2012)

Van Deursen, T., Radomirovic, S.: Attacks on RFID protocols. IACR Cryptol. ePrint Arch. 2008, 310 (2008)

Suo, H., Wan, J., Zou, C., Liu, J.: Security in the internet of things: a review. In: 2012 International Conference on Computer Science and Electronics Engineering (ICCSEE), vol. 3, pp. 648–651. IEEE (2012)

Wen, Q., Dong, X., Zhang, R.: Application of dynamic variable cipher security certificate in internet of things. In: 2012 IEEE 2nd International Conference on Cloud Computing and Intelligent Systems (CCIS), vol. 3, pp. 1062–1066. IEEE (2012)

Wang, Y., Wong, K.W., Liao, X., Xiang, T.: A block cipher with dynamic S-boxes based on tent map. Commun. Nonlin. Sci. Numer. Simul. 14(7), 3089–3099 (2009)

He, D., Chen, Y., Chen, J.: Cryptanalysis and improvement of an extended chaotic maps-based key agreement protocol. Nonlin. Dyn. 69(3), 1149–1157 (2012)

Botta, A., de Donato, W., Persico, V., Pescapé, A.: Integration of cloud computing and internet of things: a survey. Future Gener. Comput. Syst. 56, 684–700 (2016)

Marin, L., Pawlowski, M.P., Jara, A.: Optimized ECC implementation for secure communication between heterogeneous IoT devices. Sensors 15(9), 21478–21499 (2015)

Hemalatha, D., Afreen, B.E.: Development in RFID (radio frequency identification) technology in internet of things (IOT). Development 4(11) (2015)

Sicari, S., Rizzardi, A., Grieco, L.A., Coen-Porisini, A.: Security, privacy and trust in internet of things: the road ahead. Comput. Netw. 76, 146–164 (2015)

Whitmore, A., Agarwal, A., Da Xu, L.: The internet of things—a survey of topics and trends. Inf. Syst. Front. 17(2), 261–274 (2015)

Shafagh, H.: Toward computing over encrypted data in IoT systems. XRDS Crossroads: ACM Mag. Stud. 22(2), 48–52 (2015)

Bohli, J.-M., Kurpatov, R., Schmidt, M.: Selective decryption of outsourced IoT data. In: 2015 IEEE 2nd World Forum on Internet of Things (WF-IoT), pp. 739–744. IEEE (2015)

Granjal, J., Monteiro, E., Silva, J.S.: Security for the internet of things: a survey of existing protocols and open research issues. IEEE Commun. Surv. Tutor. **17**(3), 1294–1312 (2015)

Shafagh, H., Hithnawi, A., Dröscher, A., Duquennoy, S., Hu, W.: Poster: towards encrypted query processing for the internet of things. In: Proceedings of the 21st Annual International Conference on Mobile Computing and Networking, pp. 251–253. ACM (2015)

Shi, W., Kumar, N., Gong, P., Chilamkurti, N., Chang, H.: On the security of a certificateless online/offline signcryption for internet of things. Peer-to-Peer Netw. Appl. **8**(5), 881–885 (2015)

Patil, A., Bansod, G., Pisharoty, N.: Hybrid lightweight and robust encryption design for security in IoT (2015)

Kim, H., Kim, K.: Toward an inverse-free lightweight encryption scheme for IoT. In: 2014 Conference on Information Security and Cryptography (2014)

Pescatore, J., Shpantzer, G.: Securing the internet of things survey. SANS Institute, January 2014

An Inter-device Authentication Scheme for Smart Homes Using One-Time-Password Over Infrared Channel

Maninder Singh Raniyal[1], Isaac Woungang[1(✉)], and Sanjay Kumar Dhurandher[2]

[1] Department of Computer Science, Ryerson University, Toronto, ON, Canada
mraniyal@ryerson.ca, iwoungan@scs.ryerson.ca
[2] Division of Information Technology, NSIT,
University of Delhi, New Delhi, India
dhurandher@gmail.com

Abstract. Internet of Things (IoT) is an emerging paradigm which enables physical objects to operate over the Internet, and collect and share the data that describe the real physical world. In this ubiquitous environment, due to the heterogeneity of objects, communication, topology, security protocols, and the computationally limited nature of IoT objects, conventional authentication schemes may not meet the IoT security requirements since they are considered impractical, weak, or outdated. In this paper, a two-factor inter device mutual authentication scheme for smart home is proposed, where in the first level, the key exchange is performed using the Diffie-Hellman protocol and a public key cryptography in order to validate the identity of devices; and the second level relies on the use of infrared communication to distribute the One-Time Passwords (OTPs) among devices for authentication purpose. The HLPSL language is used to model the proposed protocol, and a security analysis is conducted using the SPAN (Security Protocol Animator for AVISPA (SPAN)/AVISPA (Automated Validation of Internet Security Protocol and Applications) tool, showing that the proposed scheme can achieve the goals of secrecy of secret keys and mutual authentication. A proof-of-concept in the form of a hardware design is also proposed using Raspberry-Pi, Linux Infrared Remote Control (LIRC), Infrared circuit and a public-key-infrastructure. Experimentally, it is shown that this hardware design can achieve secure device-to-device authentication.

1 Introduction

The emerging Internet of Things (IoT) paradigm is the driver for many applications in the area of smart home, smart cities, to name a few. In IoT, devices (objects) are typically grouped into clusters, and to enable secured and integrated communications across these IoT objects, the applications and objects are required to first authenticate each other, for instance, via a cloud platform, using IoT communication protocols such as Constrained Application Protocol, Message Queue Telemetry Transport, to name a few [1]. However, most of these protocols do not have inbuilt security mechanisms, or

© Springer International Publishing AG 2017
I. Traore et al. (Eds.): ISDDC 2017, LNCS 10618, pp. 95–117, 2017.
https://doi.org/10.1007/978-3-319-69155-8_7

they rely on limited inbuilt single-factor authentication security mechanisms [2]. This motivates the need for a two-factor authentication scheme for IoT. In this paper, we report on the adaptability of a particular class of authentication for IoT devices in the cloud, namely OTP.

Our literature survey reveals that most existing OTP schemes [3] have not been designed specifically for IoT, in particular smart homes. In this paper, an OTP-based inter device two factor authentication scheme is proposed, and modelled using the SPAN/AVISPAS tool [4]. Its performance in terms of achieving the secrecy of secret keys and mutual authentication is evaluated by simulation. Finally, a proof-of-concept in the form of a hardware design of the proposed authentication scheme is proposed using Raspberry-Pi, Linux Infrared Remote Control, Infrared circuit and public-key infrastructure, and validated experimentally.

The paper is organized as follows. In Sect. 2, some background on authentication for smart homes are presented. In Sect. 3, some related work are discussed. In Sect. 4, the proposed authentication scheme is described. In Sect. 5, the modelling of the proposed protocol using the High-Level Protocol Specification Language (HLPSL) is described, followed by its simulations and formal analysis using the SPAN/AVISPA tool. An informal security analysis is also presented. In Sect. 6, a proof-of-concept (in the form of a hardware solution) of the proposed authentication scheme is presented. Finally Sect. 7 concludes the paper.

2 Background on Authentication for Smart Homes

Smart Homes: The advent of IoT has changed the way that systems are used and perceived [1]. In an IoT system [1], devices can communicate with each other without the need for human intervention, and the network of these devices can manage itself. A smart home (also known as home automation) can be defined as an instance of a IoT network. It is often referred to as a home where an automated system is deployed for monitoring the temperature, doors, alarms, windows, alerts, appliances, to name a few [5]. Typically, smart home devices are equipped with sensors and some network capabilities as shown in Fig. 1.

Usually, these devices are connected to each other through a Home Gateway (HG), an interface between the home network and the Internet. In order to control the smart home system, the HG has a routing functionality and is usually connected to the user interface using a mobile software, a wall-mounted solution, to name a few. Some smart home implementations also include the use of a home server, which is responsible for authenticating the devices.

Communication Technologies: Communication technologies in a smart home environment include radio waves – which are electromagnetic waves with frequencies between 3 kHz to 300 GHz - and light waves communication – where light is used as communication medium. The former is widely accepted and has the ability to penetrate through the wall or objects, making them suitable for smart homes while the latter is rarely utilized and usually cannot penetrate through walls or objects, limiting the communication space. Common radio wave technologies include X10, Ethernet,

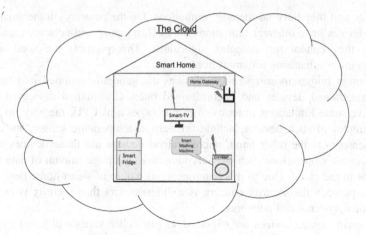

Fig. 1. Example of a smart home

RS-485, 6LoWPAN, Bluetooth LE (BLE), ZigBee, Li-Wi, and Z-Wave. On the other hand, Li-Wi is a well-known example of light waves communication [6] where communication is achieved by turning the light ON or OFF. Indeed, light-emitting diodes (LEDs), in particular Visible Light Communication (VLC) can be used as a mean to achieve light communication because of their high performance to turn the light ON or OFF. However, one of the problems encountered with the use of VLC is that it requires the light to be constantly ON for the communication to happen. In a smart home, this requirement might not be met since in the night, the lights are likely to be turned OFF. Other types of light communication include Dark visible light com-munication - which uses VLC for communication purpose - and infrared communi-cation – which uses Infrared light spectrum for the same purpose [7]. In our proposed hardware solution, we have used infrared-light for inter-device communication pur-pose. However, any other light communication medium could have been used as well.

Need for Multi-factor Authentication: Authentication is the process of confirming the identity of a subject (person, computer process, device, network connection, to name a few). It consists of asserting who a subject is (identification) and authentication itself, i.e. proving the asserted identity. Due to advancements in computing power, the development of secure and reliable authentication mechanisms has been a major research concern in the area of computer security in the recent years, especially in the IoT context such as a smart home network. One can distinguish single factor authentication schemes vs. multifactor ones. In the former, the subject is identified using only one category of patterns (or credentials) while in the latter, multiple patterns are combined and use for the same purpose. In general, to evaluate an authentication scheme, the Burrows-Abadi-Needham (BAN) logic [8] can be used in conjunction with the AVISPA [4] simulation tool, the goal being to authenticate the communicating entities and/or the key agreement between them.

In conventional authentication schemes, the client and the server have no limita-tions regarding the resources. All devices are able to run complex algorithms such as encryption; and they have no memory limitations. On the contrary, in the smart home context, devices have inherent limitations on CPU, memory and network capabilities, therefore, they cannot run complex algorithms. This prompts the need for new authentication mechanisms for smart homes.

In a smart home environment [1], devices are generally grouped into two categories: constrained devices and unconstrained ones. Constrained devices are those which have some limitations in terms of resources such as CPU, memory, to name a few. Examples of such devices include fire sensor, temperature sensor, and activity motion sensor. On the other hand, unconstrained devices are those devices that can perform complex operations such as encryption and send huge amount of data to other devices or to the cloud. Due to this heterogeneous nature of smart home devices, one needs to approach the security concern is a different way than security is tackled in conventional systems and networks.

In a smart home, devices are expected to run under various different protocols, technologies, and as discussed above, they have different resource constraints. Thus, device-to-device authentication in such environment is a challenge. Most smart home systems use wireless technologies such as Wi-Fi or Zigbee for communication purpose; and if an intruder can hold the related network packages, he/she can apply various types of attacks such as replay attack, eavesdropping, masquerading, message modification, denial-of-service, impersonation attacks [9, 10] to compromise the security of the system.

For device-to-device communication to occur, the authentication information such as password and keys are typically stored in the device's memory (or storage disk) and not in cleartext as per the recommendations made by various compliance standards including NIST [10]. Often, the sensitive information is encrypted using keys, which are often stored in their encrypted form, and a passphrase is used to protect the encrypted key, but the passphrase should also be protected as well. Therefore, the design of multi-factor authentication schemes for smart home environments has become an essential requirement. In this paper, a device-to-device two factor mutual authentication scheme for smart homes is proposed, where in the first level, the key exchange is performed using the Diffie-Hellman protocol, and a public key cryptography in order to validate the identity of devices; and in the second level, the OTP server is requested to provide the OTPs over an infrared channel, which in turn are distributed among the devices for second level authentication purpose. A proof of concept of the proposed scheme (in the form of a hardware solution) is also designed and validated.

3   Related Work

Authentication schemes for IoT environments have been intensively investigated in the recent years. Representative ones are described as follows. In [3], Madsen reports on new mechanisms and standards that can be used to authenticate IoT actors in a health care devices architecture. Related challenges and opportunities are also described. In [11], Shivraj et al. proposed an end-to-end authentication scheme for IoT based on Lamport's OTP. In their scheme, the OTP generation is modelled as a 4 steps process, namely: (1) the Setup phase - where some cryptographic parameters are involved in the PKI generation to optimize some computations over elliptic curve; (2) the Extract phase - where public and private keys are assigned to registered IoT applications and devices; (3) the Generate phase - where both the requests and data are transferred between IoT devices and a IoT cloud center using the aforementioned keys, and the required information are extracted; and (4) the Validate phase - where the OTP received at the cloud center is checked against that originally sent by the device. It is proved that the hardness of the OTP generation scheme is equivalent to solving the computational Diffie Hellman problem. In [12], Yao et al. proposed a lightweight multicast authentication scheme for small scale IoT applications based on the absorbency property of the original Nyberg's fast one-way accumulator [13]. In their scheme, the MAC is exploited to achieve such design; and in terms of security analysis, seven cardinal properties that are required by multicast authentication for resource-constraint applications are assessed and validated. In [14], Hernandez-Ramos et al. proposed a set of lightweight authentication and authorization mechanisms which can be used to assure authentication and authorization functionalities on constrained smart objects. These mechanisms are combined with some standard technologies to address different security planes of the life cycle of an IoT device within an Architectural Reference Model (ARM)-compliant security framework [15]. The suitability of the proposed framework for IoT scenarios is demonstrated through experiments, showing promising results. In [16], Sharaf-Dabbagh and Saad proposed an authentication framework for IoT objects, which uses the unique fingerprints of these objects to differentiate between normal changes in fingerprints and security attacks. In their scheme, the IoT objet set is divided into multiple hierarchies based on the types and geographic locations of the fingerprinting features. Each partition is then modelled as a set of distributions on which a learning approach is performed to extract the knowledge from the different fingerprints, thereby identifying the IoT objects. From simulations, it is found that their scheme outperforms the conventional authentication schemes by up to 8% in terms of authentication performance. In [17], Shin et al. proposed an authentication scheme for smart home networks, which uses a group key shared among the devices to encrypt and decrypt all messages from all devices. A digital DNA is also used to differentiate the devices against those pertaining to other smart home networks. The DNA is similar to a magical number generated by the authentication server or home server. However, if the group key is compromised, so will be the entire system. This scheme has been shown to be vulnerable to replay attacks since they do not use any timestamps or other mechanisms to prevent these types of attacks. In their scheme, the initial registration phase assumes that the communication channel is secure while registering a new device. In [18], Kumar et al. here proposed a short token-based authentication scheme which can be used for secure key establishment in smart home environments. In their scheme, the device registration is performed offline, which is a quite cumbersome process. This scheme is not fully protected against DoS attacks and the communication using it cannot be kept anonymous. Moreover, devices cannot communicate with each other. In [19], Santoso et al. proposed an elliptic curve cryptography (ECC)-based authentication scheme for smart homes, where the authentication mechanism involves the use of a mobile device. First, the user gets the identity information (such as device ID), and a secret key for the device, then passes them to the IoT device, which is connected automatically to the mobile device, which in turn shares this information with the gateway. Using this mechanism, the device attempts a connection to the gateway, and if the gateway has the secret key, a second level authentication process starts and a secure connection is established. However, the secret information is stored on the device itself, which is an issue. Their scheme does not keep the network anonymous, and the communication is handled via a Wi-Fi channel, which makes it vulnerable to DoS and replay attacks.

The authentication scheme proposed in this paper is fundamentally different from the above-discussed schemes by its design features. In addition, its designed hardware solution includes the use of Raspberry-Pi, Infrared circuit and the OpenSSH protocol.

4   Proposed Device-to-Device Mutual Authentication Scheme

The notations in Table 1 will be used for the design of the proposed authentication protocol.

Table 1. A-B-style-notation.

Notation	Description
D1	Client device
D2	Server device
OTP-server	OTP server that generates and send the OTPs
T1, T2, T3, T4, T5	Current timestamp
K_{D1}, K_{D2}	Public keys of D1 and D2
K'_{D1}, K'_{D2}	Private keys of D1 and D2
P	Prime number
G	primitive root modulo of P
N1, N2	Random secret numbers
SK	Secret Key generated using DH exchange
H()	Hash function
A -> B: M	A send message M to B
En{ }_K	Encryption is performed using key K
EXP	Exponent function
REQ	OTP request number
MOD	Modulus operation
OTP1, OTP2	One-Time-Password

The high-level architecture of the proposed scheme is shown in Fig. 2, where we have three devices: OTP-server, Device 1, and Device 2. Device 2 is initiating the authentication request with Device 1. Device 1 after being authenticated using a public-key infrastructure, sends a request for OTPs to the OTP-serve; The OTP-server then reply by sending the OTPs to both Device 1 and Device 2.

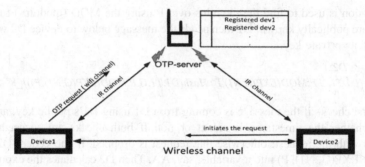

Fig. 2. High-level architecture of the proposed authentication scheme

The working of the proposed scheme consist of three phases: pre-deployment phase, deployment and registration phase, and functioning phase, described as follows.

Pre-deployment Phase: In this phase, the manufacturer presets up the device for father coming phases. First, the manufacturer builds the device along with the infrared light transceivers which will be used for infrared communication. In this process, each device gets its unique device ID, and using those IDs, devices will communicate with each other. The manufacturer then uploads the software (i.e. the operating system such as Linux or other hardening tools such as Lynis, CIS-CAT and Tiger) to a device, including the drivers for infrared light communication. The software is then configured in such a way that it is compliant with the regulations/standards such NIST [10]. Even though our focus is not on the hardening of devices, it is a good practice to harden the system in advance to protect against zero-day attacks. It is also assumed that the software is capable of updating itself frequently in a secure manner.

Deployment and Registration Phase: In this phase, all devices are registered with the OTP-server, as well as with peer devices with whom they need to authenticate in future. To register with the OTP-server, the public key of the device is stored with the OTP-server in secure manner, along with the device ID. The location of the device with respect to the OTP-server is also stored, in the form of degree of angle. One thing to point is that the devices would be facing towards the OTP-server in order for the infrared light communication to occur. In addition, devices will save the IP address information and device ID of the OTP-server. For a device, say D1, to communicate with another device, say D2, D1 needs to pre-register with D2 the same way that it has register with the OTP server.

Functioning Phase: When a device, say D1 wants to communicate with another device, say D2, D1 initiates the request for authentication. The first step is to generate a secret key which will be used for future communication. Here, the Diffie-Hellman (DH) key exchange protocol is used to generate the secret keys that will be kept secret between D1 and D2. For every new session, a different secret key will be generated for the communication. First, D1 generates a random number N1 and calculates the exponent of G to the power and N1, where G is a chosen positive integer. The result of this operation is used to find the modulus over P using the MOD (modulus) function. G and P are publically known. D1 then sends the message below to device D2 which is signed by its private key.

$D1 -> D2:$

$D1.\{D1.T1.G.P.MOD(EXP(G,N1),P).Hash(D1.T1.G.P.MOD(EXP(G,N1),P))\}\_K'_{D1}$

D2 first checks if the message is coming from D1 using D1's public key, and then checks whether the timestamp is recent or not. If both checks are succeeded, D2 continues with the request; otherwise that request is dropped. If succeeded, D2 saves the MOD(EXP(G, N1), P) into a variable, say, AA. Then D2 calculates the exponent G to the power N2 and the result is used to calculate the modulus over P. Then D2 send below message sign by its private key.

$D2 -> D1 : D2\{D2.T2.MOD(EXP(G,N2),P).Hash(D2.T2.MOD(EXP(G,N2),P))\}\_K'_{D2}$

After sending the message to D1, it computes the secret key by calculating $MOD(EXP(AA, N2), P)$ to obtain the secret key SK.

When D1 receives the message, it first check the authenticity of the message using D2's public key. Then it checks all the time stamp if it is recent. If both checks succeed, it will go further, otherwise it understands that something has gone wrong or it drops the message. If both checks succeed, it will save $MOD(EXP(G, N2), P)$ into a variable, say, BB. Then, will compute the secret key by calculating $MOD(EXP(BB, N1), P)$.

At this point, both devices have successfully shared the secret key using the DH key exchange algorithm, and the first phase of the protocol application is completed.

Upon a successful completion of phase 1, the D2 device requests the OTP-server to provide the OTPs for both devices D1 and D2. To issue such request, device D1 generates a timestamp T3 and send the below message to device D2 by signing with its private key.

$D2 -> OTP\text{-}server : D2.\{D1.D2.T3.REQ.Hash(D1.D2.T3)\}\_K'_{D2}$

After receiving the request, the OTP-server checks if the message is really sent by device D2 and it also checks if the timestamp is recent. If both conditions are met, the OTP-server continues further; otherwise, it drops the request. If both conditions were satisfied, the OTP server would generate two OTPs: OTP1 and OTP2. Then it will generate timestamp T4 and send the below message to D1 by encrypting with D1's public key.

$OTP\text{-}server -> D1 : \{T4.OTP2.OTP1\}\_K_{D1}$

Similarly, the OTP server would send the below message to D2, but keeping the OTPs order swapped and encrypted by D2's public key.

$OTP\text{-}server -> D2 : \{T4.OTP1.OTP2\}\_K_{D2}$

It should be noted that the OTPs are sent over the infrared communication within the home, which is considered a secure channel, thus, one can optionally skip the encryption part of it.

At this point, both devices, D1 and D2 have received the OTPs. The D1 device sends the hash of OTP2 to device D2; and similarly, the D2 device sends the hash of OTP1 to device D1. The communication happens securely by encrypting the message with the secret key SK.

$$D1 -> D2 : \{H(OTP2)\}\_SK$$
$$D2 -> D1 : \{H(OTP1)\}\_SK$$

Now, both the devices can authenticate each other by matching the hash received with the second OTP's hash. If both hashes match for both devices, the authentication is deemed successful, otherwise it has failed.

5 Modelling of the Proposed Authentication Scheme Using HLPSL

The SPAN/AVISPA virtual machine tool [4] (depicted in Fig. 3) is used for a formal evaluation of our proposed authentication scheme.

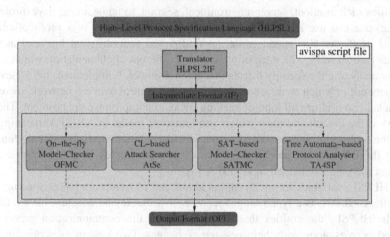

Fig. 3. High Level design of AVISPA tool [4]

It considers as the protocol (written in HLPSL format) that needs to be analyzed. Then converts it into an Intermediate format (IF) using the intrinsic HLPSL2IF translator, which in turn is passed to a specific backend tool (made of four modules, whose goal is to analyze the security of the given protocol and verify its effectiveness against various types of attacks, then check if the sessions are bounded or unbounded, and present the results in an output format (OF).

These four backend modules are:

- *On-the-fly Model-Checker (OFMC)*: This module is responsible for the protocol falsification and bounded session verification. It considers typed and untyped protocol models and have integrated various symbolic, constraint-based techniques which can be used to ensure that no attacks are lost. OFMC supports the intruder implementation who can guess weak passwords; it also provides the specification of algebraic properties of cryptographic operators. When the OFMC model specifies that the protocol is "safe", it means that all the specified goals are achieved.

- *Constraint-Logic-based Attack Searcher (CL-AtSe):* This module also performs the protocol falsification and verification. It translates the protocol specification into a set of constraints, which are then used to find the attacks; it also optimizes the branches in the protocol symbolic execution.
- *SAT-based Model-Checker (SATMC):* This module builds a propositional formula from the input, then converts it to state-of-the-art SAT solvers. If any model is found, it is translated into an attack.
- *Tree Automata based on Automatic Approximations for the Analysis of Security Protocols (TA4SP):* This module verifies the security of the protocol by approximating the intruder knowledge. For the secrecy property, the TA4SP can be used to judge whether the protocol is flawed or not.

HLPSL Syntax: As stated earlier, AVISPA considers the protocol modelled in HLPSL format as input in order to operate. HLPSL is a role based language, where all the entities such as client, server, environment, session, to name a few, have a role. For instance, one can use HLPSL to define the security properties of a protocol and the protocol itself. As also stated earlier, AVISPA has four different backend analysis modules (shown in Fig. 2), each of which has a different implementation which can be used for analyzing the security threats in a given protocol. It implements the Dolev Yao (DY) network in which an attacker model has a full control over the network, therefore, an attacker can perform all kind of hacking tricks to compromise the protocol. The DY network is the default and most widely used attacker model in AVISPA, meaning that when the tool is run, the generated output is usually interpreted as "safe" or "unsafe" against the DY attacker model. The abstract notations listed in Table 2 are used to represent the data exchanged in AVISPA [4]

In HLPSL, variables start with capital letters and constants are represented in lower case letters. HLPSL is a typed language, so each variable and constant have a unique type. In HLPSL, the entities that are involved in the communication process are modeled as roles along with their message exchanges. Two kind of roles prevail: basic and composed ones, depending on whether they represent the actions of only one agent or more. Usually, composed roles are adopted. In order to realize the required message exchanges, a session is created between the roles and the environment for all the sessions simultaneously. The key concepts of HLPSL and their syntax are as follows:

Basic Role: A protocol can easily be written in HLPSL format if the Alice-Bob (A-B) notation is used. As an example, using such notation, "A sends an encrypted message M to B, using key K to encrypt the message" is represented as:

$$A \rightarrow B : \{M\}\_K$$

Table 2. HLPSL notations.

Notation	Description
.	Associative concatenation (of messages)
:=	Initialization (of local variable) in init-section OR assignment to (primed!) local variable
'	Prime, used for referring to the next (new) value of variable in a transition
∧	Conjunction (logical AND)
=|>	Immediate transition
{ }	Set delimiter e.g. in knowledge declaration
{ }_	Encryption or signature
agent	Data-type for agents
channel (dy)	Data-type for channels. Currently only Dolev-Yao channels implemented.
def=	Indicates beginning of body of a role
hash_func	Data-type for one-way functions
exp	Exponentiation operator (prefix)
init	Indicates initialisation of local variables
inv	Inverse of a key: given a public key returns the private key
intruder_knowledge	Defines knowledge of the intruder
played_by	For basic roles: specifies which agent is playing this role
request	Used to check strong authentication (together with a witness)
witness	Used to check authentication (together with the request)
secret	Used to check secrecy

An example [4] of the syntax of a basic role declared in HLPSL is:

$$
\begin{aligned}
&role\ alice(A,B,S : agent,\\
&\qquad Kas : symmetric\_key,\\
&\qquad SND, RCV : channel\ (dy))\\
&\qquad played\_by\ A\ def=\\
&\qquad local\ State: nat, Kab: symmetric\_key\\
&\qquad init\ State := 0\\
&\qquad Transition\\
&\qquad\qquad ...\\
&end\ role
\end{aligned}
$$

In this example, Alice is a role, which should be called with parameters A, B, S as agent type, Kas as symmetric share key between A and S, Kab as symmetric shared key between A and B and SND, RCV as Dolev-Yao (dy) channels.

Transition: The system behavior in HLPSL is modelled as a `state', and each state has variables that are responsible for state transitions. A transition consists of a trigger or precondition, and an action to be performed when the trigger event occurs [4]. An example of a transition is:

> step1. State = 0 ∧ RCV({Kab'}_Kas) =|>
> State':= 2 ∧ SND({Kab'}_Kbs)

where step1 is the name of the transition. This transition specifies that if the value of the state is equal to zero and a message, which contains some value Kab' encrypted with Kas is received on a RVC channel, the transition will take place and a new state value will be set to 2 and the same value of Kab' encrypted with Kbs will be send on a SND channel.

Composed Role: This consists of basic roles that are composed together in sessions where the knowledge shared between these roles are explicitly known. Here is an example of a composed roles made of three different basic roles [4], where the symbol / \ indicates that the constituent roles are executed in parallel.

> role session(A,B,S : agent,
>   Kas, Kbs : symmetric_key) def=
> local SA, RA, SB, RB SS, RS: channel (dy)
> Composition
>   alice (A, B, S, Kas, SA, RA)
>   ∧ bob (B, A, S, Kbs, SB, RB)
>   ∧ server(S, A, B, Kas, Kbs, SS, RS)
> end role

Environment: The environment used for protocol execution is also defined as a composed type, where 'i' denotes the intruder. In the environment role, top level global constants are defined. In this top-level role, the intruder_knowledge parameter which defines the intruder's initial knowledge is also specified. Here is an example of an environment role [4]:

> role environment()
> def=
>   const a, b, s : agent,
>   kas, kbs, kis : symmetric_key
> intruder_knowledge = {a, b, s, kis}
> Composition
>   session(a,b,s,kas,kbs)
>   ∧ session(a,i,s,kas,kis)
>   ∧ session(i,b,s,kis,kbs)
> end role

Modelling the Protocol Using HLPSL: As per the above HLPSL syntax specifications [4], our proposed mutual authentication scheme protocol can be modelled as follows:

First, initially, when a device (client) wants to start communication with another device (server), it sends the request along with all parameters required for DH key exchange. This request is modelled in HLPSL as follows:

$$State=0 \land RCV(start) =|>$$
$$State':=1 \land Na':=new()$$
$$\land Timestamp':=new()$$
$$\land AA' := mod(exp(G,Na'),P)$$
$$\land$$
$$SND(A.\{A.Timestamp'.AA'.G.P.Hash(AA'.G.P.Timestamp'.A)\}\_inv(KPa))$$

Here, the state variable is initialized to 0 in the init section. Initially, the client receives a "start" message via the RCV channel to start the protocol. It first updates the state variable's new value to 1, then generates a random number, which in turn is used to generate the DH key exchange. It also generates the current timestamp (it is assumed that all the system's time is in sync). Then, it calculates the modulus of G to the power Na', where G and P are global variables, then stores that as AA', which is known to the intruder. It then calculates the hash of message. Afterwards, it sends the message by signing it with its private key. On receiving this message, the server checks if the timestamp is valid, and if validated, the server sends back its calculated value for the DH key exchange. This is modelled in HLPSL as follows:

$$State=0 \land RCV(A.\{A.Timestamp'.AA'.G.P.Hash(AA'.G.P.Timestamp'.A)\}\_inv(KPa)) =|>$$
$$State':=1 \land Nb':=new()$$
$$\land BB' := mod(exp(G,Nb'),P)$$
$$\land SND(B.\{B.Timestamp'.BB'.Hash(BB'.Timestamp'.B)\}\_inv(KPb))$$
$$\land Key' := mod(exp(AA',Nb'),P)$$
$$\land secret(Key',secret\_key, \{A,B\})$$
$$\land Req':=new()$$
$$\land SND(B.\{A.B.Timestamp'.Req'.Hash(A.B.Timestamp')\}\_inv(KPb))$$

In this specification, the state variables are local to both the client and the server.

Second, the server generates its own private random number Nb' for the DH key exchange, then calculates BB' and sends the message to the client by signing it with its private key. At this point, the server can form the secret session key Key'. Here, the *secret()* function is used to check the secrecy of the session key. The server then request the OTP-server to provide the OTPs to both the client and itself. At the same time, the client receives the message from the server. It then attempts to validate the timestamp and authenticity of the message. If the validation is successful, the client will acquire the BB' value from the server, and form a session as shown below:

$$State=1 \land RCV(B.\{B.Timestamp.BB'.Hash(BB'.Timestamp'.B)\}\_inv(KPb)) =|>$$
$$State':=2 \land Key' := mod(exp(BB',Na'),P)$$
$$\land secret(Key',secret\_key, \{A,B\})$$

Third, the OTP server attempts to validate the timestamp and the authenticity of the request. If successful, it sends the OTPs to both client and the server by encrypting them with their respective public keys as shown below:

$$State=0 \land RCV(B.\{A.B.Timestamp'.Req'.Hash(A.B.Timestamp')\}\_inv(KPb)) =|>$$
$$State':=1 \land Timestamp' := new()$$
$$\land SND(\{Timestamp'.OTP1.OTP2\}\_KPb)$$
$$\land SND(\{Timestamp'.OTP2.OTP1\}\_KPa)$$
$$\land secret(OTP1, server\_otp1, \{A,B,O\})$$
$$\land secret(OTP2, server\_otp2, \{A,B,O\})$$

It should be noted that the OTPs are sent on the light channel within the house, which is considered secure since the light cannot pass through objects such as walls. In real situations, the OTPs can be sent unencrypted because it is assumed that the intruder cannot get the hold on this light channel; however, the OTPs have been kept encrypted. Also, it should be noted that the secrecy of the OTPs is ensured by using the *secret()* function.

Forth, when both the client and the server receive the OTPs from the OTP-server, they unencrypt the message and validate the timestamp. Afterwards, the client sends OTP2 encrypted with the session key and the server sends OTP1 encrypted with the session key as well. Both the client and the server mutually authenticate each other if the encrypted hash of the received OTP rmatches with the hash of the OTP which was not sent by both entities. In the client side, to check for strong authentication, which is achieved by means of the *request()* and *witness()* functions, the following HLPSL code is used:

$$State=3 \land RCV(\{Hash(OTP1')\}\_Key) =|>$$
$$State':=4$$
$$\land witness(A,B,server\_client\_bb,\{B.Timestamp'.BB'\}\_inv(KPb).Hash(OTP1'))$$
$$\land request(A,B,client\_server\_aa,\{A.Timestamp'.AA'\}\_inv(KPa).Hash(OTP2'))$$

Now, at the server side, the server witnesses the message and OTP hash it has received by the client and request for its message and hashed OTP using the following HLPSL code.

$$State=2 \land RCV(\{Hash(OTP2)\}\_Key') =|>$$
$$State':=3 \land SND(\{Hash(OTP1)\}\_Key')$$
$$\land witness(B,A,client\_server\_aa,\{A.Timestamp'.AA'\}\_inv(KPa).Hash(OTP2'))$$
$$\land request(B,A,server\_client\_bb,\{B.Timestamp'.BB'\}\_inv(KPb).Hash(OTP1'))$$

Next, the goals of keeping OTP1 and OTP2 secret; ensuring the secrecy of the session key; and achieving mutual authentication between the client and server, is coded as follows using HLPSL:

goal

> *secrecy_of server_otp1*
> *secrecy_of server_otp2*
> *secrecy_of secret_key*
> *authentication_on client_server_key*
> *authentication_on server_client_key*

end goal

Protocol Simulation and Formal Analysis of Security Properties: The SPAN/AVISPA tool [4] is used to determine whether the proposed protocol (in HLPSL format) is secure or not in terms of authentication, secrecy, and integrity. Here, the authentication is achieved when two devices D1 and D2 can validate their identities, using OTPs, secrecy refers to ensuring that the information that is exchange between device D2 cannot be deciphered or cannot be disclosed to an unauthorized entity and only the intended receiver can decipher it; integrity refers to the fact that it is not possible for an intruder to alter or destroy the information shared by devices D1 and D2 during the communication process. This is achieved by adding a hash to the message at its source and by re-computing the hash of the message at the destination, then check for a match between the two quantities. In our proposed scheme, the session keys (which are symmetric keys) are utilized to encrypt the message and the DH key exchange is used as key exchange algorithm over an insecure channel. The simulation results of our proposed scheme are based on OFMC and CL-AtSe, the two widely-accepted AVISPA back-end tools. The SPAN gives a better understanding of the protocol and it is used to confirm whether the specification is executable or not. It also helps visualizing the protocol as shown in Fig. 4.

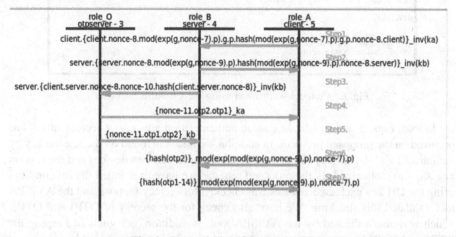

Fig. 4. Protocol Simulation in AVISPA.

Verification of Results: The two back-ends modules of AVISPA, namely OFMC and CL-ATSe reported that the proposed protocol is safe as confirmed in Figs. 5 and 6 respectively.

```
% OFMC
% Version of 2006/02/13
SUMMARY
  SAFE
DETAILS
  BOUNDED_NUMBER_OF_SESSIONS
PROTOCOL
  /home/span/span/testsuite/results/MANI.if
GOAL
  as_specified
BACKEND
  OFMC
COMMENTS
STATISTICS
  parseTime: 0.00s
  searchTime: 0.05s
  visitedNodes: 67 nodes
  depth: 8 plies
```

Fig. 5. Protocol verification using the OFMC back-end

```
SUMMARY
  SAFE

DETAILS
  BOUNDED_NUMBER_OF_SESSIONS
  TYPED_MODEL

PROTOCOL
  /home/span/span/testsuite/results/MANI.if

GOAL
  As Specified

BACKEND
  CL-AtSe

STATISTICS

  Analysed  : 21 states
  Reachable : 11 states
  Translation: 0.02 seconds
  Computation: 0.00 seconds
```

Fig. 6. Protocol verification using the CL-AtSE back-end

Indeed, Figs. 5 and 6 indicate that no authentication attack, nor secrecy attack has occurred on the proposed protocol. In addition, no attack is found on the session key by the intruder and the secrecy of the transferred message between devices and the session key are also maintained. In the proposed scheme, we have exchanged the session keys using the DH key exchange and this was checked for secrecy purpose and the AVISPA tool validated this checking. We have also check for the secrecy of OTP1 and OTP2, which was also validated by the AVISPA tool. In addition, our goals of keeping the OTP1 and OTP2 secret, ensuring the secrecy of the session key, and achieving mutual authentication between the client and the server, have been validated by the SPAN/AVISPA tool since the protocol is reported as safe.

Informal Security Analysis: Here, we discuss about some attacks and how our proposed mutual authentication scheme can be used to protect against each of them.

Eavesdropping Attack: In this attack, the eavesdropper silently listens to the communication of others without their knowledge. He/she may gain some sensitive information if not protected. In our scheme, the DH key exchange algorithm is used to construct the session keys, and the identity of the messages is signed using the private keys, which only the owner has access to. In addition, on top of it, the OTPs are sent over a light communication and an eavesdropper cannot get access to these entities after a successful authentication since all the communication entities use the session key to encrypt the data and the eavesdropper cannot make anything out of it. The session keys are generated for each session in order to maintain high security.

Masquerading/Impersonation Attack: In this kind of attack, the intruder presents himself as a genuine entity to gain the unauthorized access. Our scheme makes use of digital signature to validate the messages in the first phase, where the session keys are exchanged. Therefore, masquerading attempts will be blocked right at the first phase.

Replay Attack: In this kind of attack, the intruder first captures the data packets which can be used later to gain access to the system. To protect against this typed of attack, the current timestamp is used in our scheme, which is included in the digital signature, and it is assumed that the systems sync on time. On top of it, OTPs are used, which are randomly generated for each session.

Message Modification Attack: In this type of attack, the intruder tries to tamper the message. Our scheme uses a public key Infrastructure in its first phase to check if the message is legitimate or not. In its second phase, the hashed OTPs are sent by encrypting them with the session keys. If the message is tampered at any phase, the authentication will fail. Therefore, our scheme can be used to protect against message modification.

6 Proof of Concept

We have developed a proof-of-concept in the form of a hardware design of our authentication scheme, using three Raspberry-Pi (B+, Pi2, and Pi3) as home devices. The OTP-server is running on Raspberry-Pi3; the server is running on Raspberry-Pi-B+, and the client is running on Raspberry-Pi2. All Raspberry devices are running with the Raspbian Operating System. Each of these devices was embedded with an infrared transceiver circuit as shown in Fig. 7.

For the infrared communication, we have used an infrared emitter (IR333c LED) to send the infrared signal and the TSOP38238 as an infrared receiver. To send and receive the infrared signals, we have used the Linux Infrared Remote Control (LIRC) [21], which is meant for infrared remote communication. The LIRC package on Linux comes with multiple programs; we have used the *"irsend"* and *"irw"* programs. To configure the LIRC, a *config-file* [21] is used.

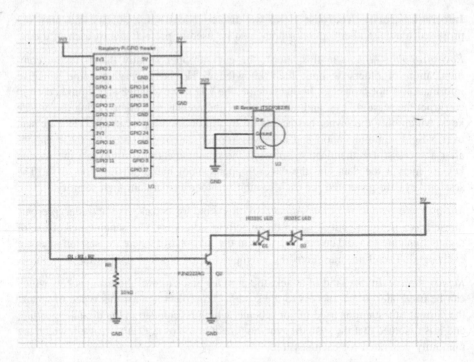

Fig. 7. Raspberry Pi Infrared trancever circuit for LIRC [20]

The OPT-server is installed with a 3D rotation device made of two SG90 Micro servo motors, which can be rotated only by 180°. To build a 3D rotation, we integrated the two servos together as shown in Fig. 8.

Fig. 8. 3D rotating servo placement.

The infrared transceiver is set on top of it to send the infrared signal in the direction that the 3D device is pointing to. The servo circuit diagram is shown in Fig. 9.

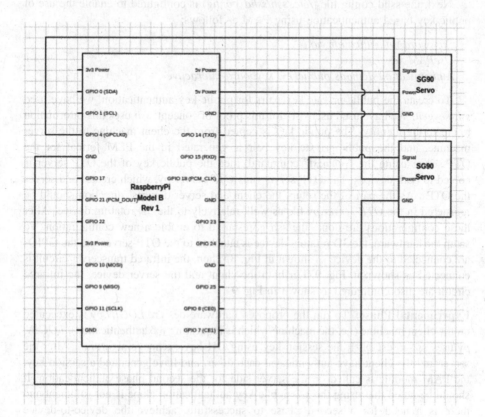

Fig. 9. 3D rotating servo circuit.

To control the servos, a program in Python is developed using the GPIO library [21]. For the first level of authentication, the OpenSSH is utilized. On the server side, a Pluggable Authentication Module (PAM) is developed, which runs on Python; for this purpose, the "python-pam" python module has been installed. This PAM module achieves an infrared communication-based OTP authentication as second level of authentication.

Setup Phase: Initially, the Raspbian OS is downloaded from [22] and installed on all the devices. Python comes by default, and the "pyopenssl" and "python-pam" python modules are installed, followed by *"lirc"* the Linux package "lirc". Next, the LIRC remote *config file* [21] is installed and the sshd PAM (/etc./pam.d/sshd) is configured in order to enable the PAM module (OTP_PAM.py) for ssh. The OTP_PAM.py is also configured using the OTP-server's IP as follows:

auth required pam_python.so   OTP_PAM.py.

Next, the sshd config file *(/etc./ssh/sshd_config)* is configured to enable the use of public-key based authentication using PAM as follows:

PasswordAuthentication no
UsePAM yes
AuthenticationMethods publickey, keyboard-interactive

To create the public-private key pairs for public-key authentication, we have used *ssh-keygen*. We have used user "pi" for this proof of concept; *ssh* uses this information to create the identity. The public key is copied from the client machine to the server machine, and the public-private key pair is generated in the PEM format for the OTP-server using the *"openssl"* command, then the public key of the OTP-server is copied to both devices. The OTP-server runs *OTP-server.py*, which creates and serves the OTPs. As the part of the setup, the client and server devices' direction should be registered in the *OTP-server.py* file as well, relatively to the 3D rotating device. After these configurations are done, the ssh is restarted to enable a new configuration. To setup the hardware, the 3D rotating device is attached to the OTP-server and the GPIOs are connected to the device as shown in Fig. 8. Then, the infrared transceiver circuit is connected as shown in Fig. 9. For both the client and the server device, the infrared circuit are also configured as shown in Fig. 9.

Experimental Phase: To run the proposed hardware design, *LOGIN.py* is executed on the client machine (i.e. the machine which is requesting the authentication). *LOGIN. py* uses *ssh* to establish the session key using DH key exchange algorithm. After the server and the client have authenticated each other, and have generated a session key, the PAM module is called on the server side for the second phase authentication. It should be noted that using the *ssh* public-key authentication alone is not sufficient and there is a need for a second phase to successfully achieve the device-to-device authentication. The PAM module figures out the information on both the client and server IPs and uses it to requests for OTPs to the OTP-server. As response, the OTP-server sends back two OTPs (one for the client and one for the server. It should be noticed thse OTPs can further be encrypted in order to strengthen the security of the proposed scheme. Both the client and the server calculates the hash of their OTPs and sends these values to each other over a Wifi channel. Then, both devices check if the hash of each other OTPs matches with the received hashed-OTP; if so, the mutual authentication has occur.

Results: For the proof of concept purpose, all the information have been recorded in log files. The experimental results are shown in Fig. 10. On the left-down of Fig. 10, the OTP-server's logs is showing which OTPs have been generated and which device requested the OTPs. The OTP-server sends the OTPs (OTP1, OTP2) to both devices, but in the opposite order. On the right-hand side of Fig. 10, the server's Syslog file is shown, where the PAM module is logging. The results are displayed by running the tail command on the Syslog file *(/var/log/syslog)*. This shows which device requested for authentication; once it asks for the OTP-server to provide OTPs, it waits till it receives

Fig. 10. OTP based mutual authentication using infrared channel.

both OTPs. It is observed that both OTPs are received over the infrared channel. It then sends the hash of OTP1 to the client over a Wifi connection and waits for the hashed OTP2. On receiving the hashed OTP2, it validates it, which is shown since it is observed that the authentication has succeeded. On left-top of Fig. 10, the client logs are shown, where *LOGIN.py* is the script used for authentication purpose. First, the public-key authentication occurs, then the OTPs (OTP2, OTP1) are received by the devices. From the server side, it receives the OTP1 hash, which is validated and the hash of OTP2 is sent back.

We have encounter an issue in the infrared emission, i.e. the LED transmission can be detected in a wide range. To fix this problem, a narrow pipe is created and foiled, which is used to the Infrared light on the infrared LED and immediately close the back side of the pipe after installation. In conducting the above experiments, two python program have been developed, namely OTP_SERVER.py and servo_controller.py to generate the OTP and send it over the infrared channel. Their pseudo-code are available on demand.

7 Conclusion

We proposed a novel two-factor mutual authentication scheme for smart homes. In its first phase, the scheme partially authenticates the devices and establishes a session key using the DH key exchange algorithm. In its second phase, OTPs are distributed over an infrared channel and the OTP hash is exchanged to achieved a complete mutual authentication of devices. Our proposed authentication scheme is formally validated using the SPAN/AVISPA tool and an informal evaluation is also described. A proof of concept of the proposed scheme (in the form of a hardware implementation using Raspberry-Pi, LIRC, infrared circuit, and servo motors, is proposed and validated by experiment, showing that the device-to-device secure authentication goal is met. As future work, it would be interesting to consider light communication such as visible light, black light, or infrared light based communication as unique medium of communication between the devices and assess the effectiveness of the proposed protocol in such context.

References

1. Dawy, Z., Saad, W., Ghosh, A., Andrews, J.G., Yaacoub, E.: Towards massive machine type cellular communications. IEEE Wirel. Commun. **24**(1), 120–128 (2017)
2. Shivraj, V.L., Rajan, M.A., Singh, M., Balamuralidhar, P.: One time password authentication scheme based on elliptic curves for Internet of Things (IoT). In: Proceedings of IEEE 5th National Symposium on Information Technology: Towards New Smart World (NSITNSW 2015), pp. 1–6, 17–19 February 2015
3. Madsen, P.: Authentication in the IoT challenges and opportunities. http://www.secureidnews.com/news-item/authentication-in-the-iot-challenges-and-opportunities. Accessed 9 Aug 2017
4. AVISPA Tool. http://www.avispa-project.org. Accessed 9 Aug 2017
5. Stobert, E., Biddle, R.: Authentication in the home. In: Workshop on Home Usable Privacy and Security (HUPS), Newcastle, UK, 24 July 2013. http://cups.cs.cmu.edu/soups/2013/HUPS/HUPS13-ElizabethStobert.pdf. Accessed 9 Aug 2017
6. PureLiFi. http://purelifi.com. Accessed 9 Aug 2017
7. Tian, Z., Wright, K., Zhou, X.: The DarkLight Rises: Visible Light Communication in the Dark. http://www.cs.dartmouth.edu/~xia/papers/mobicom16-darklight.pdf. Accessed 9 Aug 2017
8. Schneier, B.: Applied Cryptography Protocols Algorithms and Source Code in C, 2nd edn. Wiley, London (1996). ISBN 978-1-119-09672-6
9. Saxena, U., Sodhi, J.S., Singh, Y.: Analysis of security attacks in a smart home networks. In: Proceedings of 7th International Conference on Cloud Computing, Data Science and Engineering, Noida, India, 12–13 January 2017, pp. 431–436 (2017)
10. Kumar, P., Braeken, A., Gurtov, A., Iinatti, J., Ha, P.H.: Anonymous secure framework in connected smart home environments. IEEE Trans. Inf. Forensics Secur. **12**(4), 968–979 (2017)
11. Wilson, P.: Inter-device authentication protocol for the internet of things. M.Sc. thesis, Department of Electrical and Computer Engineering, University of Victoria, B.C, Canada, July 2017
12. Yao, X., Han, X., Du, X., Zhou, X.: A lightweight multicast authentication mechanism for small scale IoT applications. IEEE Sens. J. **13**(10), 3693–3701 (2013)
13. Benaloh, J., de Mare, M.: One-way accumulators: a decentralized alternative to digital signatures. In: Helleseth, T. (ed.) EUROCRYPT 1993. LNCS, vol. 765, pp. 274–285. Springer, Heidelberg (1994). doi:10.1007/3-540-48285-7_24
14. Hernandez-Ramos, J.L., Pawlowski, M.P., Jara, A.J., Skarmeta, A.F., Ladid, L.: Toward a lightweight authentication and authorization framework for smart objects. IEEE J. Sel. Areas Comm. **33**(4), 690–702 (2015)

15. Hughes, P.: ARM and Sensor Platforms Deliver an Open Source Framework for Sensor Devices, ARM. https://www.arm.com/about/newsroom/arm-and-sensor-platforms-deliver-an-open-source-framework-for-sensor-devices.php. Accessed 9 Aug 2017
16. Sharaf-Dabbagh, Y., Saad, W.: On the authentication of devices in the Internet of Things. In: Proceedings of the 17th IEEE International Symposium on World Wireless, Mobile Multimedia Networks, Coimbra, Portugal, pp. 1–3, June 2016
17. Shin, S., Yeh, H., Kim, K.: An effective device and data origin authentication scheme in home networks. In: Proceedings of 9th International Conference and Expo on Emerging Technologies for a Smarter World (CEWIT), November 5–6, Incheon, South Korea, pp. 1–5, September 2012
18. Kumar, P., Gurtov, A., Iinatti, J., Ylianttila, M., Sain, M.: Lightweight and secure session-key establishment scheme in smart home environments. IEEE Sens. J. 16(1), 254–264 (2016)
19. Santoso, F.K., Vun, N.C.H.: Securing IoT for smart home system. In: Proceedings of International Symposium on Consumer Electronics (ISCE), Madrid, Spain, pp. 1–2, 24–26 June 2015
20. Open Source Universal Remote. https://upverter.com/alexbain/f24516375cfae8b9/Open-Source-Universal-Remote/#/. Accessed 9 Aug 2017
21. Linux Infrared Remote Control. http://www.lirc.org. Accessed 9 Aug 2017
22. Raspbian Operating System. https://www.raspberrypi.org/downloads/raspbian. Accessed 9 Aug 2017

Detection and Prevention of Blackhole Attacks in Wireless Sensor Networks

Gurjinder Kaur[1(✉)], V.K. Jain[1], and Yogesh Chaba[2]

[1] Sant Longowal Institute of Engineering and Technology, Longowal, India
gurjinder13@yahoo.com
[2] Guru Jambheshwar University of Science & Technology, Hisar, India

Abstract. In recent past Wireless Sensor Network has emerged as a promising technology and has proved to be a leading motivational force for a new innovation namely Internet of Things. Due to characteristics constraints, security is one of key challenge to sustain the performance of wireless sensor networks. Blackhole attack is a major threat for Wireless Sensor Network in which an intruder absorbs the traffic intended for base station by introducing a malicious node. In this paper a new technique is proposed to detect and prevent blackhole attack in Wireless Sensor Network. The simulation results obtained with the proposed technique establishes that in the event of blackhole attack the malicious node is successfully detected and usage of proposed technique prevents the deterioration in the performance of Wireless Sensor Network.

Keywords: Wireless sensor network · Sensor node · Blackhole attack

1 Introduction

Due to ease of use of attributes such as small and low cost sensors deployment Wireless Sensor Networks (WSNs) are turning out to be a promising technology [1] in various fields including healthcare, industrial monitoring, environmental data record, automobile, military applications, home automation, fire detection [2] and many more. Generally, in WSNs sensor nodes (SNs) are connected to one or several base stations known as sinks. These base stations or sinks have mission to collect information circulating on the network, and store them or send them directly via an Internet or a GSM connection. One of major constraint in the working of WSNs is energy/power. The major chunk of energy in WSNs is consumed for communication of sensed data. In order to limit the consumption of energy during communications WSNs need protocols with effective routes.

Routing in WSNs is very challenging due to the inherent characteristics that distinguish these networks from other wireless networks like mobile ad hoc networks or cellular networks [3]. Routing protocols in WSNs are broadly divided into three categories [4]: flat network protocols, hierarchical protocols and location based protocols. In flat networks all nodes have same capability of sensing and routing data, while location-based protocols utilize position information to relay the data to the desired

© Springer International Publishing AG 2017
I. Traore et al. (Eds.): ISDDC 2017, LNCS 10618, pp. 118–126, 2017.
https://doi.org/10.1007/978-3-319-69155-8_8

regions rather than the whole network. The intent of hierarchical protocols is to save energy used for routing data to base station by individual nodes. A solution is to use clustering, which divides networks in many clusters as shown in Fig. 1. In each cluster, a cluster head is elected and this cluster head collects data from the sensor nodes of the cluster and transmits the data to sink node. The election of the cluster head is made by choosing a node with the higher energy or residual energy. The objective is to extend the life of WSN by reducing the number of data exchanges.

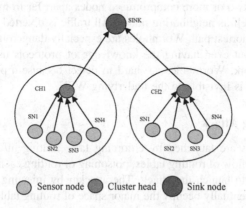

Fig. 1. Normal data flow in WSN with two clusters and one sink node

2 Attacks in WSN

Security is a crucial issue in WSNs. The solutions used in conventional adhoc networks cannot be applied in WSNs because of their specific characteristics such as limited-power, lower-bandwidth, shorter-range radios [5–10]. These characteristics of WSNs make them more vulnerable to security attacks. The attacks in WSNs can be classified as external and internal attacks, active and passive attacks or attacks at different layers. Some common and most dangerous attacks are as discussed below:

2.1 Sybil Attack

Sybil attack is a typical identity spoofing attack in which an attacker illegally presents multiple MAC identities. To participate in network communication by hiding itself, an attacker can spoof as a normal legitimate sensor or as a base station to obtain unauthorized privileges or resources of the WSN. Spoofing attacks are usually the basis of further cross-layer attacks that can cause serious consequences. For example, Sybil attacks may expose legitimate information to the adversary or provide wrong information for routing to launch false routing attacks.

2.2 Greyhole Attack

In greyhole attack the attacker selectively forwards the information to next node. In case of sensor nodes, non critical data is transmitted to base station to prove the integrity but critical data is absorbed. Such kind of attack is more difficult to detect and can easily disrupt the performance of whole WSN.

2.3 Wormhole Attack

In wormhole attack two or more compromised nodes apart far from each other form a tunnel posing themself as neighboring nodes. All traffic is diverted through the tunnel considering it as a shortest path Wormholes are especially dangerous because they can cause damage without even having the knowledge of protocols used or the services offered in the network. Wormholes are hard to detect because a private, out-of-band channel is used that is invisible to the underlying WSN.

2.4 False Routing Attack

False routing attacks are launched by enforcing false routing information. Different approaches like overflow of routing tables, poisoning of routing cache and poisoning of tables may be used to launch the attack. The attacker by injecting a large volume of void information, eventually occupy the major space of routing table of a normal node and cause overflow.

2.5 Blackhole Attack

The blackhole attack is one of the hazardous security threats that exploit integrity of WSNs. The blackhole node absorbs all the traffic directed to it by refusing forward packets to intended nodes. Hence, the throughput of a particular area especially the neighboring nodes around the attacker is dramatically decreased. The performance of a WSN is influenced by the location of blackhole nodes on the network.

After extensive literature survey it is found that balckhole attack is one of the severe attacks prevalent in WSNs and there is need of some effective strategies to prevent and detect blackhole attacks in WSNs.

3 Existing Methodologies

A lot of research has been done in order to figure out the flaws in existing system against blackhole attack. Different algorithms have been proposed based on checking agents and multiple base stations, multipath routing, trust based mechanisms and cryptographic techniques.

A technique for detection of malicious node based on the time intervals of data shared by sensor nodes to cluster head (CH) and by CH to base station is presented by Lal [11]. Two different scenarios of blackhole attack viz within a cluster and among the clusters have been considered. Cluster head selection is based on Optimized Weight Based Clustering algorithm. Cluster head maintain a table via assigning IDs and

Sequence number to all nodes present in the cluster. Base stations are responsible for detection of malicious cluster heads via maintaining a table having assigned IDs and Sequence number for each cluster. The detection of malicious node is done by keeping check on the time intervals of data shared by sensor nodes to CH and by CH to base station. If data is not received any CH and base station after a defined interval of time the node is considered as malicious.

Prathapani [12] presented the use of intelligent agents called Honeypots to detect blackhole attacks in WSN's. The Honeypots generate dummy route request packets to lure and trap blackhole attackers. It has been demonstrated that honeypot based detection model aids in increase of throughput in a wireless mesh networks with blackhole nodes and has a high detection rate and low false positive rate.

Misra [13] proposed an efficient technique based on the deployment of spatially diverse multiple base stations in the network to mitigate black hole attacks. The technique is applied on flat wired networks where all sensor nodes are directly attached to base station. The routes between base stations and sensor nodes are established by using TinyOS beacons.

A methodology based on mobile agent is presented by Sheela [14] to tackle blackhole attack in WSNs. The proposed scheme applies multiple BS by using mobile agents to overcome the impact of blackhole attack. The applied mobile agent is a program segment which is self-controlling. A simulation based model is also presented to recover from blackhole attack in WSNs.

Jian [15] proposed a hierarchal secure routing protocol against black hole attack using symmetric key cryptography. In hierarchal secure routing protocol network is divided into different groups organized as a tree with each group leader as the root of the tree. After inter-group shared key and intra-group shared key establishment, black hole attacks are detected locally. For detection of cooperative black hole attack a randomized data acknowledgement scheme is proposed.

Tripathi [16] proposed an energy efficient window based scheme to detect misbehavior in WSN. Most of the computations are done at base station only. The base station has data of all the cluster heads as well as residual energy of all the nodes it watches the behavior of all nodes to detect the malicious node.

4 Detection and Prevention Methodology for Blackhole in WSN

Blackhole attack is a kind of denial of service in nature. Blackhole attacks are easy to constitute and they are capable of undermining network effectiveness by absorbing all the traffic directed to it that leads to decrease in network performance. In cluster based WSN, blackhole node make itself appear more attractive to prove the candidature of being a cluster head by advertising as it has a highest energy. After becoming a CH blackhole node starts dropping data packets intended for base station causing considerable effect on quality of service parameters. The placement/position of malicious nodes has significant impact on severity of blackhole attack.

In cluster based WSN a normal flow of data is shown in Fig. 1 and data flow under blackhole attack is represented in Fig. 2. Each cluster having four number of sensor nodes including a CH responsible to transmit data to base station. Sink node is not receiving any data from CH of cluster 1 even though cluster 1 is receiving data from the sensor nodes associated with it. CHs have always higher possibility of becoming a blackhole node because effectiveness of attack is multiplied by blocking a large amount of data. Blackhole attack has severe impact on performance of WSN especially the end-to- end delay and throughput. So to sustain the efficiency of WSN it becomes very important to detect and prevent Blackhole attack.

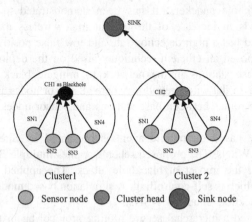

Fig. 2. WSN under blackhole attack

Wireless Sensor Network consists of numerous sensors possessing the ability to communicate among each other. Each individual sensor node has the capability of performing routing and network management. While transmitting sensed information security and efficient use of energy are prime concerns in WSNs. Cluster based structure of WSN is most energy efficient way to transmit sensed data to sink node. LEACH is most commonly used clustering algorithm that allows dynamic selection of cluster heads in order to preserve energy of all sensor nodes in WSNs. LEACH is divided into number of rounds for selecting cluster heads. The election of cluster head is rotation based and is repeated after a fix amount of time. In process of electing a cluster head, there are considerable chances that a compromised node will present itself a suitable candidate with having maximum energy and appropriate distance from sink node in order to acquire considerable data and disrupt the performance of WSN.

In cluster based networks, a CH is responsible to transmit all the data of a cluster to base station. A compromised CH may badly affect the efficiency of single hop WSN. In multihop WSN, the blackhole CH placed near to base station can harm more as compare to blackhole CH placed far from base station.

After a comprehensive review of literature it has been found that maximum damage in the working of WSN is done when a malicious node get selected as CH. Hence there is need of an efficient algorithm which should ensure that a malicious node does not become the CH.

In this paper an algorithm for detection and prevention of blackhole attack in WSN is proposed. The proposed algorithm follows an iterative procedure to ensure that a malicious node is not selected as CH. The broad procedure of the proposed algorithm is elaborated herewith:

- Sink node will maintain the information of all sensor nodes.
- The responsibility of **election of CHs** lies with the Sink node.
- In first round of election of CH:
  - The sensor node having maximum residual energy is selected as CH.
  - If two or more nodes possess same amount of residualenergy then the sensor node having optimal distance from sink node will be elected as CH.
- In the subsequent rounds of CH election following two scenarios are taken care off:
  - It is checked that if a node already elected as CH is again advertising same maximum residual energy level as presented in round 1 then it will be marked as suspicious blackhole sensor node because as communication proceeds the energy level of CH node should decrease.
  - If a node already elected as CH is showing slight decrease in residual energy level, then its ratio of decrease in energy level will be compared with ratio of decrease in energy level of other CHnodes. The wide variation in the ratio of decrease in energy level will be considered as suspicious and node may be declared as blackhole.
- Sink node will maintain the information of all elected CHs with their associated sensor nodes.
- Sink node waits a t_i amount of time to receive data from CHs.
- If a CH is not responding after the lapse of $t_i$time, sink node will declare that CH as a blackhole node.
- Sink node will assign a new CH to all sensor nodes earlier associated with the blackhole CH.

The procedure will be executed iteratively for **maxr** number of rounds. The pseudo code of the proposed algorithm is listed below:

```
Start ( )
for (r=1;r<=maxr;r++)
      {
            if (r=1)then
               {
      Call Select CH ( )
               }
            else
               {
      if (CH advertises maximum residual energy level same as in r=1)
                  {mark as suspicious blackhole sensor node}
            endif
            if (level of decrease in residual energy level of a CH is odd in comparison
                  to decrease in residual energy level of other CH's)
                  {mark as suspicious blackhole sensor node}
            endif
      Call Select CH ( )
      }
      endif
```

After lapse of t₁ waiting time check whether all CHs have sent data.

```
if (CH is not responding with data after the lapse of t₁time)
    {mark as suspicious blackhole sensor node}
endif
Call Select CH ( )  // Assign a new CH to all sensor nodes earlier associated with
                         the blackholeCH
}
endfor
}
Stop

Select CH ( )
{
for (i=1;i<=n;i++)   // n is number of sensor nodes
    {
    Select SNᵢ with maximum residual energy as CH
            if (two nodes have same level of residual energy)
            {Select SNᵢ having optimal distance from sink node as CH}
            endif
    }
endfor
}
```

5 Simulation and Result Analysis

The performance of WSN under blackhole attack has been evaluated using QualNet 5.02 network simulator. The simulation area is set 1000 m × 1000 m flat areas. CBR is used as data traffic application with multiple source and destination. Simulation scenario consists of six clusters with five sensor nodes in each including CH and a PAN coordinator (sink node). The sink node used is a fully functioned device without any energy constraint and other remaining nodes are the devices having limited constraints like storage, energy and power. Simulation is performed by deploying one CH as blackhole. The proposed algorithm is implemented on WSN against blackhole attack. The simulation time is 200 s. The performance is measured on the basis of metrics like throughput and end-to-end delay.

In Fig. 3 the variation has been presented for all three cases i.e. network without blackhole, with blackhole and after implementing proposed algorithm. It is clear that the throughput decreases effectively after deploying blackhole attack. The proposed algorithm is able to procure throughput almost same as without blackhole attack.

Average end-to-end delay of the data packets is defined as the interval between the data packet generation time and the time of arrival of last bit at the destination. Figure 4 shows the increase in end to end delay while network is under blackhole attack. After implementing the proposed algorithm the value of end to end delay decreases near to the value of without blackhole attack.

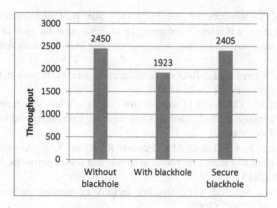

Fig. 3. Throughput of network

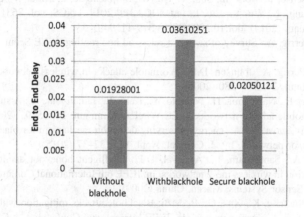

Fig. 4. End to End Delay of network

6 Conclusion

Blackhole attack degrades the performance of WSN drastically. The proposed methodology handles the blackhole attack in WSN efficiently both when malicious node is acting as CH as well as when it is trying to be elected as CH. The simulation results obtained with the proposed technique establishes that in the event of blackhole attack the malicious node is successfully detected and usage of proposed technique prevents the deterioration in the performance of WSN. In future the proposed technique may be extended to detect blackhole in multihop WSNs.

References

1. Martins, D., Guyennet, H.: Wireless sensor network attacks and security mechanisms: a short survey. In: 13th International Conference on Network-Based Information Systems (2010)

2. Antoine-Santoni, T., Santucci, J.F., Gentili, E.D., Costa, B.: Using wireless sensor network for wildfire detection: a discrete event approach of environmental monitoring tool. In: First International Symposium on Environment Identities and Mediterranean Area, Corte-Ajaccio, France (2006)
3. Al-Karaki, J.N., Kamal, A.E.: Routing techniques in wireless sensor networks: a survey. IEEE Wireless Commun. **11**, 6–28 (2004)
4. Singh, H., Singh, D.: Taxonomy of routing protocols in wireless sensor networks: a survey. In: IEEE 2nd International Conference on Contemporary Computing and Informatics, Noida, India, pp. 822–830 (2016)
5. Ahmed, A., Bakar, K.A., Channa, M.I., Haseeb, K., Khan, A.W.: A survey on trust based detection and isolation of malicious nodes in ad-hoc and sensor networks. Frontiers Comput. Sci. **9**, 280–296 (2015)
6. Deng, H., Li, W., Agrawal, D.P.: Routing security in wireless ad-hoc networks. IEEE Commun. Mag. **40**, 70–75 (2002)
7. Gao, H., Wu, R., Cao, M., Zhang, C.: Detection and defense technology of blackhole attacks in wireless sensor network. In: Sun, X., Qu, W., Stojmenovic, I., Zhou, W., Li, Z., Guo, H., Min, G., Yang, T., Wu, Y., Liu, L. (eds.) ICA3PP 2014. LNCS, vol. 8631, pp. 601–610. Springer, Cham (2014). doi:10.1007/978-3-319-11194-0_53
8. Hu, Y.C., Perrig, A.: Survey of secure wireless ad hoc routing. IEEE Secur. Priv. **2**, 28–39 (2004)
9. Hu, Y.-C., Perrig, A., Johnson, D.B.: Wormhole attacks in wireless networks. IEEE J. Sel. Areas Commun. **24**, 370–380 (2006)
10. Kannhavong, B., Nakayama, H., Nemoto, Y., Kato, N., Jamalipour, A.: A survey of routing attacks in mobile ad hoc networks. IEEE Wireless Commun. **14**, 85–91 (2007)
11. Lal, C., Shrivastava, A.: An energy preserving detection mechanism for blackhole attack in wireless sensor networks. Int. J. Comput. Appl. **115**, 32–37 (2015)
12. Prathapani, A., Santhanam, L., Agrawal, D.P.: Intelligent honeypot agent for blackhole attack detection in wireless mesh networks. In: IEEE 6th International Conference on Mobile Adhoc and Sensor Systems, Macau, China (2009)
13. Misra, S., Bhattarai, K., Xue, G.: BAMBi: Blackhole attacks mitigation with multiple base stations in wireless sensor networks. In: IEEE International Conference on Communications (ICC), Kyoto, Japan (2011)
14. Sheela, D., Srividhya, V.R., Begam, A., Anjali, Chidanand, G.M.: Detecting black hole attacks in wireless sensor networks using mobile agent. In: International Conference on Artificial Intelligence and Embedded Systems (ICAIES 2012), Singapore (2012)
15. Jian, Y., Madria, S.K.: A hierarchical secure routing protocol against black hole attacks in sensor networks. In: IEEE International Conference on Sensor Networks, Ubiquitous, and Trustworthy Computing (SUTC'06), Taichung, Taiwan (2006)
16. Tripathi, M., Gaur, M.S., Laxmi, V., Sharma, P.: Detection and countermeasure of node misbehaviour in clustered wireless sensor network. ISRN Sen. Netw. **2013**, 1–9 (2013)

Detection of Online Fake News Using N-Gram Analysis and Machine Learning Techniques

Hadeer Ahmed[1(✉)], Issa Traore[1], and Sherif Saad[2]

[1] ECE Department, University of Victoria, Victoria, BC, Canada
meresger.hs@gmail.com, itraore@ece.uvic.ca
[2] School of Computer Science, University of Windsor, Windsor, ON, Canada
Sherif.SaadAhmed@uwindsor.ca

Abstract. Fake news is a phenomenon which is having a significant impact on our social life, in particular in the political world. Fake news detection is an emerging research area which is gaining interest but involved some challenges due to the limited amount of resources (i.e., datasets, published literature) available. We propose in this paper, a fake news detection model that use n-gram analysis and machine learning techniques. We investigate and compare two different features extraction techniques and six different machine classification techniques. Experimental evaluation yields the best performance using Term Frequency-Inverted Document Frequency (TF-IDF) as feature extraction technique, and Linear Support Vector Machine (LSVM) as a classifier, with an accuracy of 92%.

Keywords: Online fake news · Text classification · Online social network security · Fake news detection · N-gram analysis

1 Introduction

In the recent years, online content has been playing a significant role in swaying users decisions and opinions. Opinions such as online reviews are the main source of information for e-commerce customers to help with gaining insight into the products they are planning to buy.

Recently it has become apparent that opinion spam does not only exist in product reviews and customers' feedback. In fact, fake news and misleading articles is another form of opinion spam, which has gained traction. Some of the biggest sources of spreading fake news or rumors are social media websites such as Google Plus, Facebook, Twitters, and other social media outlet [1].

Even though the problem of fake news is not a new issue, detecting fake news is believed to be a complex task given that humans tend to believe misleading information and the lack of control of the spread of fake content [2]. Fake news has been getting more attention in the last couple of years, especially since the US election in 2016. It is tough for humans to detect fake news. It can be argued that the only way for a person to manually identify fake news is to have a vast knowledge of the covered topic. Even with the knowledge, it is considerably hard to successfully identify if the information in the article is real or fake. The open nature of the web and social media in

© Springer International Publishing AG 2017
I. Traore et al. (Eds.): ISDDC 2017, LNCS 10618, pp. 127–138, 2017.
https://doi.org/10.1007/978-3-319-69155-8_9

addition to the recent advance in computer science simplify the process of creating and spreading fake news. While it is easier to understand and trace the intention and the impact of fake reviews, the intention, and the impact of creating propaganda by spreading fake news cannot be measured or understood easily. For instance, it is clear that fake review affects the product owner, customer and online stores; on the other hand, it is not easy to identify the entities affected by the fake news. This is because identifying these entities require measuring the news propagation, which has shown to be complex and resource intensive [3]. Trend Micro, a cyber security company, analyzed hundreds of fake news services provider around the globe. They reported that it is effortless to purchase one of those services. In fact, according to the report, it is much cheaper for politicians and political parties to use those services to manipulate election outcomes and people opinions about certain topics [4, 5]. Detecting fake news is believed to be a complex task and much harder than detecting fake product reviews given that they spread easily using social media and word of mouth.

We present in this paper an n-gram features based approach to detect fake news, which consists of using text analysis based on n-gram features and machine learning classification techniques. We study and compare six different supervised classification techniques, namely, K-Nearest Neighbor (KNN), Support Vector Machine (SVM), Logistic Regression (LR), Linear Support Vector Machine (LSVM), Decision tree (DT) and Stochastic Gradient Descent (SGD). Experimental evaluation is conducted using a dataset compiled from real and fake news websites, yielding very encouraging results.

The remaining sections are structured as follows. Section 2 is a review of related works. Section 3 introduces our proposed approach and model. Section 4 presents the experiments conducted to evaluate our proposed fake news detection model. Section 5 makes concluding remarks and discusses future work.

2 Related Works

Research on fake news detection is still at an early stage, as this is a relatively recent phenomenon, at least regarding the interest raised by society. We review some of the published work in the following. In general, Fake news could be categorized into three groups. The first group is fake news, which is news that is completely fake and is made up by the writers of the articles. The second group is fake satire news, which is fake news whose main purpose is to provide humor to the readers. The third group is poorly written news articles, which have some degree of real news, but they are not entirely accurate. In short, it is news that uses, for example, quotes from political figures to report a fully fake story. Usually, this kind of news is designed to promote certain agenda or biased opinion [6].

Rubin et al. [7] discuss three types of fake news. Each is a representation of inaccurate or deceptive reporting. Furthermore, the authors weigh the different kinds of fake news and the pros and cons of using different text analytics and predictive modeling methods in detecting them. In this paper, they separated the fake news types into three groups:

- Serious fabrications are news not published in mainstream or participant media, yellow press or tabloids, which as such, will be harder to collect.
- Large-Scale hoaxes are creative and unique and often appear on multiple platforms. The authors argued that it may require methods beyond text analytics to detect this type of fake news.
- Humorous fake news, are intended by their writers to be entertaining, mocking, and even absurd. According to the authors, the nature of the style of this type of fake news could have an adverse effect on the effectiveness of text classification techniques.

The authors argued that the latest advance in natural language processing (NLP) and deception detection could be helpful in detecting deceptive news. However, the lack of available corpora for predictive modeling is an important limiting factor in designing effective models to detect fake news.

Horne et al. [8] illustrated how obvious it is to distinguish between fake and honest articles. According to their observations, fake news titles have fewer stop-words and nouns, while having more nouns and verbs. They extracted different features grouped into three categories as follows:

- Complexity features calculate the complexity and readability of the text.
- Psychology features illustrate and measure the cognitive process and personal concerns underlying the writings, such as the number of emotion words and casual words.
- Stylistic features reflect the style of the writers and syntax of the text, such as the number of verbs and the number of nouns.

The aforementioned features were used to build an SVM classification model. The authors used a dataset consisting of real news from BuzzFeed and other news websites, and Burfoot and Baldwin's satire dataset [9] to test their model. When they compared real news against satire articles (humorous article), they achieved 91% accuracy. However, the accuracy dropped to 71% when predicting fake news against real news.

Wang et al. [10] introduced LIAR, a new dataset that can be used for automatic fake news detection. Thought LIAR is considerably bigger in size, unlike other data sets, this data set does not contain full articles, it contains 12800 manually labeled short statements from politicalFact.com.

Rubin et al. [11] proposed a model to identify satire and humor news articles. They examined and inspected 360 Satirical news articles in mainly four domains, namely, civics, science, business, and what they called "soft news" ('entertainment/gossip articles'). They proposed an SVM classification model using mainly five features developed based on their analysis of the satirical news. The five features are Absurdity, Humor, Grammar, Negative Affect, and Punctuation. Their highest precision of 90% was achieved using only three combinations of features which are Absurdity, Grammar, and Punctuation.

3 Proposed Approach and Models

3.1 N-gram Model

N-gram modeling is a popular feature identification and analysis approach used in language modeling and Natural language processing fields. N-gram is a contiguous sequence of items with length n. It could be a sequence of words, bytes, syllables, or characters. The most used n-gram models in text categorization are word-based and character-based n-grams. In this work, we use word-based n-gram to represent the context of the document and generate features to classify the document. We develop a simple n-gram based classifier to differentiate between fake and honest news articles. The idea is to generate various sets of n-gram frequency profiles from the training data to represent fake and truthful news articles. We used several baseline n-gram features based on words and examined the effect of the n-gram length on the accuracy of different classification algorithms.

3.2 Data Pre-processing

Before representing the data using n-gram and vector-based model, the data need to be subjected to certain refinements like stop-word removal, tokenization, a lower casing, sentence segmentation, and punctuation removal. This will help us reduce the size of actual data by removing the irrelevant information that exists in the data.

We created a generic processing function to remove punctuation and non-letter characters for each document; then we lowered the letter case in the document. In addition, an n-gram word based tokenizer was created to slice the text based on the length of n.

Stop Word Removal

Stop words are insignificant words in a language that will create noise when used as features in text classification. These are words commonly used a lot in sentences to help connect thought or to assist in the sentence structure. Articles, prepositions and conjunctions and some pronouns are considered stop words. We removed common words such as, *a, about, an, are, as, at, be, by, for, from, how, in, is, of, on, or, that, the, these, this, too, was, what, when, where, who, will,* etc. Those words were removed from each document, and the processed documents were stored and passed on to the next step.

Stemming

After tokenizing the data, the next step is to transform the tokens into a standard form. Stemming simply is changing the words into their original form, and decreasing the number of word types or classes in the data. For example, the words "Running", "Ran" and "Runner" will be reduced to the word "run." We use stemming to make classification faster and efficient. Furthermore, we use Porter stemmer, which is the most commonly used stemming algorithms due to its accuracy.

3.3   Features Extraction

One of the challenges of text categorization is learning from high dimensional data. There is a large number of terms, words, and phrases in documents that lead to a high computational burden for the learning process. Furthermore, irrelevant and redundant features can hurt the accuracy and performance of the classifiers. Thus, it is best to perform feature reduction to reduce the text feature size and avoid large feature space dimension. We studied in this research two different features selection methods, namely, Term Frequency (TF) and Term Frequency-Inverted Document Frequency (TF-IDF). These methods are described in the following.

Term Frequency (TF)

Term Frequency is an approach that utilizes the counts of words appearing in the documents to figure out the similarity between documents. Each document is represented by an equal length vector that contains the words counts. Next, each vector is normalized in a way that the sum of its elements will add to one. Each word count is then converted into the probability of such word existing in the documents. For example, if a word is in a certain document it will be represented as one, and if it is not in the document, it will be set to zero. Thus, each document is represented by groups of words.

TF-IDF

The Term Frequency-Inverted Document Frequency (TF-IDF) is a weighting metric often used in information retrieval and natural language processing. It is a statistical metric used to measure how important a term is to a document in a dataset. A term importance increases with the number of times a word appears in the document, however, this is counteracted by the frequency of the word in the corpus.

One of the main characteristics of IDF is it weights down the term frequency while scaling up the rare ones. For example, words such as "the" and "then" often appear in the text, and if we only use TF, terms such as these will dominate the frequency count. However, using IDF scales down the impact of these terms.

3.4   Classification Process

Figure 1 is a diagrammatic representation of the classification process. It starts with preprocessing the data set, by removing unnecessary characters and words from the data. N-gram features are extracted, and a features matrix is formed representing the documents involved. The last step in the classification process is to train the classifier. We investigated different classifiers to predict the class of the documents. We investigated specifically six different machine learning algorithms, namely, Stochastic Gradient Descent (SGD), Support Vector Machines (SVM), Linear Support Vector Machines (LSVM), K-Nearest Neighbour (KNN) and Decision Trees (DT). We used implementations of these classifiers from the Python Natural Language Toolkit (NLTK).

We split the dataset into training and testing sets. For instance, in the experiments presented subsequently, we use 5-fold cross validation, so in each validation around 80% of the dataset is used for training and 20% for testing.

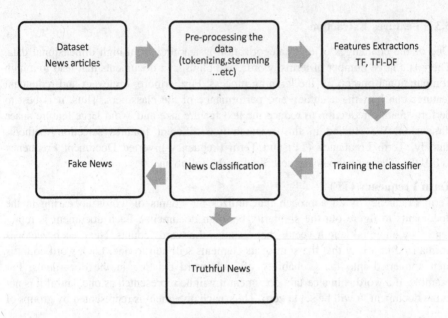

Fig. 1. Classification process

Assume that $\Delta = [d_i]_{1 \leq i \leq m}$ is our training set consisting of m documents d_i.

Using one of the feature extraction techniques (i.e., TF or TF_IDF), we calculate the feature values corresponding to all the terms/words involved in all the documents in the training corpus and select the p terms $t_j(1 \leq j \leq p)$ with the highest feature values. Next, we build the features matrix $X = [x_{ij}]_{1 \leq i \leq m, 1 \leq j \leq p}$, where:

$$\begin{cases} x_{ij} = feature(t_j) \ if \ t_j \in d_i \\ x_{ij} = 0 \ otherwise \end{cases}$$

In other words, x_{ij} corresponds to the feature extracted (using TF or TF-IDF) for term t_j for document d_i. Such value is null (0) if the term is not in the document.

4 Experiments

4.1 Dataset

The field of fake news detection is a relatively new area of research. Hence, few public datasets are available. We used in this work primarily a new dataset collected by our team by compiling publicly available news article. We also tested our model on the data set Horne and Adali [8], which is accessible to the public.

Our new dataset was entirely collected from real world sources[1]. We collected news articles from Reuters.com (News website) for real news articles. As for the fake news, they were collected from a fake news dataset on kaggle.com. The collector of the data set collected fake news items from unreliable web sites that Politifact (a fact checking organization in the USA) has been working with Facebook to stamp out. We used 12,600 fake news articles from kaggle.com and, 12,600 truthful articles. We decided to focus only on political news article because these are currently the main target of spammers. The news articles from both fake and truthful categories happened in the same timeline, specifically in 2016. Each of the articles length is bigger than 200 characters.

For every article, the following information is available:

- Article Text
- Article Type
- Article label (fake or truthful)
- Article Title
- Article Date

4.2   Experiments Procedure

We run the aforementioned machine learning algorithms on the dataset, with the goal of predicting whether the articles are truthful or fake. The experiments started by studying the impact of the size (n) of n-grams on the performance. We started with unigram ($n = 1$), then bigram ($n = 2$), then steadily increased n by one until reaching n = 4. Furthermore, each n value was tested combined with a different number of features.

The experiments were run using 5-fold cross validation; in each validation round the dataset is divided into 80% for training and 20% for testing.

The algorithms were used to create learning models, and then the learned models were used to predict the labels assigned to the testing data. Experiment results were then presented, analyzed and interpreted. In the start of our research, we applied our model on a combination of news articles from different years with a broader variety of political topics. Our model achieved 98% accuracy when using this type of data. Thus, we decided to collect our data set so we can require fake and real articles from the same year and even same month. Furthermore, we decided to limit the scope of the articles. Thus we only focused on news articles that revolve around the 2016 US elections and the articles that discuss topics around it. In total, we picked 2000 articles from real and fake articles we collected, 1000 fake articles and 1000 real articles. The 2,000 articles represent a subset of the dataset described in the previous section that focuses only politics.

4.3   Experiments Results

We studied two different features extraction methods, TF-IDF, and TF (described earlier), and varied the size of the n-gram from n = 1 to n = 4. We also varied the number of features p (i.e., top features selected), ranging from 1,000 to 50,000. Tables 1, 2, 3, 4, 5 and 6 show the obtained results.

---

[1] http://www.uvic.ca/engineering/ece/isot/datasets/index.php.

Table 1. SVM accuracy results. The second row corresponds to features size. Accuracy values are in %.

N-Gram Size	TF-IDF				TF			
	1000	5000	10,000	50,000	1000	5000	10,000	50,000
Uni-gram	84.0	86.0	84.0	84.0	85.0	72.0	69.0	69.4
Bi-Gram	78.0	73.0	67.0	54.0	68.0	51.0	47.0	47.0
Tri-Gram	71.0	59.0	53.0	48.0	53.0	47.0	53.0	47.0
Four-Gram	55.0	37.0	37.0	45.0	47.0	48.0	40.0	47.0

Table 2. LSVM Accuracy results. The second row corresponds to the features size. Accuracy values are in %.

N-Gram Size	TF-IDF				TF			
	1000	5000	10,000	50,000	1000	5000	10,000	50,000
Uni-gram	89.0	89.0	89.0	92.0	87.0	87.0	87.0	87.0
Bi-gram	87.0	87.0	88.0	89.0	86.0	83.0	82.0	82.0
Tri-gram	84.0	85.0	86.0	87.0	86.0	84.0	84.0	79.0
Four-gram	71.0	76.0	76.0	81.0	70.0	70.0	70.0	61.0

Table 3. KNN Accuracy results. The second row corresponds to the features size. Accuracy values are in %.

N-Gram Size	TF-IDF				TF			
	1000	5000	10,000	50,000	1000	5000	10,000	50,000
Uni-gram	79.0	83.0	82.0	83.0	77.0	70.0	68.0	68.0
Bi-gram	67.0	65.0	68.0	64.0	62.0	55.0	51.0	45.0
Tri-gram	73.0	68.0	65.0	67.0	76.0	63.0	57.0	46.0
Four-gram	69.0	68.0	68.0	58.0	67.0	54.0	56.0	43.0

Table 4. DT Accuracy Results. The second row corresponds to the features size. Accuracy values are in %.

N-gram Size	TF-IDF				TF			
	1000	5000	10,000	50,000	1000	5000	10,000	50,000
Uni-gram	88.0	88.0	89.0	89.0	83.0	88.0	88.0	80.0
Bi-gram	85.0	85.0	85.0	84.0	84.0	87.0	87.0	84.0
Tri-Gram	86.0	86.0	87.0	85.0	86.0	86.0	84.0	86.0
Four-gram	74.0	74.0	71.0	74.0	67.0	67.0	70.0	67.0

Table 5. SGD Accuracy Results. The second row corresponds to the features size. Accuracy values are in %.

N-gram Size	TF-IDF				TF			
	1000	5000	10,000	50,000	1000	5000	10,000	50,000
Uni-gram	88.0	86.0	88.0	89.0	87.0	86.0	89.0	85.0
Bi-gram	86.0	85.0	87.0	86.0	85.0	84.0	85.0	84.0
Tri-gram	84.0	85.0	86.0	86.0	85.0	85.0	87.0	87.0
Four-gram	70.0	72.0	74.0	80.0	72.0	73.0	72.0	78.0

Table 6. LR Accuracy Results. The second row corresponds to the features size. Accuracy values are in %.

N-Gram Size	TF-IDF				TF			
	1000	5000	10,000	50,000	1000	5000	10,000	50,000
Uni-gram	83.0	89.0	89.0	89.0	89.0	89.0	83.0	89.0
Bi-gram	87.0	87.0	88.0	88.0	87.0	85.0	86.0	86.0
Tri-gram	86.0	85.0	88.0	87.0	83.0	83.0	83.0	82.0
Four-gram	70.0	76.0	75.0	81.0	68.0	67.0	67.0	61.0

From the results obtained in our experiments, Linear-based classifiers (Linear SVM, SDG, and Logistic regression) achieved better results than nonlinear ones. However, nonlinear classifiers achieved good results too; DT achieved 89% accuracy. The highest accuracy was achieved using Linear SVM as 92%. This classifier performs well no matter the number of feature values used. Also with the increase of n-gram (Tri-gram, Four-gram), the accuracy of the algorithm decreases. Furthermore, TF-IDF outperformed TF. The lowest accuracy of 47.2% was achieved using KNN and SVM with four-gram words and 50,000 and 10,000 feature values.

We conducted additional experiments by running our model on the dataset of Adali and Horne [8], consisting of real news from BuzzFeed and other news websites, and satires from Burfoot and Baldwin's satire dataset. We obtained 87% accuracy using n-gram features and LSVM algorithm when classifying fake news against real new, which is much better than the 71% accuracy achieved by the authors on the same dataset.

5 Conclusion

The problem of fake news has gained attention in 2016, especially in the aftermath of the last US presidential elections. Recent statistics and research show that 62% of US adults get news on social media [12, 13]. Most of the popular fake news stories were more widely shared on Facebook than the most popular mainstream news stories [14]. A sizable number of people who read fake news stories have reported that they believe them more than news from mainstream media. Dewey [15] claimed that fake news played a huge role in the 2016 US election and that they continue to affect people opinions and decisions.

In this paper, we have presented a detection model for fake news using n-gram analysis through the lenses of different features extraction techniques. Furthermore, we investigated two different features extraction techniques and six different machine learning techniques. The proposed model achieves its highest accuracy when using unigram features and Linear SVM classifier. The highest accuracy score is 92%.

Fake news detection is an emerging research area with few public datasets. We run our model on an existing dataset, showing that our model outperforms the original approach published by the authors of the dataset. In our future work, we will run our model on the few other publicly available datasets, such as the LIAR dataset which was released only recently, after we completed the current phase of our research [10].

References

1. The Verge: Your short attention span could help fake news spread (2017). https://www. theverge.com/2017/6/26/15875488/fake-news-viral-hoaxes-bots-information-overload-twitter-facebook-social-media. Accessed 16 Aug 2017
2. Lemann, N.: Solving the Problem of Fake News. The New Yorker (2017). http://www. newyorker.com/news/news-desk/solving-the-problem-of-fake-news

3. Schulten, K.: Skills and Strategies—Fake News vs. Real News: Determining the Reliability of Sources. The Learning Network (2017). https://learning.blogs.nytimes.com/2015/10/02/skills-and-strategies-fake-news-vs-real-news-determining-the-reliability-of-sources/. Accessed 16 Aug 2017

4. Levin, S.: Pay to sway: report reveals how easy it is to manipulate elections with fake news. The Guardian (2017). https://www.theguardian.com/media/2017/jun/13/fake-news-manipulate-elections-paid-propaganda

5. Gu, L., Kropotov, V., Yarochkin, F.: The fake news machine, how propagandists abuse the internet and manipulate the public. In: 1st ed. [pdf] Trend Micro, p. 81 (2017). https://documents.trendmicro.com/assets/white_papers/wp-fake-news-machine-how-propagandists-abuse-the-internet.pdf?_ga=2.117063430.1073547711.1497355570–1028938869.1495462143

6. Schow, A.: The 4 Types of 'Fake News'. Observer (2017). http://observer.com/2017/01/fake-news-russia-hacking-clinton-loss/

7. Rubin, V.L., Chen, Y., Conroy, N.J.: Deception detection for news: three types of fakes. In: Proceedings of the 78th ASIS&T Annual Meeting: Information Science with Impact: Research in and for the Community (ASIST 2015). Article 83, p. 4, American Society for Information Science, Silver Springs (2015)

8. Horne, B.D., Adali, S.: This just in: fake news packs a lot in title, uses simpler, repetitive content in text body, more similar to satire than real news. In: the 2nd International Workshop on News and Public Opinion at ICWSM (2017)

9. Burfoot, C., Baldwin, T.: Automatic satire detection: are you having a laugh? In: Proceedings of the ACL-IJCNLP 2009 Conference Short Papers, 4 August 2009, Suntec, Singapore (2009)

10. Wang, W.Y.: Liar, Liar Pants on fire: a new Benchmark dataset for fake news detection. arXiv preprint (2017). arXiv:1705.00648

11. Rubin., Victoria, L., et al.: Fake news or truth? Using satirical cues to detect potentially misleading news. In: Proceedings of NAACL-HLT (2016)

12. Gottfried, J., Shearer, E.: News use across social media platforms. Pew Res. Cent. 26 (2016)

13. Gottfried, J., et al.: The 2016 presidential campaign–a news event that's hard to miss. Pew Res. Cent. 4 (2016)

14. Silverman, C., Singer-Vine, J.: Most americans who see fake news believe it, new survey says. BuzzFeed News (2016)

15. Dewey, C.: Facebook has repeatedly trended fake news since firing its human editors. Washington Post (2016)

Security Protocol of Social Payment Apps

Jasmeen Saini[✉]

New York Institute of Technology, Vancouver, Canada
Ahmed.Awad@nyit.edu

Abstract. Social Payment Apps have now become an integral part of individual's life and business operations because of its reliability, easiness, and pace of transferring money. However, with the development of new technology, the security related issues have also increased drastically. In this research, many problematic issues have been observed in various apps that are in use these days. Both technical and social vulnerabilities were observed, that would allow an adversary to steal individual's credential information or leak it. Moreover, a usable and secure payment guidelines and steps will be provided to make a better payment application which will gain users' trust and e-commerce business. To measure the performance of the used payment app, one needs to dive off the boat in order to understand the flaws. Venmo, Google Wallet, and Apple Pay are the key apps that are analyzed and risks are observed in relation to social engineering. Moreover, a secure payment protocol using one-time password tokenization method is proposed that will keep transactions more secure. This research enlightens the security challenges and possible mitigations to prevent data breaches.

Keywords: Tokenization · Social engineering · PCI-DSS compliance · Social payment apps · Security · Payment protocol · Private key · Public key

1 Introduction

These days fascination has led to the inception of new types of payment services that are blending capabilities with social networking. This new type is termed as "Social Payment App". The good examples of this blend of service are [1] 'PayPal', 'Venmo', 'Google Wallet', 'Apple Pay' and much more, that lets you request, pool and pay money with your friends.

The social payment apps are directly connected to either user's bank account or debit/credit card detail and turn into a website or an app. The money is withdrawn or deposited to the account as per user's choices [1]. These apps are now capitalized in businesses nowadays as they have the ability to integrate loyalty and incentive programs [2].

Social payment applications bring new opportunities and with them, the new risks are evolved eventually with the growth of vulnerability and threat. With the advancement of technology, people always seek for an ease, flexibility and of course security while exchanging money on social apps. Social payment transactions can be

© Springer International Publishing AG 2017
I. Traore et al. (Eds.): ISDDC 2017, LNCS 10618, pp. 139–150, 2017.
https://doi.org/10.1007/978-3-319-69155-8_10

more exposed to risk as several users are linked to each other in performing payment service. This multi-user transaction environment is favorable to exploitation by adversaries using technological attacks if appropriate preventive measures are not established throughout the whole payment system [3]. As the technology advances, digital hacking is also growing at the same pace.

To retain high-security standards, it is imperative for service providers of social payment apps to consider this as a major parameter. Assuming that system or user's phone are somehow undermined then an adversary can easily access the bank information or can easily manipulate the payments on the app. With the emergence of the new market, it would be a challenge to step ahead along with customer education, service providers, payment methods and fraud detections and preventions for the mitigation of security risks [4].

About Project

The analysis is performed on different social payment apps such as Venmo, Google Wallet and Apple pay that are currently used among users because of their services at the intersection of the payment process and social network. The standard laws related to mobile payment security are also compared. Finally, the issues found in these social payment apps that violate security, such as fraudulent transactions or information leakage of users whose access must be restricted are improved using possible solutions.

2 Related Work

Customers now carry mobile phones more often than a wallet or purse. Making payment through mobile payment apps is much easier service that has been issued to the customer but security and privacy risks are major barriers to adoption. The major concern is about hacking or intercepting of personal data. At the point when customers or users are offered a protected online payment condition, customers don't have to give cash each time they want to split a bill or make a purchase.

In the year 2014, Venmo app was used for security research. Kraft and his team [5] researched technical and social vulnerabilities and found several issues in the application. They analyze the issues at payment processing position and at social networking. They looked for bugs that could allow others to steal the money of another person. Moreover, they gave some considerable suggestions for the improvement of application.

The researchers initially downloaded the APK file of the Android version of Venmo and then used dex2jar for decompiling of a file. Later on, they tried to figure out apps process and their payment system which resulted in them finding a private API endpoint.

Another group in the year 2016 also researched on this social payment apps security. Khandekar and her team [6] analyze Square Cash and highlight its flaws. In order to find risks and security issues, they tried different methods to inspect issues in this application. They researched on every aspect such as security checking, authentication, authorization and other related issues.

This group initially retrieved APK file and unpacked it. Later they convert the obtained .dex file through reverse engineering into a jar file using dex2jar. The recovered jar file was decompiled using a decompiler and source code. They proposed a secure payment protocol as an improvement method and provide some useful guidelines that could help in building a secure protocol.

Jawale and Park [7] analyze the possible security concerns and vulnerabilities in Apple Pay. They relate their work with other social payment apps such as Google Wallet, Samsung Pay, PayPal, and AliPay. In their findings, they found some security concerns regarding transactions and payment data that deal directly with the users and their credential information.

Moreover, researchers even analyzed and suggested the best possible ways to make the system more reliable along with the implementation to overcome security flaws.

Roland and Langer [8] performed the relay attack on Google Wallet to understand its functionality and security issues. To compare this with Apple Pay, Margraf and his team [8] performed similar actions on Apple Pay to determine components needed for functionality and transaction security issues.

After analyzing security parameters both in Apple Pay and Google Wallet, they demonstrated that security vulnerabilities are more exploited in later in contrast to the former.

3 Analysis

3.1 Risk Assessment of Social Payment Apps

3.1.1 "Venmo"

Venmo is a widely used social payments application that has provided a frictionless way among friends to pay each other cashless such as sharing rent or splitting bills and anything else. Venmo is fast, casual, convenient and trendy. It has allowed users to connect with their friends, send payments, charge other users, and publicize their transactions to other users under various privacy settings [5].

Venmo was acquired by PayPal which is owned by eBay. It prominently assures its security by using the encryption on all connections with the help of SSL (Secure Socket Layer) basically called as bank-grade security (used by leading banks and governmental agencies) to secure users' transactions or access to their personal data information.

Ben Kraft and his team [5] reverse engineered their private API to analyze issues that violate Venmo's security. In their findings, they disclose the leakage of information about transactions during API call and sending and receiving spoofed messages. Moreover, in their testing, they found Venmo's security policy more unsecured as they were able to make fake accounts and send payments to non-friend users too.

Venmo took a heat when security holes were revealed after a user's account was defrauded to a huge amount of money. It's been studied that Venmo's interface and social networking interface made it vulnerable to social engineering attacks [9].

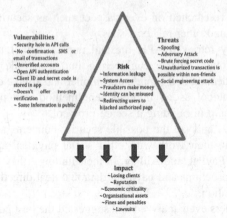

Vulnerabilities
~Security hole in API calls
~No confirmation SMS or email of transactions
~Unverified accounts
~Open API authentication
~Client ID and secret code is stored in app
~Doesn't offer two-step verification
~ Some information is public

Risk
~Information leakage
~System Access
~Fraudsters make money
~Identity can be misused
~Redirecting users to hijacked authorized page

Threats
~Spoofing
~Adversary Attack
~Brute forcing secret code
~Unauthorized transaction is possible within non-friends
~Social engineering attack

Impact
~Losing clients
~Reputation
~Economic criticality
~Organisational assets
~Fines and penalties
~Lawsuits

Apart from this Venmo still does not hold some basic security feature such as two-factor authentication [10] or any notifications when a password is changed or account is added. These issues have not trickled down yet which is a big problem.

3.1.2 "Google Wallet"

Google wallet is another peer-to-peer social payment app which is developed and owned by Google itself. Both the debit card details and bank account information are linked to the Google account and could be used in both Android and iOS system. The funds are added to the Google account and then could be used accordingly such as transferring to another account or paying directly whenever one makes a purchase [11].

Though Google assures 100% security coverage but still there are some major concerns that must be taken into account. On Android devices, Google run pseudo open ecosystem due to which the device makers and carriers get the ability over custom versions of firmware and give access to the third-party application. This simply explains the lack of control of Google on running devices. In the year 2012, a security flaw was uncovered in which an adversary could view all credential information of user's digital wallet on a device. This could be made possible with Brute force attack uncovering PIN code associated user's Google Wallet [12].

Since Google Wallet stores credential information but officials claimed that the data is encrypted and an attacker will not be able to get access as the information is never shown in the app. Moreover, this social payment app uses host card emulation rather than tokenization to obtain a secure connection using Near Field Communication chip.

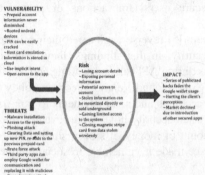

VULNERABILITY
~Prepaid account information never diminished
~Rooted android devices
~PIN can be easily cracked
~Host card emulation- Information is stored in cloud
~Use implicit intent
~Open access to the app

Risk
~Losing account details
~Exposing personal information
~Potential access to account
~Stolen information can be monetized directly or sold underground
~Gaining limited access to the system
~Cloning magnetic stripe card from data stolen wirelessly

IMPACT
~Series of publicized hacks fades the Google wallet usage
~Hurting the client's perception
~Market declined due to introduction of other secured apps

THREATS
~Malware installation
~Access to the system
~Phishing attack
~Clearing Data and setting up new PIN, re-adds to the previous prepaid card
~Brute force attack
~Third party apps can employ Google wallet for communication and replacing it with malicious
~Eavesdropping attack

Due to effective fraud reduction, all major credit card companies, banks, and corporations are backing this new technology. With the addition of a layer of security, there will always be a chance of some form of a security breach due to some unnoticeable vulnerability [13].

3.1.3 "Apple Pay"

Apple Pay is another social payment app or digital wallet that uses iOS devices including iPhone, Apple Watch, iPad, and Mac. In order to get rid of credit/debit cards or PIN/magnetic stripe transaction, Apple designs this solution with additional Two-factor authentication contactless transaction method. It allows a user to initialize payments and transfer money between user, merchant and card issuer.

It's aim is to replace wallet and prevent people from digging into purse or wallet to look for credit cards and debit cards [14]. It uses NFC technology and can be used at any NFC-based contactless payment POS terminal.

Apple somehow put emphasis on security to gain the trust of iPhone users and assuring the owners that payment information and transaction is safe and secure than their physical wallet [14]. It's hard to define the difference between Google Wallet and Apple Pay but if a single point of failure is considered then Google Wallet lags behind.

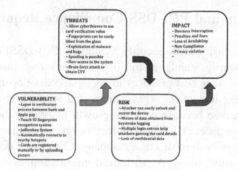

Though Apple pay possesses some vulnerability, still they are more secure than credit cards. Apple has a partnership with many major banks to handle transactions. For the security problems identified, it has to keep in mind that security measures such as passwords or fingerprint scanners are always on edge of risk.

3.2 Potential Security Issues in Social Payment Apps

Surprisingly, money is social which is considered for buying or selling products. These days mobile and social networks have become a funnel for online payment which offers great business deals to financial industries and gives rise to new security threats as well. In this study risk assessment is analyzed by considering confidentiality, availability, and integrity as principle areas. Social payment apps link directly to the individual's bank account/credential information and thus require highest security standards. If systems or personal phones are compromised, hackers could easily access information of users and manipulate payments [15].

On the surface, all social payment apps use security policies such as Secure Socket Layer to protect their customers' information by encrypting data, hashing passwords and verifying links with banks and other users in order to protect it from snooping.

As discussed in the analysis the possible threats are Verification Lapse, Unauthorized/Fake accounts (Open access), Malware/Virus (DOS attack). Moreover, some of the apps don't use two-factor authentication and do not even notify when changes are made in the account. A phishing scam is another effective attack that somehow attempts to steal information from customers. Some other security concerns that can be traced generally are Human Error when a personal device (mobile phones) are hacked and other could be using Public Wi-Fi which gives hackers to access unsecured data [16].

Contactless technology, in general, presents new risks and frauds interconnected with finance, technology, legal and compliance and of course users. These challenges require a clear focus on risk and governance to overcome this issue. All social payment apps have some vulnerability so do the processors, and even the trusted credit card in the wallet. Vendors who have created such apps are diligently working to figure out risk factors and mitigation techniques for it.

4 Scope Problem and PCI DSS Compliance Requirements

The Payment Card Industry Data Security Standards (PCI DSS) develops and maintains information security standards for organizations that manage payment data security. PCI DSS provides best practices to social app developers or manufacturers.

PCI DSS has a big impact on organizations and is much more challenging than most organizations realize because with the growth of organizations the information also spread at the same pace. PCI DSS requirements/guidelines are important to follow the credibility and security purposes of a company. Companies dealing with PCI DSS struggles to follow a pattern [17]. As with most information security issues, PCI DSS compliance starts with the information of an individual. It is not limited to payment card data but to any kind of data that involves confidential information. In order to deal with PCI DSS, strategic planning needs to be followed not tactical (Fig. 1).

Objectives of PCI DSS [18]:

1. Building and maintaining a Secure Network and protecting cardholder data.
2. Implementing strong access control measures and maintaining security policies.
3. Preventing account data from being intercepted when entered into a mobile device.
4. Preventing account data from compromise while processed or stored within the mobile device.
5. Preventing account data from interception upon transmission out of the mobile device.
6. Preventing unauthorized device access and escalation of privileges.
7. Protection against malware and known vulnerabilities.
8. Confirming secure coding, engineering, and testing.
9. Detection of theft or loss of data and able to report events on server side.

Fig. 1. Payment card industry security standards

The main focus of above objectives is to show direction on how to secure social payment processes along with the payment environment itself and how to prevent it from being intercepted during a transaction or being compromised on mobile devices while processing or storage, by giving training to developers in the emerging market.

Venmo protects user data with firewalls as stated on their webpage [19]. To protect user's cardholder data, Venmo follows all PCI requirements and guidelines such as encrypting data transmission of cardholder in all types of networks.

Google Wallet has a PCI standards level of one, which is the highest a business can achieve [20]. They submit a quarterly network scan after testing security breaches in their payment infrastructure and then send an attestation of compliance form to the Council to inform them that they've met the security requirements, such as protecting IDs, passwords, personal information of customer or using a firewall configuration.

Apple's new token-based system has definitely changed the environment. The specific way of designing new security system and keeping customer's privacy, resonate across the market [21]. Apple Pay worked on enhancing the security for the transactions that are directed through it. The multiple ways of protection such as fingerprint identification, dedicated chip to hold payment information, and a single-use payment "token" offer security that is today's need for transactions. Apple Pay is a leading, developed and promising app but still need to maintain PCI DSS requirements like point-to-point encryption for protection of data.

5 Recommendations

The Payment Card Industry wants the cardholder data that includes credit card numbers and other identity information, to be protected. In short, privacy is the main challenge as it deals with user's confidential information. The ongoing battle between security vendors and adversaries regarding a loss of sensitive data is a big problem and is likely to be worse for established companies. In order to lower this exposure, the practice of tokenization can be used.

5.1 Rate Limiting Mechanism

Social payment apps have numerous benefits when it comes to the ease of use and security. All the payment transactions are protected under the security policies followed by payment app companies whether it's encryption or repellence of malware. To prevent fraudsters brute forcing the secret codes or card verification value code the 'rate limiting mechanism' [22] is one of the suggested solutions. Not all apps require adopting this, but apps like Apple Pay and Venmo need this implementation. This mechanism will simply shut down the system after 3 incorrect tries and user will have to wait for 24 h before retrying for next time.

5.2   Tokenization

These social apps are currently working on smart phones under secured protocol but still facing security issues. The tokenization is used to protect it by replacing sensitive information with modified data from which it is improbable that an adversary could recover the sensitive information. This technology provides secure and good protection to the information.

Tokenization converts the plaintext message into a token. The tokenization server replaces the plaintext with the encrypted one. The security provided by a tokenization system is essentially unrelated to the difficulty an attacker has in converting a token into the corresponding plaintext. This is probably so hard that it's essentially impossible. Instead, other aspects of a tokenization system will always be much easier to exploit, and these are where we should focus our attention.

5.3   One Time Password

One-time passwords are passwords that are only valid for a single or small number of transactions. This contrasts with conventional passwords which are valid for many transactions as users are reluctant to voluntarily change passwords frequently. Since OTPs are only valid for a limited number of users, an attacker has a smaller window of time to gain access to resources guarded by such a password because any previously stolen passwords will likely have become invalid. As with traditional passwords, one-time passwords are vulnerable to man-in-the-middle attacks [23].

By observing the OTP before it is successfully received by the authenticator, an attacker has a valid password. Because of this undesirable property, both OTPs and conventional passwords must travel securely. Typically, the one-time password is generated by a hardware device that the person desiring to be authenticated carries to promote use across many physically distant domains. The hardware implements an algorithm that generates passwords in a specific manner that the authenticator knows. The hardware device will often display the password on a small screen for a user to type into the authenticator.

6   Proposed Secured Payment Protocol

Since not every application is using all of the above recommendations, it is hard to say which app is more secure and safer. After analyzing extensively possible security issues in them, we designed a proposed secured protocol that helps mitigate possible security flaws up to some extent. The proposed secured payment protocol for social payment apps is comprised of following stages using both tokenization and one-time password:

Proposed Scenario

- Sender shares his information with a server such as ID, receiver's detail, and witness value W, private key P, generated using Diffie–Hellman assumption, and request for receiver's ID to initiate a transaction.

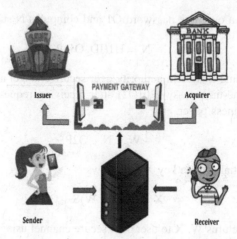

- To initiate transaction sender will be provided with one-time password token which will be used to compute ID.
- The server checks the authorization of both senders' from issuer and receivers' from acquirer and responds accordingly to transaction request made by a sender with required details like receiver's ID.
- It further calculates witness W using receiver's one-time password token after receiver accepts the request.
- Once sender computes W, it calculates private key X.
- To get authentication, the sender sends an encrypted authentication request to server and server further send it to the payment gateway.
- Payment gateway contacts issuer and acquirer financial organizations for withdrawal and transfer of the amount from respective accounts after verifying their tokens, encrypted form of credit/debit card details, generated using the tokenization method.
- Payment gateway has all required parameters to calculate private and public keys, so as to decrypt messages. On response to these authentication requests, payment gateway sends an encrypted response which is recovered by a server and later by sender.

Stage 1: Issuing a One-time password token

Sender and receiver will be issued a 6-digit token once he tried to log in. This one-time password token is sent as SMS or email. Token generator will generate a random token for particular time period.

Stage 2: Self-generating key

In proposed protocol, a self-certified public key is generated based on identity and one-time password. As per Diffie–Hellman assumption, internal mechanism in sender's end device generates a nonsingular elliptic curve E defined over a finite field Fq of characteristic p such that Fq is used with base point generator P of prime order n. It chooses a key pair (S, Pk), where Pk = SP. The related parameter Pk is public key while S is secret key [24].

Private Key Generation

- Sender chooses a one-time password O1 and computes N such that

$$N = H1(ID, O1)P \tag{1}$$

- ID, O1 are sending to system authority over secure channel and request receiver to exchange his one-time password (O2) after receiving request message and calculates W as a witness payer.

$$W = N + O2P \tag{2}$$

- It computes partial private key X as follows

$$X = H2(ID, W)S + O2 \tag{3}$$

- Finally Server returns W, X to user over secure channel using which Secret Key Sk can be calculated

$$Sk = X + H1(ID, O1) \tag{4}$$

Public Key Extraction

- From Eq. (4) we obtain

$$Sk = X + H1(ID, O1)$$

- Multiply Prime number P on both sides

$$SkP = XP + H1(ID, O1)P$$

- Using value of X from Eq. (3)

$$SkP = H2(ID, W)SP + O2P + H1(ID, O1)P$$

- As per Eq. (1), N = H1(ID, O1)P

$$SkP = H2(ID, W)SP + O2P + N$$

- As per Eq. (2), N + O2P = W

$$SkP = H2(ID, W)SP + W$$

- As Pk = SP

$$SkP = H2(ID, W)Pk + W$$

- Public key is

$$Pk = (SkP-W)/H2(ID, W)$$

Stage 3: Transaction Completion

Payment gateway now has both public key and private key that are computed as above. These keys are used for the decryption of information sent by sender and details related to it. The payment gateway holds all the parameters and thus contact sender's issuer and receiver's acquirer for encrypted authentication request and responds to server and later to sender for the completion of transaction.

7   Conclusion

In this paper, security analysis of various social payment applications is done in various factors. It has been observed that these apps are secured and reliable. However, in order to improve the level of security, a new payment protocol was introduced called as self certified key generation payment protocol using one-time password tokens to establish a link between two participants for sharing a key. Using this protocol, user can send or receive money without any third-party involvement for key generation which reduces various types of security attacks, provide user anonymity and secure tokenized transaction. This proposal will help in future developments in secured social payment apps.

References

1. Social Payment (n.d.). http://www.investopedia.com/terms/s/social-payment.asp. Accessed 16 Feb 2017 from Investopedia
2. 5 Major Benefits of Mobile Payments (2012). https://www.americanexpress.com/us/small-business/openforum/articles/5-major-benefits-of-mobile-payments/. Accessed from Open Forum
3. Mobile Payments: Risk, Security and Assurance Issues. ISACA, Meadows (2011)
4. Pegueros, V.: Security of Mobile Banking and Payments. SANS (2012)
5. Kraft, B., Mannes, E., Moldow, J.: Security Research of a Social Payment App (2014)
6. Khandekar, S., Liang, J., Razaque, A., Amsaad, F., Abdulgader, M.: Security research of a social payment app and suggested improvement. Commun. Appl. Electron. **4**, 14–21 (2016)
7. Park, A.S.: A security analysis on apple pay. In: European Intelligence and Security Informatics Conference, pp. 160–163, New York (2016)
8. Margraf, M., Lange, S., Otterbien, F.: Security evaluation of apple pay at point-of-sale terminals. IEEE (2016)
9. Griswold, A.: Venmo Money, Venmo Problems (2015). http://www.slate.com/articles/te chnology/safety_net/2015/02/venmo_security_it_s_not_as_strong_as_the_company_wants_you_to_think.html. Accessed from Slate

10. Campbell-Dollaghan, K.: Should You Worry About the Security of Apps Like Venmo? (2015). http://lifehacker.com/which-online-money-transfer-service-is-the-most-secure-16889 12343/1688958375. Accessed from Life Hacker

11. Kumparak, G.: TechCrunch Review: Google Wallet (2011). Accessed from https://techcr unch.com/2011/09/19/techcrunch-review-google-wallet/

12. Westervelt, R.: 10 Reasons Why Apple Pay Beats Google Wallet on Security (2014). Accessed from http://www.crn.com/slide-shows/security/300074128/10-reasons-why-apple-pay-beats-google-wallet-on-security.htm

13. Hanavan, P.: Let's Address the Security Concerns with Apple Pay and Google Wallet (2015). Accessed from http://www.truemerchant.com/lets-address-the-security-concerns-with-apple-pay-and-google-wallet/

14. Apple Pay (n.d.). https://www.macrumors.com/roundup/apple-pay/. Accessed from MacRumors

15. Abaitua, A.G.: The Emergence of Social Payment Apps (2016). Accessed from http://blogs. icemd.com/blog-moma-trends-mobile-payments/the-emergence-of-social-payment-apps/

16. Rampton, J.: Your Security Concerns About Using Mobile Payment Are Valid (2016). https://www.entrepreneur.com/article/282722. Accessed from Entrepreneur

17. Williams, B.R.: How tokenization and encryption can enable PCI DSS compliance. Inf. Secur. Tech. Rep. **15**, 160–165 (2010)

18. Technologies, E.: PCI Mobile Payment Acceptance Security Guidelines for Developers (2012)

19. Venmo. Web. https://venmo.com/about/security/

20. Parker, M. (n.d.): Is Your Debit Card Information Safe With Google Wallet? http://smallbusiness.chron.com/debit-card-information-safe-google-wallet-64981.html. Accessed from Chron

21. Getzelman, M.: Apple Pay and PCI Compliance (2014). https://www.coalfire.com/The-Coalfire-Blog/November-2014/Apple-Pay-and-PCI-Compliance. Accessed from Coalfire

22. Fox-Brewster, T.: Here's Proof Apple Pay Is Useful For Stealing People's Money (2016). https://www.forbes.com/sites/thomasbrewster/2016/03/01/apple-pay-fraud-test/#44a0fb7946c6. Accessed from Forbes

23. Schneier, B.: Two-Factor Authentication: Too Little, Too Late (2005). https://www.schneier. com/essays/archives/2005/04/two-factor_authentic.html. Accessed from Schneier on Security

24. Li, W., Wen, Q., Su, Q., Jin, Z.: An efficient and secure mobile payment protocol for restricted connectivity scenarios in vehicular ad hoc network. Comput. Commun. **35**, 188–195 (2012)

Spectral-Spatial Classification of Hyperspectral Imagery Using Support Vector and Fuzzy-MRF

Sumit Chakravarty[1](✉), Madhushri Banerjee[2], and Sonali Chandel[3]

[1] Department of Electrical Engineering, Kennesaw State University, Marietta, GA, USA
schakra2@kennesaw.edu
[2] Georgia Gwinnett College, Lawrenceville, GA, USA
[3] New York of Institute of Technology, Nanjing, China

Abstract. Hyper-Spectral Image (HSI) classification is one of the essential problems in hyperspectral image processing. It has been researched extensively and has resulted in a variety of publications. A key approach investigated in recent years incorporates both spectral and spatial characteristics to analyze the hyperspectral data. In this paper we have presented our proposed approach to improve the accuracy of HSI classification. Support Vector Machines have been used to classify spectral characteristics of images in conjunction with Markov Random Fields that classify HSI using spatial means. However, this current technique of combining them does not enforce smoothness in spatial and spectral analyses. We ensure finer segmentations in the results by adding our innovative approach of including Fuzzy-Markov Random Field to spectral classification. The 'fuzziness' promotes smoother transitions among classified pixels while preserving region integrity. Results show the efficacy of our approach.

Keywords: Hyperspectral imagery · Support Vector Machines · Fuzzy image processing · Markov Random Fields

1 Introduction

In recent years, immense research efforts have been devoted to hyperspectral image classification. Given a set of pixel vectors of a hyperspectral image, the goal of classification is to assign a unique label to each pixel-vector so that it can be represented by a given class. Although classification can be either supervised or unsupervised, due to its better performance supervised classification has received far more audience. Various classification techniques have been proposed that label a pixel on the basis of its spectral properties alone, with no attention to labels which are assigned to neighboring pixels [1]. A prominent method among such supervised spectral classification technique is the Support Vector Machines. However, in remote sensing images the pixels in the neighborhood are likely to be assigned the same labels, because imaging sensors acquire significant portions of energy from adjacent pixels and also because ground cover types generally occur over a region that is large compared to the size of a pixel [2].

© Springer International Publishing AG 2017
I. Traore et al. (Eds.): ISDDC 2017, LNCS 10618, pp. 151–161, 2017.
https://doi.org/10.1007/978-3-319-69155-8_11

Thus there has been a significant trend to incorporate spatial information into the erst-while spectral classification techniques.

Among the approaches of spectral classification with rudimentary spatial coverage has been [1]. Here SVM spectral technique has been applied at multiple spatial resolutions and depending on the variation among the SVM results of multiple layers, segmentation procedure is carried out. In [2] spectral spatial classification is targeted by incorporating Spatial Markov Random Field based regularization to the SVM generated spectral classification results. This work was extended in [3] by adding another spectral classified called the Multilogistic Regression (MLR) in tandem with the SVM. The MLR learns the spectral class probabilities generated by the SVM and has the effect of smoothening and refining the SVM predictions. Another extension in this direction has been [4], the research here performs gradient on the principal component of hyperspectral imagery and thereby get the edge information. The edge pixel are then provided higher weights. In [5] a different direction is undertaken. Instead of performing spectral classification, wavelet based spectral compression is carried out thereby generating compressed spatial scenes. Grayscale morphology is thereupon performed and resultant data is stacked back into the hyperspectral imagery. This results in an augmented hyperspectral cube incorporating spatial context. Use of texture from invariant moments have been used in [6]. Feature vector from texture and spectral are then used for classification. Other approaches include DNA encoding [7], super pixel approach [8] minimum spanning tree [9], and window patch based spectral kernel-classification technique [10].

From the above survey we see that the field of spectral spatial classification as applied to hyperspectral scenario has been well exploited. Numerous techniques haven been presented using the MRF model for spatial regularization, but besides a very few, no work has been done to exploit the inherent MRF structure. The well-known MRF energy structure considers neighborhood energy as well as likelihood energy. This paper's main contribution is to exploit the neighborhood prior of the MRF by incorporating nonlinearity in terms of the fuzzy median filtering approach. By incorporating such advanced novelty we bring a new outlook to application of MRF based spectral spatial classification for Hyperspectral Imagery. In the following sections we provide background information on the relevant techniques used in our approach, followed by the architecture of our novel method and finally end with presentation of comparative results and conclusions.

2   Materials and Methods

2.1   Data Sets

The scene for testing our algorithm was gathered by AVIRIS sensor over the Indian Pines test site in North-western Indiana in the late nineties. It consists of a square image of 145×145 pixels and 224 spectral reflectance bands in the wavelength range 0.4–2.5×10^{-6} m. This scene is a subset of a larger one. The Indian Pines scene contains two-thirds agriculture, and one-third forest or other natural perennial vegetation [13]. Other than the agricultural content, there are two major dual lane highways, a rail line, as well as some low density housing, other built structures also embedded in the scene. Since the scene is taken in June some of the crops present, corn, soybeans, are in early stages of growth with less than 5% coverage, hence there is significant similarity in their spectral signatures. The ground truth available is designated into sixteen classes and is not all mutually exclusive. Typically reduced data band image is used by removing bands covering the region of water absorption: [104–108], [150–163], 220. The resultant image has 200 bands. Indian Pines data are available through Purdue University's MultiSpec site [14].

2.2   Framework

In this section, we detail our process. We first perform probabilistic SVM pixel wise classification in the first step. The results of the spectral classification is supplied as an input to spatial processing. Markov Random Field has been used in past as spatial operator. One of the main contributions of this paper is to use Fuzzy Markov Random Field to smoothly classify the pixels. We first provide the details for the key techniques, namely probabilistic SVM and Fuzzy Filtering and Markov Random Fields. We then detail how these techniques are implemented in our paper.

2.2.1   Probabilistic Support Vector Machines

We refer to the reference [15] for the details of probabilistic SVM. For a pixel, we need to know the a posteriori probabilities that the pixel belongs to each of the K classes yi (i = 1, 2,..., K) given that the pixel has the feature vector $xk \in$ Rd (k = 1, 2,..., N); where d and N are the numbers of bands and pixels of input image respectively. With the probability, $p(yi|xk)$, we can write a discriminant function as: $xk \in yi$ if $p(yi|xk) > p(yj|xk)$.

$$\forall j = i. \tag{1}$$

Various classification techniques are introduced to process hyperspectral data, however we suggest to use support vector machine (SVM) for this purpose [16, 17]. SVM originally do not provide class probability estimates, while in [17] two previous techniques are proposed for this purpose based on combining all pairwise comparisons. We use one which is implemented in the LIBSVM library [18]. The approach used is to first perform binary SVMs for each class in one-against-all fashion. So for K classes we generate K binary SVM models. These models are then used to predict the probability of every pixel being a member of a particular class. The resultant probabilities from all classes generate the conditional probability of the pixel for each class $p(xk|yi)$ for $xk \in$ Rd (k = 1, 2,..., N) and yi (i = 1, 2,..., K).

2.2.2   Fuzzy Image Filtering

The effect of Markov Random Field is to perform spatial regularization. It considers pixel neighborhoods called Cliques and calculates prior potentials. The potential generating functions weigh pixel similarity much more than dissimilarity. While this enables image smoothening, it tends to make the image-edges week and over smoothens them. For above reasons, we reinforce edges in Markov priors before MRF processing. We choose Fuzzy based edge reinforcement, which forms one of the key contributions of this paper. Fuzzy edge enhancement works on window regions which in our case are Markov cliques. Membership functions play important role in fuzzy logic and are used to calculate the fuzziness in a fuzzy set. For our case we use Trapezoid and Gaussian membership function on grey scale differences. The functions are defined below:

$$T_{rz}F(\Delta y_k; r, s, t, u) = \begin{cases} 0 & (\Delta y_k < r) or (\Delta y_k > u) \\ \frac{z-r}{s-r} & r \leq \Delta y_k \leq s \\ 1 & s \leq \Delta y_k \leq t \\ \frac{u-z}{u-t} & t \leq \Delta y_k \leq u \end{cases} \tag{2}$$

Where r, s, t and u are various parameters of the trapezoidal Membership Function for Fig. 1(a).

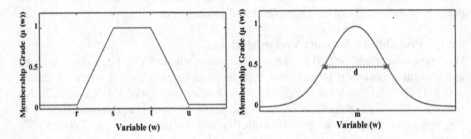

Fig. 1. Graphical example of Trapezoid (left) and Gaussian (right) membership functions

The details of the Gaussian (shown in Fig. 1(b)) Membership Function are

$$GF(\Delta y_k; m, d) = e^{-\frac{(\Delta y_k - m)^2}{2d^2}} \tag{3}$$

where m and d are the mean and variance.

And Δy_k represents the respectively the deviation of the representative measure of the prior within a window $y(k)$, wherein the window size is denoted by the variable k. Using the 'fuzzied' input (by application of the membership functions), and a set of fuzzy rules [13], and fuzzy output membership functions, we generate an '*Edgeness*' factor for the clique region. This term can be added to the prior data very much like *High Boosting* effect in image processing, thereby producing edge enhanced prior for MRF processing.

2.2.3   Markov Random Field
The last step of this proposed approach is to utilize the Markov Random Field (MRF) for spatial regularization. The MRF technique considers spatial neighborhood of a pixel and its likelihood probability for belonging to any particular class. Based on

the pixel's class probability and spatial consistency, MRF generates local energy given by:

$$U(\mathbf{x}_i) = U_{spectral}(\mathbf{x}_i) + U_{spatial}(\mathbf{x}_i)$$
$$U_{spectral}(\mathbf{x}_i) = -\ln\{P(\mathbf{x}_i|y_i)\}$$
$$U_{spatial}(\mathbf{x}_i) = \sum_{\mathbf{x}_i \in N_i} \beta(1 - \delta(y_i - y_j)) \tag{4}$$

where, $P(xi|yi)$ is the conditional likelihood of observation **xi** belonging to class $yi, (i = 1,\dots,N)$, and N_i is the neighborhood of observation $\mathbf{x}_i$. β is the control parameter and $\delta(.,.)$ is the Kronecker delta function. It is to be noted here that the likelihood probabilities are generated based on the input from the spectral classification step. The local energy for each observation is then used in an optimization framework to generate the class prediction for the observation for minimum global energy of the image. We use the ICM algorithm for calculation of the optimality.

2.3   Architecture of Proposed Method

Traditionally Hyperspectral Imagery has been classified using spectral techniques. This is due to the significant spectral information available for harnessing. For our dataset we have 220 bands available for processing. The spectral signatures however do not consider their neighborhoods. This leads to 'pixelated' classifications, and significant absence of smoothness in the results. This becomes even more important as modern hyperspectral sensor are able to generate high resolution data and thereby provide 'spatial consistency'. Recent research approaches have addressed this issue and have published multiple techniques of utilizing spatial information. Among then use of Markov Random Field (MRF) regularization scheme is by far most significant, due to its extreme flexibility and applicability. The MRF approach enables us to enrich the model further. Recent venue of research on MRF have focused on developing advanced neighborhood energy criteria. The advancement proposed in this paper, which also makes it of the key contributions, is to incorporate fuzzy edge enhancement into the energy the energy criteria. As previously elaborated in Sect. 2.2.2, by performing fuzzy edge enhancement on the neighborhood cliques of the MRF model, we ensure that the energy term is not biased by smoothness maintaining region consistency and enforces spatial regularization on the MRF results. So, the effect of incorporating the fuzzy filtering into the spatial prior formulation of the Markov Random Field is the changed spectral and spatial energy function, given by:

$$U_{spectral}(\mathbf{x}_i) = -\ln\{P(\mathbf{x}_i|y_i'(k))\}$$
$$U_{spatial}(\mathbf{x}_i) = \sum_{\mathbf{x}_j \in N_i} \beta(1 - \delta(y_i'(k) - y_j'(k))) \tag{5}$$

$y'(k) = y(k) + Edgeness[y(k)]$ *(refer Sect. 2.2.2)*.

We will see in the experiment section that this enables smoother class segmentations. The flowchart of the proposed algorithm is shown below in Fig. 2.

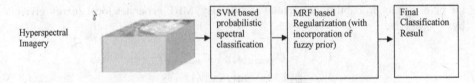

Fig. 2. Flow chart of the FuzzySVMMRF algorithm's workflow.

3 Results and Discussion

3.1 Results and Comparison with Previous Techniques

In this section we provide the results of the application of our new algorithm and compare it with current results. The results show that our approach generates significant improvement in smoothness of the result and better group uniformity than the current approaches of classification. Next, we present the table of comparative results between the spectral classification (using SVM), the spectral spatial classification using SVMMRF and finally our FuzzySVMMRF technique. In order to compare the results, we calculate the amount of variance in the output results of each of the three comparative algorithms (Fig. 3).

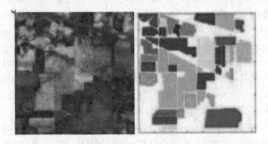

Fig. 3. False color Indiana Pines image and its ground truth map

To better study the variance we select 7 groups out of the total sixteen groups. The choice of selection is based on group size and the uniqueness of their spectral signatures. Figure 4 shows the considered groups, with their group number represented by false color (jet) image.

For the above seven groups, we use the two commonly used criteria of measuring variability, namely, standard deviation and range. The result from the three algorithms under consideration for all the seven groups are presented in the Table 1. From the result we clearly see that our novel method (FuzzySVMMRF) quite often outperform the previous two techniques with respect to preserving smoothness within each group. Markov based techniques can also be applied iteratively, with each iteration incrementing the spatial regularity. As the performance for all the Markov processes deteriorate with increased iteration we do not expand in this direction. We also ensure that the distinction among the ground truth groups are maintained amongst the comparative methods. Figure 5 shows the mean values for each of the seven groups as result of the three algorithms in discussion.

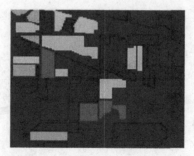

Fig. 4. False color image of the seven groups under consideration.

Table 1. Comparison among the three techniques (SVM, SVMMRF, FuzzySVMMRF for 1 iteration of the MRF-ICM algorithm)

	Grp1	Grp2	Grp3	Grp4	Grp5	Grp6	Grp7
Standard deviation per group							
SVM	1.3716	2.8767	1.2457	1.2124	1.2203	1.9327	1.5901
SVMMRF	1.3398	2.5322	1.4772	1.3587	1.4344	1.9891	1.6521
FuzzySVMMRF	1.1911	1.324	1.1866	1.286	1.3462	2.1172	2.101
Range per group							
SVM	3.7248	6.2009	3.3293	3.2441	3.5724	4.5493	4.0629
SVMMRF	3.3906	5.8531	3.5477	3.4423	3.726	4.9742	4.2277
FuzzySVMMRF	2.9532	3.2711	2.8774	3.1161	3.5267	5.0399	5.1419

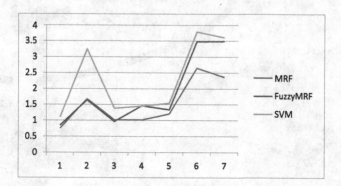

Fig. 5. Mean values of each of the seven ground truth groups for the three algorithms.

From Fig. 5 we see that all the algorithms are able to maintain the distinction between the groups. it is to be noted that our algorithm outperforms MRF technique as it provides much more variablity for the mean signatures than MRF technique.

Finally we present visual images for the SVM results and the two MRF based techniques. As is seen from Fig. 6, our method is able to maintain better smoothness as well as region consistency. Narrow regions like roads on the top right segment of the image (highlighted by black oval) are preserved by our technique like MRF, it also

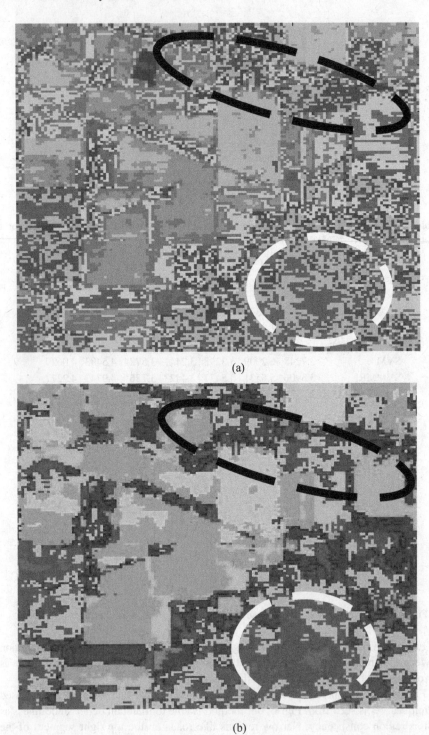

(a)

(b)

Fig. 6. Representative images of the final classification for (a) SVM (b) SVMMRF (c) FuzzySVMMRF

(c)

Fig. 6. (*continued*)

does much better in maintaining region segments like in the bottom right of the image (highlighted by white circle). Thus the efficacy of our approach is clearly visible.

3.2   Conclusion

The results of hyperspectral image spectral-spatial classification using a novel method is proposed in this paper. The result of spectral classification using probabilistic approach is augmented using spatial regularization. Extending from generic Markov Random Field, this paper presents a new fuzzy based neighborhood prior energy term for the MRF. This advanced MRF is better able to perform classification and maintain class smoothness as well as region consistency as evidenced from the presented experimentation.

References

1. Arai, M., Okumura, K., Satake, M., Shimizu, T.: Proteome-wide functional classification and identification of prokaryotic transmembrane proteins by transmembrane topology similarity comparison. Protein Sci. **13**, 2170–2183 (2004)

2. He, M., Imran, F.M., Belkacem B., Mei, S.: Improving hyperspectral image classification accuracy using Iterative SVM with spatial-spectral information. In: 2013 IEEE China Summit and International Conference on Signal and Information Processing, Beijing, pp. 471–475 (2013). doi:10.1109/ChinaSIP.2013.6625384

3. Khodadadzadeh, M., Rajabi, R., Ghassemian, H.: A novel approach for spectral-spatial classification of hyperspectral data based on SVM-MRF method. In: 2011 IEEE International Geoscience and Remote Sensing Symposium, Vancouver, BC, pp. 1890–1893 (2011). doi:10.1109/IGARSS.2011.6049493

4. Khodadadzadeh, M., Li, J., Plaza, A., Ghassemian H., Bioucas-Dias, J.M.: Spectral-spatial classification for hyperspectral data using SVM and subspace MLR. In: 2013 IEEE International Geoscience and Remote Sensing Symposium - IGARSS, Melbourne, VIC, pp. 2180–2183 (2013). doi:10.1109/IGARSS.2013.6723247

5. Borhani, M., Ghassemian, H.: Hyperspectral image classification based on spectral-spatial features using probabilistic SVM and locally weighted Markov random fields. In: 2014 Iranian Conference on Intelligent Systems (ICIS), Bam, pp. 1–6 (2014). doi:10.1109/IranianCIS.2014.6802573

6. Quesada-Barriuso, P., Argüello, F., Heras, D.B.: Spectral–spatial classification of hyperspectral images using wavelets and extended morphological profiles. IEEE J. Sel. Top. Appl. Earth Obs. Remote Sens. 7(4), 1177–1185 (2014). doi:10.1109/JSTARS.2014

7. Kumar, B., Dikshit, O.: Spectral–spatial classification of hyperspectral imagery based on moment invariants. IEEE J. Sel. Top. Appl. Earth Obs. Remote Sens. 8(6), 2457–2463 (2015). doi:10.1109/JSTARS.2015.2446611

8. Ma, A., Zhong, Y., Zhao, B., Jiao, H., Zhang, L.: Spectral-spatial DNA encoding discriminative classifier for hyperspectral remote sensing imagery. In: 2015 IEEE International Geoscience and Remote Sensing Symposium (IGARSS), Milan, pp. 1710–1713 (2015). doi:10.1109/IGARSS.2015.7326117

9. He, Z., Shen, Y., Zhang, M., Wang, Q., Wang, Y., Yu, R.: Spectral-spatial hyperspectral image classification via SVM and superpixel segmentation. In: 2014 IEEE International Instrumentation and Measurement Technology Conference (I2MTC) Proceedings, Montevideo, pp. 422–427 (2014). doi:10.1109/I2MTC.2014.6860780

10. Poorahangaryan, F., Ghassemian, H.: Spectral-spatial hyperspectral classification with spatial filtering and minimum spanning forest. In: 2015 9th Iranian Conference on Machine Vision and Image Processing (MVIP), Tehran, pp. 49–52 (2015). doi:10.1109/IranianMVIP.2015.7397502

11. Wang, J., Jiao, L., Wang, S., Hou, B., Liu, F.: Adaptive Nonlocal Spatial-Spectral Kernel for Hyperspectral Imagery Classification. IEEE J. Sel. Top. Appl. Earth Obs. Remote Sens. 9(9), 4086–4101 (2016). doi:10.1109/JSTARS.2016.2526604

12. Yu, H., Gao, L., Li, J., Zhang, B.: Spectral-spatial classification based on subspace support vector machine and Markov random field. In: 2016 IEEE International Geoscience and Remote Sensing Symposium (IGARSS), Beijing, pp. 2783–2786 (2016). doi:10.1109/IGARSS

13. Izhar, et. al.: Fuzzy logic based edge detection for noisy images. Tech. J. 20(SI)(II(S)) (2015). University of Engineering and Technology (UET) Taxila, Pakistan

14. Baumgardner, M.F., Biehl, L.L., Landgrebe, D.A.: 220 band AVIRIS hyperspectral image data set: june 12, 1992 indian pine test site 3. Purdue University Research Repository (2015). doi:10.4231/R7RX991C

15. https://engineering.purdue.edu/~biehl/MultiSpec/hyperspectral.html

16. Vapnik, V., Chervonenkis, A.: The necessary and sufficient conditions forconsistencyin the empirical risk minimization method. Pattern Recogn. Image Anal. 1(3), 283–305 (1991)

17. Melgani, F., Bruzzone, L.: Classification of hyperspectral remote sensing images with support vector machines. IEEE Trans. Geosci. Remote Sens. **42**(8), 1778–1790 (2004)

18. Wu, T.-F., Lin, C.-J., Weng, R.C.: Probability estimates for multi-class classification by pairwise coupling. J. Mach. Learn. Res. **5**, 975–1005 (2004)

19. Chang, C., Lin, C.: LIBSVM: a library for support vector machines (2009). http://www.csie.ntu.edu.tw/~cjlin/libsvm

20. Chang, C.-I.: Hyperspectral Data Exploitation: Theory and Applications. Wiley, New York (2007)

21. Richards, J.A., Jia, X.: Remote Sensing Digital Image Analysis, 4th edn. Springer, Heidelberg (2006)

Infant Monitoring System Using Wearable Sensors Based on Blood Oxygen Saturation: A Review

Pardeep Singh[✉], Gurpreet Kaur, and Daljeet Kaur

Eternal University, Baru Sahib, India
Pardeepl3@yahoo.com

Abstract. This paper investigates the monitoring of infants using wearable sensor networks technologies based on blood oxygen saturation. Wearable sensors are suitable for the diagnostic and monitoring of "applications". Their miniaturization as well as that of electronic circuits play a vital role in the development of wearable systems. On the other hand, bBood oxygen content is now considered as one of the vital signs for infant monitoring based on temperature, respiratory rate, heart rate, and blood pressure. One of the main advantages of pulse oximetry is that measurements are taken non-invasively through optical measurements. The system consists of a sensor module, a monitor, and an alarm. The sensor is to be placed on a peripheral tissue bed such as the child's ankle. The monitor should be able to receive telemetric data through a signal from a sensor. The monitor and an alarm could be placed in a different room, for instance, the parents room. The alarm must sound if an abnormal level of oxygen or pulse rate is detected. This paper reports on the usability of such monitoring system. This paper discusses on a general architecture for infant monitoring system using wireless body area network based on oxygen saturation.

Keywords: Wireless sensor networks · Pulse oximetry · Sensor module · Monitor

1 Introduction

In the literature, several care systems have been developed for monitoring the health status of elderly people, but these systems are not necessarily applicable to infants since infants are most likely at a great risk of death and such risk cannot be predicted in advance using the above-mentioned systems. In addition, it has been reported [1] that most such systems are not necessary suitable for monitoring the oxygen blood content. These drawbacks have prompted the research community to investigate the design of systems capable of monitoring the infant's oxygen saturation. In such system, a wireless sensor device can be placed on the thin part of the patient's body-earlobe, across a foot or fingertip or on the infant body part, then used for monitoring the amount of oxygen carried in the patient's body. In such systems, a monitor component is designed to receive the signal from the sensor component, and an alarm is incorporated, whose function is to raise some sounds whenever some abnormal changes

© Springer International Publishing AG 2017
I. Traore et al. (Eds.): ISDDC 2017, LNCS 10618, pp. 162–168, 2017.
https://doi.org/10.1007/978-3-319-69155-8_12

occur in the patient's blood saturation level [1]. In the recent years, several devices and sensors have been developed for clinical research and health monitoring. Meanwhile, several wearable sensor devices have also emerged as sensing technologies, which have high accuracy in terms of measurements. Examples of these are baby vest which includes fully-integrated sensors for measuring various body conditions of infant. In [2], a monitoring system was developed, which can be used to monitor the breathing, fever and volume of a baby sleeping in the crib. In [3], a wearable hardware gadget was developed, which can be used to capture the biological status of the baby such as motion, temperature and heart rate. In [4], an infant monitoring system was developed, which can be used to monitor the exhaled air from an infant, in order to reduce the potential risks of the Sudden Infant Death Syndrome (SIDS). In such system, which includes a sensor network to monitor the heart rate, temperature and humidity under clinical observation and home condition, CO_2 sensors are placed around the cradle in order to check the carbon dioxide level. Considering the resulting output, it is possible to detect unusual infant's respiration. Indeed, an alarm is raised if something unusual happens. In [5], a monitoring system based on GSM networks was developed, which are suitable for measuring the heart rate and blood pressure using a transmitter and a receiver. Sensors are placed on the infant's chest and the above-mentioned parameters are sensed and the results are reported to a microcontroller. The data is received by the GSM module and send to the server, which makes them available via a Web browser. Typically, the use of such system typically triggers an audible alarm/message so that immediate actions can be taken whenever a problem occur.

2 Existing Infant Monitoring Systems

Several monitoring systems for infant monitoring have been proposed in the literature [1]. Here, our focus is on systems based on the ZigBee technology such as the one depicted in Fig. 1, which are mainly used for collecting and transferring the monitoring information using temperature sensor and heart beat sensor. In fact, Zigbee is low-cost and low-powered network deployed for controlling and monitoring the applications. In such system, the network is usually operated in a mode where the battery power is conserved all the time. The considered system consists of five modules, namely the data acquisition module, the data processing module, the health status detection module, the wireless communication module and the power supply module. The data acquisition module collects the data from the infant by using various types of sensors. The data processing module includes some data processing methods such as A/D conversion, feature extraction and few data processing algorithms. The health status detection module is usually meant for comparing the results obtained from the sensors. In determining the health status of the infant, a threshold is usually predefined. The wireless communication module is meant to achieve the transmission of information between infants, the base station, and the parents, which are the three entities usually involved in the communication. The power supply module provides the necessary energy for the entire system. There exist at least one coordinator for the network, which is responsible for handling and storing the information while performing the receiving and transmitting data operations. In such system, Zigbee routers act as intermediary devices that permit the data to pass to/from other devices. Zigbee operates in two modes, namely, beacon mode and non-beacon mode. In a beacon mode, the coordinators and routers continuously monitor the active state of incoming data, yielding more power consumption. In this mode, the routers and coordinators are always in the active mode because at any time, any node can wake up and communicate. In a non-beacon mode, when there is no data communication from the end-devices, the routers and coordinators enter into the so-called sleep state. Periodically, the coordinator wakes up and transmits the beacons to the routers in the network whenever it is deemed necessary. All nodes in this network are connected as a star topology and a central node is assigned the role of network controller.

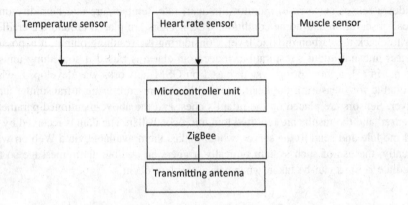

Fig. 1. Block diagram of the transmitting section

Based on specific targeted requirements, the system's hardware can be modified to deploy more sensors. Typically, when the measured data exceeds the allowable normal range, the system triggers an alarm message to the concerned healthcare professionals. Furthermore, the system depicted in Fig. 1 is meant to measure different physical parameters of an infant using three different sensors. The microcontroller receives the signals from the sensors and processes them before sending them to a ZigBee transmitter module. This transmitter module then transmits the signal, which is received at the other end by the receiving antenna of the ZigBee receiver as illustrated in Fig. 2.

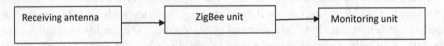

Fig. 2. Block diagram of the receiving section

Next, the receiver antenna receives the data sent by the transmitting antenna and the data are sent to a Monitoring unit for display.

3 System Design

In a nutshell, a wireless sensor network can be defined as a set of autonomous sensor nodes that are meant to monitor the physical conditions such as sound, temperature, and pressure. These sensors communicate the data directly to a centralized processing station, as well as with the base station. A sensor node is typically composed of four basic components, namely, a sensing unit, a transceiver unit, and a power unit as shown in Fig. 3.

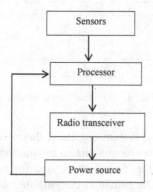

Fig. 3. Components of a wireless sensor network

In the above-mentioned infant monitoring system, the use of a wireless sensor module (as shown in Fig. 4) is to monitor the important signs of the infant such as respiration rate, body temperature, and blood pressure. The output of these deployed pressure sensors is then converted into digital signals using an analog to digital converter (ADC). These signals are processed using a microcontroller and the resulting output is transferred via a wireless module to the monitor.

In the monitoring module of Fig. 4, the body part activity and facial expression of the infant are taken into consideration and various sensors such as wet sensors are placed on the infant to monitor its respiration rate and other vital signs. This module consists of a cradle made of sensor nodes. The infant is placed in the cradle and sensors are placed on various parts of the cradle and the infant's body (for instance, his foot or ear lobe). An embedded application is invoked to process the information collected by these sensors. While doing so, an alert message is trigger if something abnormal occurs. It should be noted that the sensors motes that are used to monitor the oxygen in the infant's body transmit the data in pulse intervals once every second, and the frequency of the generated waveforms is analyzed and sent wirelessly to a microcontroller which processes them. Other key components of the infant monitoring system depicted in Fig. 4 include: (1) the respiration rate sensors – example applications of these sensors in practice are given in [6, 7]; temperature sensors – which typically fall in two categories, namely those that produce a voltage as indicator and those that generate other types of physical responses that should be converted into a voltage for measurement purpose [8]. Well-known examples of such sensors include

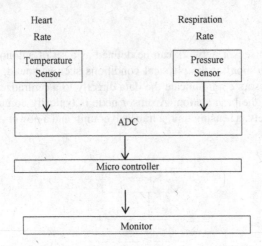

Fig. 4. Wireless sensor module

thermocouples, resistance temperature detectors, thermistors, infrared, and semiconductor sensors [9]. In using the aforementioned monitoring system, a pulse oximeter is also involved (as shown in Fig. 5), which is used for measuring how much of the hemoglobin in the blood of the patient is carrying the oxygen. This is referred to as measuring the oxygen saturation level (Spo_2) [10]. This is done by measuring the absorption of different wavelengths of light that undergo preferential absorption by the oxyhemoglobin or the deoxyhemoglobin [11].

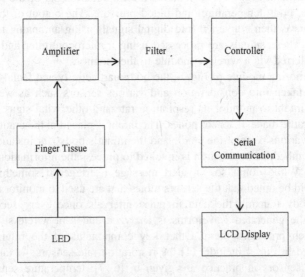

Fig. 5. Block diagram of the pulse oximeter

The heart rate is determined by measuring the elapsed time between peaks of the IR signal [11]. The pulse oximeter used for measuring the blood oxygen saturation and heart rate consists of sensors (see Fig. 5), a led driver, a microcontroller, and a LCD module [12, 13]. The signals from the sensors are amplified and sent to the microcontroller which then measures their levels. Next, the data is sent from the microcontroller to the LCD module. In this system, two types of light are considered, one referred to as transmitted light and the other referred to as reflected light. Both types of lights include probes, transmittance probe, and reflectance probe. Transmittance probe are composed of two LED's on one side and a light detector on the other side. Thus, the tissue which needs to be analyzed for blood saturation and heart rate is placed between the two types of light. On the other hand, the reflectance probe consists of two LED's and a light detector on the same side. Thus, it can be placed over any body tissue of the infant. The light is then emitted with the help of LED and passes through the body tissues and the same light is reflected by the bone, then is detected. In this process, the use of the reflectance probe is more complex than that of the transmittance probe.

4   Conclusion

This paper has provided a review of sensor systems for infants, including monitoring methods and techniques based on some of the recent research on wireless sensor networks' applications. As future work, the following points will be explored: (1) illustrating the proposed infant monitoring system using a case scenario which involves data collection and analysis; (2) qualitative comparison of existing state-of-the-art infant monitoring systems, including a discussion on metrics or measurements methods which can be used to evaluate the above-discussed sensor systems for infants; and (3) Discussion on how the collected data could be used for analytics or insights.

References

1. Linti, C., Horter, H., Osterreicher, P., Planck, H.: Sensory baby vest the monitoring of infants. In: Proceedings of International Workshop on Wearable and Implantable Body Sensor Networks, Cambridge, MA, USA, pp. 135–137, 3–5 Apr 2006
2. Luzon, R.:Infant Monitoring System. US Patent Publication, No. US 2002/0057202 A1, 16 May 2002
3. Chen, W., Dols, S., Oetomo, S.B., Feijs, L.: Monitoring body temperature of newborn infants at neonatal intensive care units using wearable Sensors. In: Proceedings of the Fifth International Conference on Body Area Networks, Corfu Island, Greece, pp. 188–194 (2010)
4. Saadatian, E., Iyer, S.P., Lihui, C., Newton Fernando, O.N.N., Hideaki, N., Cheok, A.D., Madurapperuma, A.P., Ponnampalam, G., Amin, Z.: Low cost infant monitoring and communication system. In: Proceedings of the IEEE International Conference Publication, Science and Engineering Research, 5–6 Dec 2011
5. Meihua, X., Yu, F., Fangjie, Z., Qian, Z.: A remote medical monitoring system based on GSM network. In: Proceedings of IET International Conference on Wireless Mobile and Computing (CCWMC), Shanghai, China, 7–9 Dec 2009. doi:10.1049/cp.2009.1970

6. Al-Dasoqi, N., Mason, A., Shaw, A., Al-Shamma'a, A.I.: Preventing cot death for infants in day care. In: Report of *RF* and Microwaves Group, General Engineering Research Institute, Liverpool John Moores University Byrom Street, Liverpool, L3 3AF, UK (2000)
7. Passport Respiration Rate Sensor. http://store.pasco.com/pascostore/showdetl.cfm?&DID=9&Product_ID=53778&Detail=1. Accessed 21 Aug 2017
8. Research-on-Sensing-Human   Affect.   http://affect.media.mit.edu/areas.php?id=sensing. Accessed 21 Aug 2017
9. Temperature-Sensors. http://www.mstarlabs.com/sensors/temperature.pd.f. Accessed 21 Aug 2017
10. Oximetric-probe. http://www.favoriteplus.com/blog/pulse-oximetry-probe. Accessed 21 Aug 2017
11. Samuell, S.P., Thilagavth, B.: Embedded Based Low Cost Pulse Oximeter. IOSR J. Electron. Commun. Eng. (IOSR-JECE), ISSN: 2278-8735, Vol. 9, Issue 1, Version IV, January 2014
12. Behbahani, S., Pishbin, M.A.: New oxygenation method based on pulse oximeter. Am. J. Biomed. Eng. **2**(4), 185–188 (2012)
13. Watthanawisuth, N., Lomas, T., Wisitsoraat, A., Tuantranont, A.: Wireless wearable pulse oximeter for health monitoring using zigbee wireless sensor network. In: IEEE Transactions On Electronics and Computer Technology, Vol. 2, Issue 3, July 2010

Network Behavioral Analysis for Zero-Day Malware Detection – A Case Study

Karim Ganame[⊠], Marc André Allaire, Ghassen Zagdene,
and Oussama Boudar

StreamScan Inc, 2300 Sherbrooke East, Montreal, QC H2K 1E5, Canada
info@streamscan.io

Abstract. The number of cyber threats is constantly increasing. In 2013, 200,000 malicious tools were identified each day by antivirus vendors. This figure rose to 800,000 per day in 2014 and then to 1.8 million per day in 2016! The bar of 3 million per day will be crossed in 2017. Traditional security tools (mainly signature-based) show their limits and are less and less effective to detect these new cyber threats. Detecting never-seen-before or zero-day malware, including ransomware, efficiently requires a new approach in cyber security management. This requires a move from signature-based detection to behavior-based detection. We have developed a data breach detection system named CDS using Machine Learning techniques which is able to identify zero-day malware by analyzing the network traffic.

In this paper, we present the capability of the CDS to detect zero-day ransomware, particularly WannaCry.

Keywords: Network behavior analysis · Ransomware · Artificial intelligence · Machine learning · Zero-day threat · Compromise detection

1 Introduction

Signature-based malware detection systems struggle with the identification zero-day malware, as by design such systems rely on known malware patterns. In contrast, behavioral systems can potentially detect such malware.

One of the latest malware that has challenged the capability of existing malware detection systems is the WannaCry ransomware. The damage caused by WannaCry is a testimony to its ability to evade most current malware detection systems, which in general rely on signature models.

CDS [2] is an advanced malware detection system that uses behavioral features and heuristics models, combined with machine learning techniques to detect both known and novel forms of malware.

In this paper, we analyze the behavior of the WannaCry ransomware, and study the capacity to successfully detect it.

The paper provides a sneak peek on malware analysis and detection using real-world industry scale appliance.

The rest of the paper is structured as follows. Section 2 gives an overview of CDS. Section 3 provides an outline of the WannaCry ransomware. Section 4 presents the

© Springer International Publishing AG 2017
I. Traore et al. (Eds.): ISDDC 2017, LNCS 10618, pp. 169–181, 2017.
https://doi.org/10.1007/978-3-319-69155-8_13

analysis of WannaCry ransomware using CDS. Section 4 discusses related technologies. Section makes concluding remarks.

2 CDS Overview

CDS (Compromise Detection System) is a new generation of data breach detection system that incorporates behavioral analysis to detect the most evasive malware, persistent threats and zero-day exploits.

The CDS operates in a systematic way by:

1. Collecting network packets entering and going out of the network;
2. Analyzing network packets for detecting malware, data breach and malware related activities, and feeding the processed packets to an alerting module and to a learning module.
3. Determining a normal behaviour of the computer network with machine learning algorithms for allowing detection of any deviation from normal behaviour of the computer network;
4. Storing information about the normal behaviour of the computer network and signatures of known malware, and feeding such information to an analysis module and a learning module;
5. Correlating results obtained from steps (2) and (3) to reduce false positive in a behaviour detection phase; and
6. Creating an alert upon detection of malware, data breach, and malware related activities over the computer network.

The CDS can be configured in **active mode** to take action when a compromise or abnormal behavior is detected in a network. Thus, the CDS can:

- Interact with a firewall to block the source of a compromise.
- Interact with a Network Access Control (NAC) when a computer is infected or displays suspicious behavior. This will result in the isolation of compromised device from the network.

The CDS has at least two modes of operation:

Standalone mode

In the standalone mode, all the components of the modules are integrated in the same system acting as a unique appliance being physical or virtual.

Distributed mode

In the distributed mode, different data collection modules are connected to each segment of a computer network and forward collected data to a centralized analysis module of the system.

Figures 1, 2 3 depict the CDS dashboard. The dashboard shows the number of compromised and suspicious devices. The administrator can also see the latest alerts that were generated, as shown in Fig. 2.

Impacted devices are classified by priority (LOW, MEDIUM, HIGH). Thus, when an alert is generated, the security administrator knows which devices they must focus

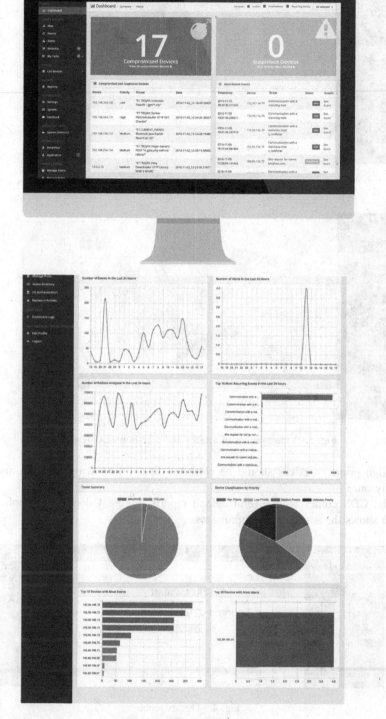

Fig. 1. CDS Dashboard

Fig. 2. Example of alerts generated by the CDS

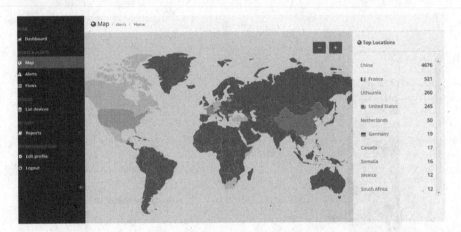

Fig. 3. View sources of attacks and compromises, by country

on. High priority devices should be corrected first, followed by Medium and Low priority ones.

The CDS comes with several default reports. Figure 4 depicts a sample report which shows the sources of compromises.

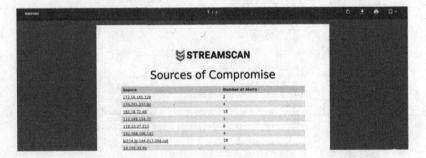

Fig. 4. Threats report

3   WannaCry Ransomware

WannaCryptor, also known as WannaCry, is a ransomware [1] that surfaced on Friday May 12th and instantly made international headlines. This great media attention is due to the ravages caused by this ransomware (crippled hospitals in the UK, massive infections at FedEx, Vodafone, Renault, etc.) as well as its capacity to propagate in a way that was never seen before. In fact, more than 200,000 computers spread over 150 countries were infected between May 12th and May 14th, 2017.

WannaCry targets files with specific extensions on the infected computers to encrypt them. These extensions include but are not limited to .doc, .docx, .xls, .xlsx, .ppt, .pptx, .pst, .ost, .msg, .eml, .vsd, .vsdx, .txt, .csv, .rtf, .pdf.

3.1   Definitions

To fully understand the scope and operation of WannaCry, it is important to get familiar with the following concepts and definitions.

Ransomware
A ransomware is a type of malicious software (malware) that encrypts data, mainly files, on the infected machine and demands a ransom to decrypt the affected data.

Computer Worm
A computer worm is a malicious program similar to a computer virus due to its malicious effect (it usually causes damage to the system it infects). The difference between them lies in the method of propagation. A computer worm does not require a user interaction to propagate as it only needs the available resources on the system to accomplish that. Therefore, an infected machine could potentially infect dozens if not hundreds of other machines.

Zero-Day Malware
A **zero-day** malware refers to a new generation of malicious tool that just appeared. Conventional security tools based on signatures (i.e. antivirus, intrusion detection or prevention systems, SIEM) are not capable of detecting this type of cyber threat.

TOR
Internet protocol used to anonymize conversations or communications over the Internet.

WannaCry = Ransomware + ComputerWorm

The particularity of WannaCry lies in the fact that it is a ransomware that uses a worm to spread. In order to infect new targets and spread, WannaCry exploits a critical vulnerability that affects the Windows operating system [3]. A Microsoft hotfix has been available since March 14th, 2017, about a month before the major incident caused by WannaCry.

For information, the vulnerability exploited by WannaCry concerns the SMB protocol (Server Message Block) [4] and can lead to remote computer code execution.

Almost all non-updated Windows versions, from Windows XP to Windows 10, are vulnerable.

4 Analysis of WannaCry Ransomware Using CDS

4.1 Methodology

To analyze WannaCry, we have set up a confined test environment where a Windows 7 computer has been infected (IP = 192.168.0.186). The network traffic generated by the infected computer was then captured for analysis purposes.

We have established two (2) network configurations for our analysis. In the first configuration, the infected host had access to the Internet while in the second configuration, the host did not have access to the Internet.

Two (2) variants of the WannaCry ransomware were analyzed: the first version, which appeared on May 12th, 2017 and the second, which appeared a few days later. The purpose of the analysis of the second variant was to obtain an idea of its degree of variation with respect to the initial version (i.e. new functionalities).

1. *Version 1 analyzed (original WannaCry version)*

   File name: WannaCry.EXE
   HashSHA256:
   ed01ebfbc9eb5bbea545af4d01bf5f1071661840480439c6e5babe8e080e41aa
   Hash MD5: 84c82835a5d21bbcf75a61706d8ab549

2. *Version 2 analyzed*

   File name: mssecsvc.exe
   Hash SHA256:
   24d004a104d4d54034dbcffc2a4b19a11f39008a575aa614ea04703480b1022c
   Hash MD5: db349b97c37d22f5ea1d1841e3c89eb4

4.2 Dynamic Analysis of WannaCry

Once infected with the first version of WannaCry (original version), the Windows 7 host scans the local network as well as randomly generated IP addresses for vulnerable systems. The scans are done on the 445 port (associated with the SMB service). If the connection is established, WannaCry executes the EternalBlue [5] exploit to infect the machine.

One of the main behaviors of the original WannaCry version is that before encrypting the infected host hard disk and scanning the Internet for vulnerable systems, it sends a DNS query to the following domain: **ifferfsodp9ifjaposdfjhgosurijfaewr-wergwea.com**. Figure 5 depicts sample network traffic capture showing a DNS query initiated to the randomly generated domain name.

As a reminder, the registration of this domain name by Malwaretech, an English researcher, fortunately slowed down the spread of the ransomware. Indeed, as we have seen in our analysis, the original version of WannaCry does not run if it does not

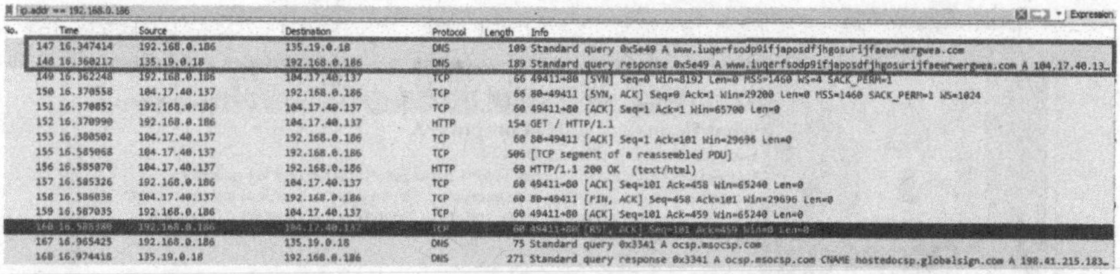

Fig. 5. DNS query initiated to the randomly generated domain name

receive a response to its DNS query. This domain name acts as a "kill switch". The registration of the domain name **ifferfsodp9ifjaposdfjhgosurijfaewrwergwea.com** therefore severely limited the impact of WannaCry.

Another feature of WannaCry is that it installs a TOR client on the infected machine to communicate with remote malicious servers. This makes all communications (any encryption key exchange, messages, etc.) anonymous and encrypted.

A word on the domain ifferfsodp9ifjaposdfjhgosurijfaewrwergwea

At a glance, one notices that this domain name is generated randomly (*random-generated domain*). However, it has been randomly generated only once and is the same for all copies of WannaCry version 1.

The use of randomly generated domain names is a widely used technique by several malicious tools (including malware command and control units- also known as C&C). This method makes it difficult to track C&C servers because the number of randomly generated domain names can be as high as 50,000 per day (in the case of the Conficker malware) and an infected computer can send queries to about 500 domains.

In general, queries to a randomly generated domain name is an indicator of compromise or suspicious behavior of a computer.

4.2.1   What to Remember About the Behavior of the Original Version of WannaCry When It Is Executed in an Environment with Internet Access

- If the DNS query to the domain www.iuqerfsodp9ifjaposdfjhgosurijfaewrwergwea. com is successful, the execution of the ransomware ends and the hard disk of the infected host is not encrypted.
- If the DNS query fails, the hard disk is encrypted.

4.2.2   What to Remember About the Behavior of the Original Version of WannaCry When the Test Is Performed in an Environment Without Internet Access

- The DNS query to www.iuqerfsodp9ifjaposdfjhgosurijfaewrwergwea.com domain fails. WannaCry runs and encrypts the hard disk of the infected host. After infection, WannaCry displays on the user's screen as shown in Fig. 6.

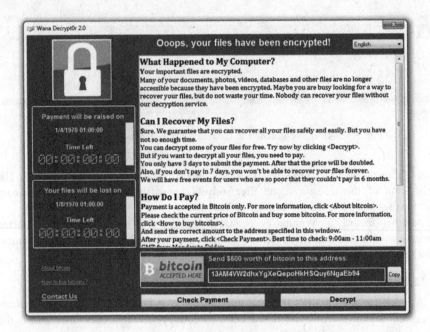

Fig. 6. Screen displayed after infection of a host by WannaCry

- WannaCry then attempts to connect to TOR [6] routers without success. As shown in Fig. 7, the ransomware keeps going by running thousands of scans on external addresses to port 445, the port exploited by the SMB vulnerability in order to potentially find other vulnerable Windows hosts to infect (confers multiple SYN requests initiated by the infected host whose IP address is 192.168.0.168).

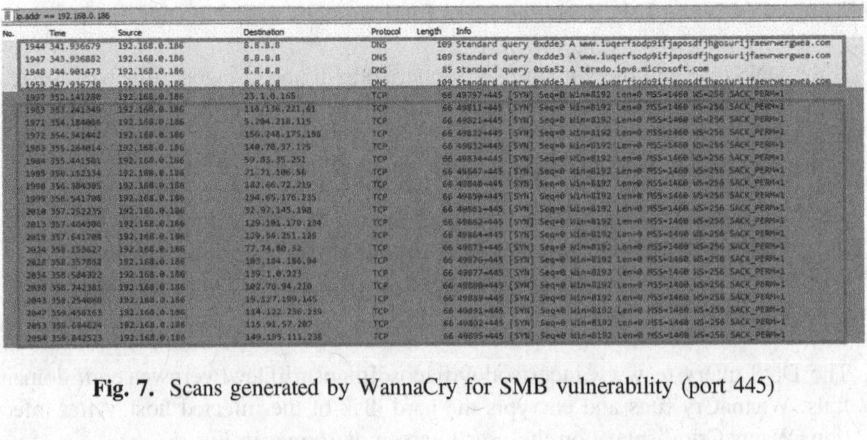

Fig. 7. Scans generated by WannaCry for SMB vulnerability (port 445)

4.3 Capacity of the CDS to Detect WannaCry

4.3.1 Detection of the Original Version of WannaCry

By analyzing the network packets generated by the WannaCry-infected Windows 7 machine, the Domain Generated Detection module of the CDS generated an alert when that machine sent the DNS request to the domain www.iuqerfsodp9ifjaposdfjhgosur ijfaewrwergwea.com. This CDS module uses Domain Generation Algorithms (DGA) [7] to detect domain names of this kind.

As shown in Fig. 8, CDS was able to detect the first version of WannaCry on day 0 of its expansion, on Friday, May 12, 2017. CDS provides the ability to view or download all of the network packets that generated the alert in PCAP format. The downloaded PCAP file could be read by tools such as Wireshark [8] or Tcpdump [9] (depicted by Fig. 10).

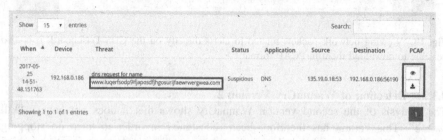

Fig. 8. Detection of WannaCry by the CDS

The CDS Signature Detection Module also detected WannaCry, after updating, following the availability of the SNORT [9] signatures, as shown by Fig. 9.

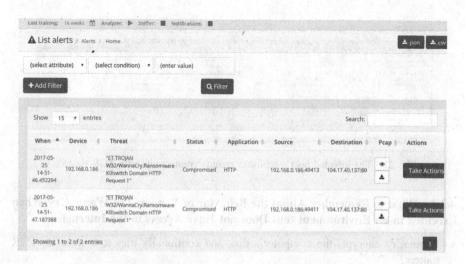

Fig. 9. Alerts generated by the CDS signature detection module

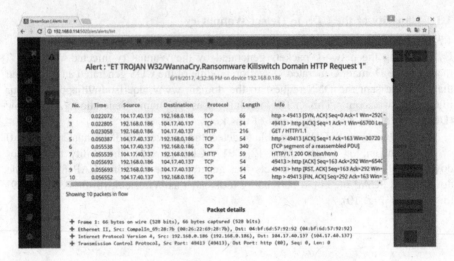

Fig. 10. Viewing network packets related to alerts directly on the CDS Dashboard. It is also possible to download them in PCAP format.

4.3.2 Detection of WannaCry Version 2

The analysis of the second version WannaCry shows that it does not have a "kill switch". This variant has therefore been redesigned in order to have no stopping condition. We also found that this version does not have a "worm" function, which explains why it does not try to propagate by scanning other computers to exploit the SMB vulnerability.

The particularity of this version of WannaCry is that it continuously initiates queries to TOR routers. One notices the use of randomly generated domain names in queries, as shown in the traffic samples in Figs. 11 and 12.

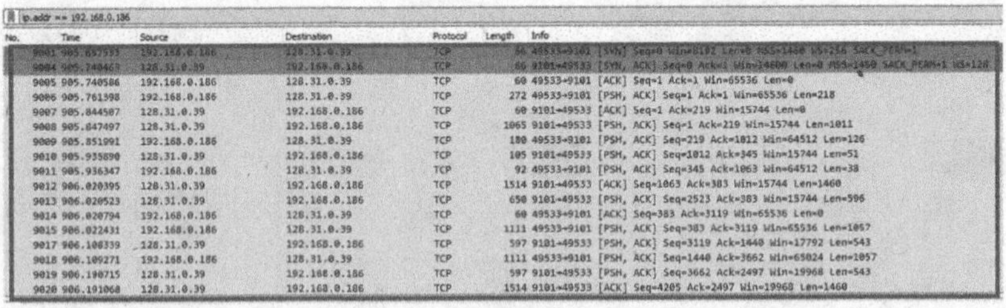

Fig. 11. The infected host establishes remote connections with TOR routers.

4.3.2.1 What to Remember About the Behavior of Version 2 of WannaCry When Executed in an Environment that Does not Have Access to the Internet

- WannaCry encrypts the computer's disk and continually tries to connect to TOR routers.

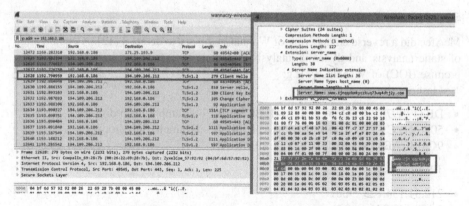

Fig. 12. Identification of random generated domain in TOR traffic

4.3.2.2 What to Remember About the Behavior of Version 2 of WannaCry When It Is Executed in an Environment with Internet Access

- WannaCry encrypts the computer disk and connects to remote digital routers.

4.3.2.3 Capacity of the CDS to Detect Version 2 of WannaCry

As with the first WannaCry version, the CDS is able to detect version 2, always relying on its Domain Name Detection module by analyzing TOR requests.

5 Related Work

In this section, we briefly discuss related malware detection technologies in industry handled the wannaCry ransomware threat.

5.1 AlienVault Evaluation

AlienVault Unified Security Management (USM) is a well-known Security Information and Event Management tool (SIEM) which seems to have a capability to detect zero-day malware (using behavioral monitoring) according to the company. However, to detect WannaCry, AlienVault released an IDS signature (ET EXPLOIT Possible ETERNALBLUE MS17-010 Echo Response) to the USM users [11]. This IDS signature was made available on 18 April 2017 (3 weeks before WannaCry surfaced.). Even if the IDS signature was available before WannaCry surfaced, this cannot be considered as a zero-day detection approach because only updated USM were able to detect WannaCry.

5.2 McAfee Approach to Detect WannaCry

McAfee did a reverse engineering of WannaCry binary to detect it [12]. A combination of static analysis and dynamic analysis was done to extract the Indicators of Compromise (IOC) of WannaCry. E.g:

Hashes

- DB349B97C37D22F5EA1D1841E3C89EB4 – Example main dropper
- 509C41EC97BB81B0567B059AA2F50FE8 – Example Sub dropper
- 9C514CAB458488A082070560C40D9DAB

IP Addresses

- 212.51.134.123 :9001
- 5.199.142.236 : 9001
- 197.231.221.221:9001

5.3 FireEye Approach to Detect WannaCry

FireEye used an agent (FireEye Exploit Guard) to monitor ransomware activities on end points in order to detect WannaCry [13]. Exploit Guard uses a combination of observations to detect WannaCry: executable file created in temporary folder suspiciously, suspicious process starting from temp folder, registry entry creation, etc.

A centralized console is used to view the security activities occurring on the network.

6 Conclusion

Detecting zero-day ransomware will remain a big challenge for the cyber security community. A disruptive and pragmatic approach needs to be taken in order to face to the explosion of cyber threats. The CDS is our response to this new challenge. Unlike sandboxing solutions, the CDS does not need to extract the binaries of malware to decide there is an infection. The behavioral analysis of the network flows using Machine Learning [14, 15] is sufficient for it to make decisions.

During its evaluation, the CDS proved that it is a powerful tool which is able to detect zero-day ransomware like WannaCry.

In active mode, the CDS could interact with a firewall to block the source of a compromise. In the case of WannaCry, the CDS can block the IP of the infected computer, which would isolate it from the network and prevent it from scanning other computers for propagation. It has a web-based GUI for viewing security alerts and events; the corresponding network flow is dumped as a pcap file for each alert. Comprehensive reports may be generated from this information. These resources help security administrators during investigations, and in determining the impact of a security incident.

References

1. Gazet, A.: Comparative analysis of various ransomware virii. J. Comput. Virol. **6**(1), 77–90 (2010)
2. CDS Compromise Detection System. https://www.streamscan.io/cds Accessed 07 Aug 2017
3. Microsoft Security Bulletin MS17-010. https://technet.microsoft.com/en-us/library/security/ms17-010.aspx
4. Simple Message Bloc. https://msdn.microsoft.com/en-us/library/windows/desktop/aa365233 (v=vs.85).aspx. Accessed 07 Aug 2017
5. EthernalBlue: https://packetstormsecurity.com/files/142169/ETERNALBLUE-2.2.0-Windows-2008-R2-SMBv1-Zero-Day-Exploit.html. Accessed 07 Aug 2017
6. TOR: https://www.torproject.org/about/overview.html.en. Accessed 07 Aug 2017
7. Antonakakis, M., et al.: From Throw-Away traffic to bots: detecting the rise of DGA-Based malware. USENIX security symposium, Vol. 12 (2012)
8. Wireshark. https://www.wireshark.org. Accessed 07 Aug 2017
9. TCPDUMP: www.tcpdump.org
10. SNORT Intrusion Detection System. https://www.snort.org/. Accessed 07 Aug 2017
11. Alienvault Detecting WannaCry Ransomware. http://www.infosec-cloud.com/wp-content/uploads/2017/05/AlienVault-Detect-WannaCry-Ransomware-white-paper.pdf. Accessed 07 Aug 2017
12. McAfee Labs Threat Advisory, Ransom-WannaCry. https://kc.mcafee.com/resources/sites/MCAFEE/content/live/PRODUCT_DOCUMENTATION/27000/PD27077/en_US/McAfee_Labs_WannaCry_May_24.pdf. Accessed 07 Aug 2017
13. FireEeye Endpoint Security Detect Prevent WannaCry. https://www.fireeye.com/blog/products-and-services/2017/05/fireeye-endpoint-security-detect-prevent-wannacry.html
14. Zhao, D., Traore, I.: P2P botnet detection through malicious fast flux network identification. In: 7th International Conference on P2P, Parallel, Grid, Cloud, and Internet Computing - 3PGCIC 2012, 12–14, Victoria, BC, Canada, November 2012
15. Gu, G., et al.: BotMiner: clustering analysis of network traffic for protocol-and structure-independent botnet detection. In: USENIX Security Symposium, Vol. 5(2) (2008)

Author Index

Printed in the United States
by Bookmasters

Printed in the United States
By Bookmasters